Noel Brehony had a career as a Durham and post-doctoral resear— the early years of the People's Der events there until unity in 1990. Middle East Institute at SOAS and has been chairman of the Middle East Association and the Council for British Research in the Levant and President of the British Society of Middle East Studies. He is currently chairman of the British Yemeni Society.

'Noel Brehony is a veteran commentator on that oxymoron of a place, known as modern Yemen. With much of this book based on his direct experience of the country, Brehony has produced a work that manages to be comprehensive and critical, but never disdainful. An important addition to our knowledge of an increasingly important, yet vulnerable country.'
Philip Robins, Reader in Middle East Politics and Faculty Fellow, St Antony's College, University of Oxford

'A timely account of an important period in Yemen's modern history.'
Ginny Hill, freelance journalist and Associate Fellow, Middle East and North Africa Programme, Chatham House

'The fascinating story of how a small nationalist movement overturned Britain's plans for South Arabia and established the only Marxist republic in the Arab world has never been told as well, as comprehensively and as authoritatively as in this lively account by someone who combines scholarly skill with first-hand observation and interviews with many of the key actors of the day. This is a major contribution to the literature on South Arabia's political history, and an excellent read as well!'
Gerd Nonneman, Professor of International Relations and Middle East Politics, University of Exeter

'No one is better placed than Dr Brehony to write a history based on interviews with many of the surviving protagonists and close study of the sources. He has a deft feel for the politics of the era and places the tale of the PDRY neatly into its regional context. If you want to understand the southern dimension to the various conflicts that currently threaten to turn a unified Yemen into a failed state, you could not find a better guide to the background and underlying issues than Noel Brehony.'
Michael Crawford CMG, Consulting Senior Fellow on the Middle East and South Asia at the International Institute of Strategic Studies, London

'*Yemen Divided* is an accessible and well-informed account of the rise and fall of the People's Democratic Republic of Yemen. The book is particularly valuable for its thoughtful and at times colourful account of the ideas, personalities, and leadership disputes that moulded the trajectory of the country. Not only is it an important read for understanding the history of the PDRY, but also a timely work that offers critical insights into the historical legacies and personalities that are currently shaping political instability and growing secessionist demands in the former South Yemen.'
April Longley Alley, PhD, independent consultant and Yemen specialist

'Such precision, illustrated by numerous anecdotes with interesting maps and appendices, is likely to turn this book into a classic. The book is informative in regard to the sensitive issue of contemporary southern secessionist movements. It helps historians – as well as social scientists, journalists and diplomats – to navigate the complex genealogies, organizations, regional kinships, and hundreds of individuals that have played, and continue to play, an active role in southern Yemen ... Noel Brehony's volume constitutes a timely contribution to today's urgent debates and raises a number of relevant questions: What can Southerners learn from past experiences and mistakes? To what extent will such a legacy, culminating in the failure of the People's Democratic Republic of Yemen, hamper any future attempt to recreate an independent South?'
Laurent Bonnefoy, Institut français du Proche-Orient, Beirut

YEMEN DIVIDED

The Story of a Failed State in South Arabia

Noel Brehony

I.B. TAURIS
LONDON · NEW YORK

To Jennifer

New paperback edition published in 2013 by I.B.Tauris & Co Ltd
6 Salem Road, London W2 4BU
175 Fifth Avenue, New York NY 10010
www.ibtauris.com

Distributed in the United States and Canada Exclusively by Palgrave Macmillan
175 Fifth Avenue, New York NY 10010

First published in hardback in 2011 by I.B.Tauris & Co Ltd

Copyright © Noel Brehony, 2011, 2013

The right of Noel Brehony to be identified as the author of this work has been asserted by the author in accordance with the Copyright, Designs and Patents Act 1988.

All rights reserved. Except for brief quotations in a review, this book, or any part thereof, may not be reproduced, stored in or introduced into a retrieval system, or transmitted, in any form or by any means, electronic, mechanical, photocopying, recording or otherwise, without the prior written permission of the publisher.

ISBN: 978 1 78076 491 7

A full CIP record for this book is available from the British Library
A full CIP record is available from the Library of Congress

Library of Congress Catalog Card Number: available

Typeset in Garamond by Charles Peyton
Printed and bound in Great Britain by CPI Antony Rowe, Chippenham
from camera-ready copy edited and supplied by the author

Front Panel Image: Mud Tower, Hadhramaut, Yemen, 2007 © Bridget Cowper-Coles
Back Panel Image: Al Hajjara in the Haraz Mountains, Northern Yemen © Franco Pecchio

CONTENTS

Illustrations	vii
Preface and Acknowledgements	ix
Abbreviations	xi
Outline Chronology	xiii
Maps	xvi
Introduction	xix

PART A: FROM SOUTH ARABIA TO SOUTH YEMEN

1. South Arabia in 1967	3
2. The National Liberation Front Takes Power	14
3. From PRSY to PDRY via the Glorious Corrective Move	31

PART B: THE SALMIN YEARS

4. Structures and Leadership in the Early 1970s	53
5. The PDRY's Internal and External Policies in the Salmin Years	64
6. Who Leads – the President or the Party? The Downfall of Salmin	86

PART C: THE STRUGGLE FOR POWER

7. The Presidency of Abd al-Fattah Isma'il and the Formation of the Yemeni Socialist Party	105
8. Ali Nasir Muhammad as Supreme Leader	122
9. Policies in the Ali Nasir Years	137

PART D: FROM THE PDRY TO THE REPUBLIC OF YEMEN

10. Fracturing the Regime: The Events of January 1986 — 151
11. Unity or Reform? — 168
12. Union Without Unity — 183

PART E: DID THE PDRY FAIL?

13. Could an Independent South Yemen Return? — 201

APPENDICES — 213

Appendix A: The Principal Tribes in Lahij, Abyan and Shabwa — 215
Appendix B: List of Prominent Personalities — 218

Notes — 221
Select Bibliography — 240
Index — 250

ILLUSTRATIONS

The author would like to thank Dar al-Ayyam in Aden and Ali Nasir Muhammad for permission to use the photographs, which appear in Ali Nasir Muhammad's book Aden: History and Civilizations *(Abu Dhabi, 2002, in Arabic).*

Figure 1   Mentors and rivals: George Habbash, Nayif Hawatmah, Ali Nasir Muhammad, Muhsin Ibrahim, Ahmad Haydarah Sa'id, Ali Antar and Muhammad Ali Ahmad.

Figure 2   Muhammad Salih Muti'a, Ali Nasir Muhammad, Abd al-Fattah Isma'il and Salim Rubayya Ali (Salmin) celebrating a peasants' uprising to seize land in 1970.

Figure 3   Salim Rubayya Ali (Salmin), Abd al-Fattah Isma'il, Ali Nasir Muhammad and Ali Antar.

Figure 4   Salim Rubayya Ali (Salmin) with Muhammad Salih Ubad (Muqbil) and Muhammad Ali Ahmad, in Abyan.

Figure 5   Ali Abdullah Salih and Ali Salim al-Bidh sign the Aden unity agreement.

PREFACE AND ACKNOWLEDGEMENTS

I have long wanted to write the story of the People's Democratic Republic of Yemen (PDRY). I was fortunate to be a diplomat in Aden in the early 1970s, when it was possible to view what was happening in this new state, and it was still possible to meet its leaders and its people. It was fascinating to see a Marxist regime being created from what seemed to be unpromising and unlikely material. After leaving Aden I tried for the rest of the PDRY's existence to follow events there up to union in 1990. When I first started research for this book, the PDRY seemed like a piece of twentieth-century history: it was an interesting experiment, a mere interlude in the long history of Yemen. However, in the course of writing the book there have been new calls for the establishment of a decentralized region, or even an independent state, on the lands of the former PDRY. In interviews with South Yemenis I have asked about the past, and they have often talked about the present and future. In writing the book I have tried to keep in mind that the experience of the PDRY might have lessons for all those interested in the future of Yemen.

I have had help from a large number of Yemenis, some of whom have asked me not to name them. I would like to thank all those who have helped so generously. Among those I can name are Ali Nasir Muhammad, Haydar al-Attas, Salim Salih Muhammad, Muhammad Ali Ahmad, Abd al-Aziz al-Dali, Muhammad Sa'id Abdullah (Muhsin), Abdullah al-Asnaj, Mundai al-Afifi, Farooq al-Hakimi, Sinan Abu Luhum, Ali Muhsin Hamid, Muhammad bin Dohry, Yassin Sa'ld Nu'man, Hassan Ba'um, Rashid al-Kaff, Mohsen Alaini, Abd al-Jalil Gailani, Shaf'al Umar, Abd al-Aziz al-Quaiti, Lutfi Shatara, Khalid Yamani, Matahir Mus'id Muslih, Ahmad Abdullah Muhammad Hassani, Sulaiman Nasir Mas'ud, Professor Abd al-Aziz al-Tarb and Sharif Haydar al-Habili. I would also like to thank the late Fred Halliday, the outstanding scholar of the PDRY, for his encouragement and for providing some of his papers. John Shipman has been an invaluable source of support, helping me to get in touch with south Yemenis, providing advice, and reading many of the chapters in draft. Helen Lackner has also been very helpful, and has often put me right when I have been too harsh in my judgements on the PDRY. I am grateful to others who have provided advice and read chapters in draft, including Stephen Day, Michael Crawford, Muhammad Bin Dohry and Rashid al-Kaff. I would like to thank Peter Hinchcliffe for helping with the pre-1967 history. The London Middle East Institute at SOAS allowed me to become a Research Associate and I am grateful to Bob Springborg, the former director of LMEI, for all his support. Roland Popp has allowed me to see his as yet unpublished paper based on examination of the former East German intelligence (STASI) archives. Charles Peyton has given me a great deal of assistance in preparing the book for publication. Finally, I am grateful to my wife Jennifer, not just for being so understanding about the amount of time I have put into the book, but for reading and correcting its contents.

In acknowledging this help, I should nevertheless make it clear that I am responsible for the accuracy of its contents and the judgements it offers.

The PRSY government divided the country into six provinces shortly after independence, and named First Province, Second Province, and so on. The names were changed in 1980 to Aden (First Province), Lahij (Second), Abyan (Third), Shabwa (Fourth), Hadhramaut (Fifth) and Mahra (Sixth). I have used the latter names throughout. I have used the term 'northerner' to refer to South Yemeni politicians mostly from Aden who were born in north Yemen, following the practice of southern-born politicians from the late 1970s.

I have used the simplest method of transliterating Arabic into English. The only symbol I have used is ', representing 'ayn when it appears in the middle of words. I have tried to be as consistent as possible, but have used well-known transliterations such as 'Hadhramaut' where necessary, or in references where I have stuck with the transliterations used by the original authors. I have referred to Ali Nasir Muhammad, but to Gamal Nasser.

ABBREVIATIONS

ACC	Arab Cooperation Council
ATUC	Aden Trade Union Congress (existing in the last years of British rule in Aden)
CPSU	Communist Party of the Soviet Union
EAP	Eastern Aden Protectorate
FLOSY	Front for the Liberation of South Yemen
FRA	Federal Regular Army
GPC	General People's Congress
HBL	Hadhrami Bedouin Legion
MAN	Movement of Arab Nationalists
NDF	National Democratic Front
NF	National Front
NFPO	The National Front Political Organization
NLF	National Liberation Front
OLOS	Organization for the Liberation of the Occupied South
PDF	Popular Defence Forces (PDRY armed forces)
PDFLP	Popular Democratic Front for the Liberation of Palestine
PDRY	People's Democratic Republic of Yemen (1970–90)
PDU	People's Democratic Union (Communist Party)
PFLOAG	Popular Front for the Liberation of Oman and the Arabian Gulf
PFLP	Popular Front for the Liberation of Palestine
PLO	Palestine Liberation Organization
PORF	Popular Organization for Revolutionary Forces
PRSY	People's Republic of South Yemen (1967–70)
PSP	People's Socialist Party (founded by Abdullah al-Asnaj, a leader of the ATUC)
RDP	Revolutionary Democratic Party
ROY	Republic of Yemen (the united Yemen from 1990)

SPC	Supreme People's Council
UPONF	United Political Organization of the National Front
WAP	Western Aden Protectorate
YAR	Yemen Arab Republic (1962–90)
YPUP	Yemeni People's Unity Party
YSP	Yemen Socialist Party

OUTLINE CHRONOLOGY

1959 Formation of the Federation of South Arabia.
1962 Overthrow of Imam and proclamation of Yemen Arab Republic.
Egyptian forces arrive in YAR.
1963 Foundation of the National Liberation Front.
Aden joins the Federation of South Arabia.
Radfan campaign; revolution begins on 14 October.
1964 Britain announces it will grant independence to the Federation in 1968, retaining its base.
1965 First NLF Congress.
1966 Second and Third NLF Congresses. NLF joins and then leaves FLOSY.
Britain decides to abandon its military base.
1967 NLF and FLOSY fight for Aden.
NLF takes control of large parts of the country outside Aden.
June War sees defeat of Egypt and withdrawal of forces from YAR.
Suez Canal closes.
South Yemen becomes independent as People's Republic of South Yemen.
NLF becomes NF.
1968 Fourth NF Congress.
Qahtan al-Sha'bi's victory over the left.
1969 Glorious Corrective Move.
Overthrow of Qahtan al-Sha'bi.
New Presidential Council: Salim Rubayya Ali (Salmin) as Chairman, Abd al-Fattah Isma'il as secretary general of the NF, and Muhammad Ali Haytham as prime minister.
1970 Proclamation of the People's Democratic Republic of Yemen.
National Reconciliation in the YAR.

1971	Resignation of Muhammad Ali Haytham.
	Ali Nasir Muhammad becomes prime minister.
1972	Fifth NF Congress.
	The 'Seven Glorious Days'.
	Border war between PDRY and YAR.
	Cairo and Tripoli agreements on unity of the YAR and PDRY.
1973	October Ramadan (Yom Kippur) War.
1974	Ibrahim al-Hamdi becomes president of the YAR.
1975	Sixth NF Congress and the Unification Congress.
	Merger of NF with People's Democratic Union and the Popular Vanguard Party (al-Tali'a).
1977	President al-Hamdi murdered; al-Ghashmi succeeds him.
1978	Assassination of President al-Ghashmi.
	Execution of Salim Rubayya Ali in Aden.
	Ali Abdullah Salih becomes president of the YAR.
	NF becomes Yemeni Socialist Party; first Conference of the YSP
	Abd al-Fattah Isma'il becomes secretary general of YSP and chairman of the Presidium.
	Formation of Northern Branch of YSP.
1979	Border war between YAR and PDRY.
	Kuwait agreement on unity.
1980	Abd al-Fattah Isma'il resigns and leaves for Moscow.
	Second 'Exceptional' YSP Conference.
	Ali Nasir Muhammad becomes president, secretary general of the YSP and prime minister.
	Iraq attacks Iran, leading to war that lasts until 1988.
1982	Establishment of General People's Congress in the YAR.
1985	Haydar al-Attas becomes prime minister.
	Return of Abd al-Fattah Isma'il from Moscow.
	Third YSP Congress.
1986	Failure of coup attempt by Ali Nasir Muhammad leads to virtual civil war.
	Ali Nasir defeated and leaves for YAR with 30,000 of his followers. Haydar al-Attas becomes president, Ali Salim al-Bidh secretary general, and Yassin Sa'id Nu'man prime minister.
1987	Fourth YSP Congress.
1988	Meetings between YAR and PDRY leaders to discuss unity.
	Creation of Joint Economic Zone.
1989	Fall of the Berlin Wall.
	PDRY and YAR sign unity agreement.

1990	Proclamation of the Republic of Yemen with Ali Abdullah Salih as president and Ali Salim al-Bidh as vice president.
	Haydar al-Attas made prime minister.
	Iraq occupies Kuwait.
	Saudi Arabia expels 800,000 Yemenis.
1993	First parliamentary elections.
	Ali Salim al-Bidh leaves permanently for Aden.
1994	Ali Abdullah Salih and Ali Salim al-Bidh sign Document of Pledge and Accord.
	Civil war starts.
	Proclamation of the Democratic Republic of Yemen.
	Civil War ends in decisive victory for the northern forces.
	Al-Bidh and al-Attas leave Yemen.

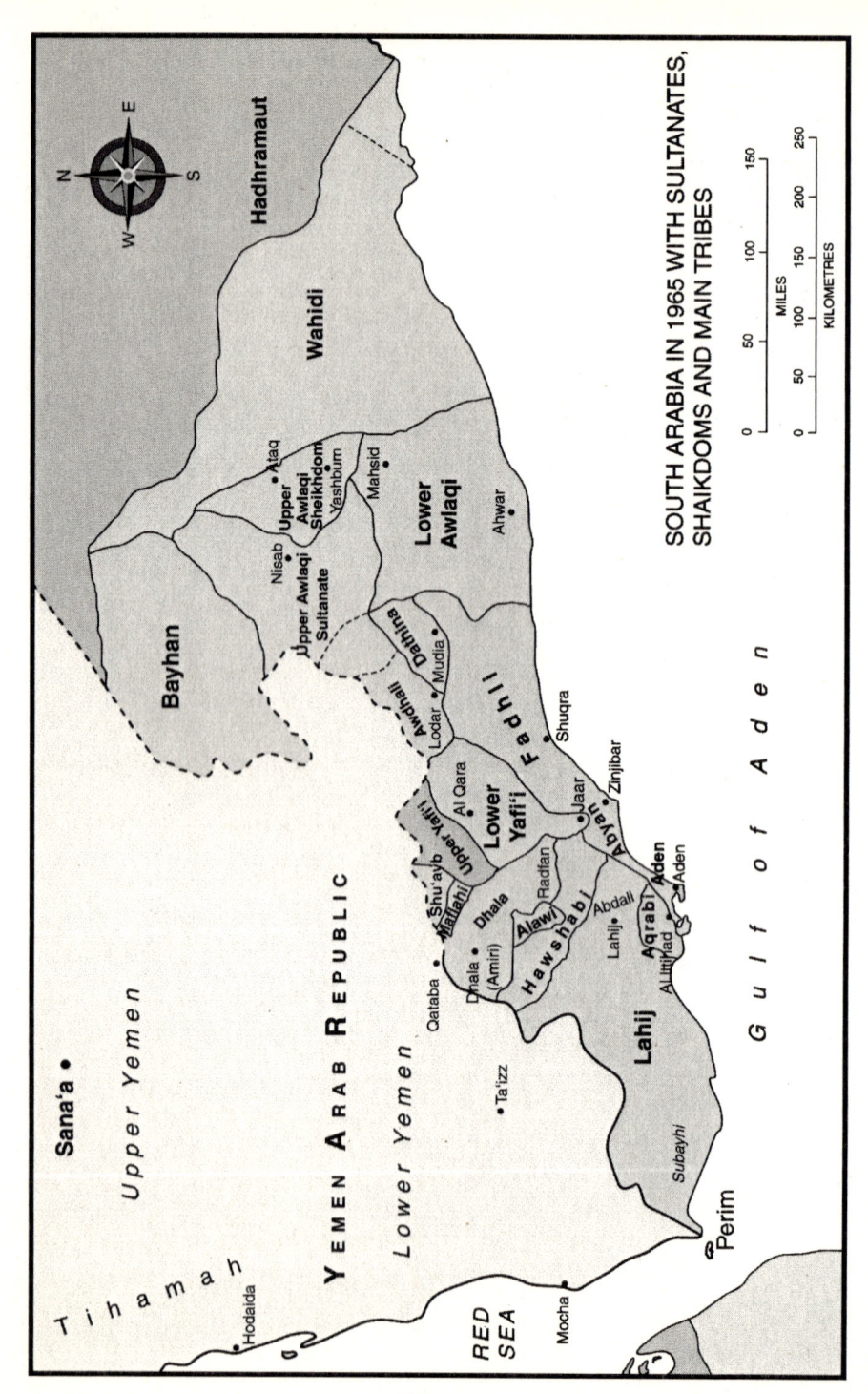

Map A

Map B

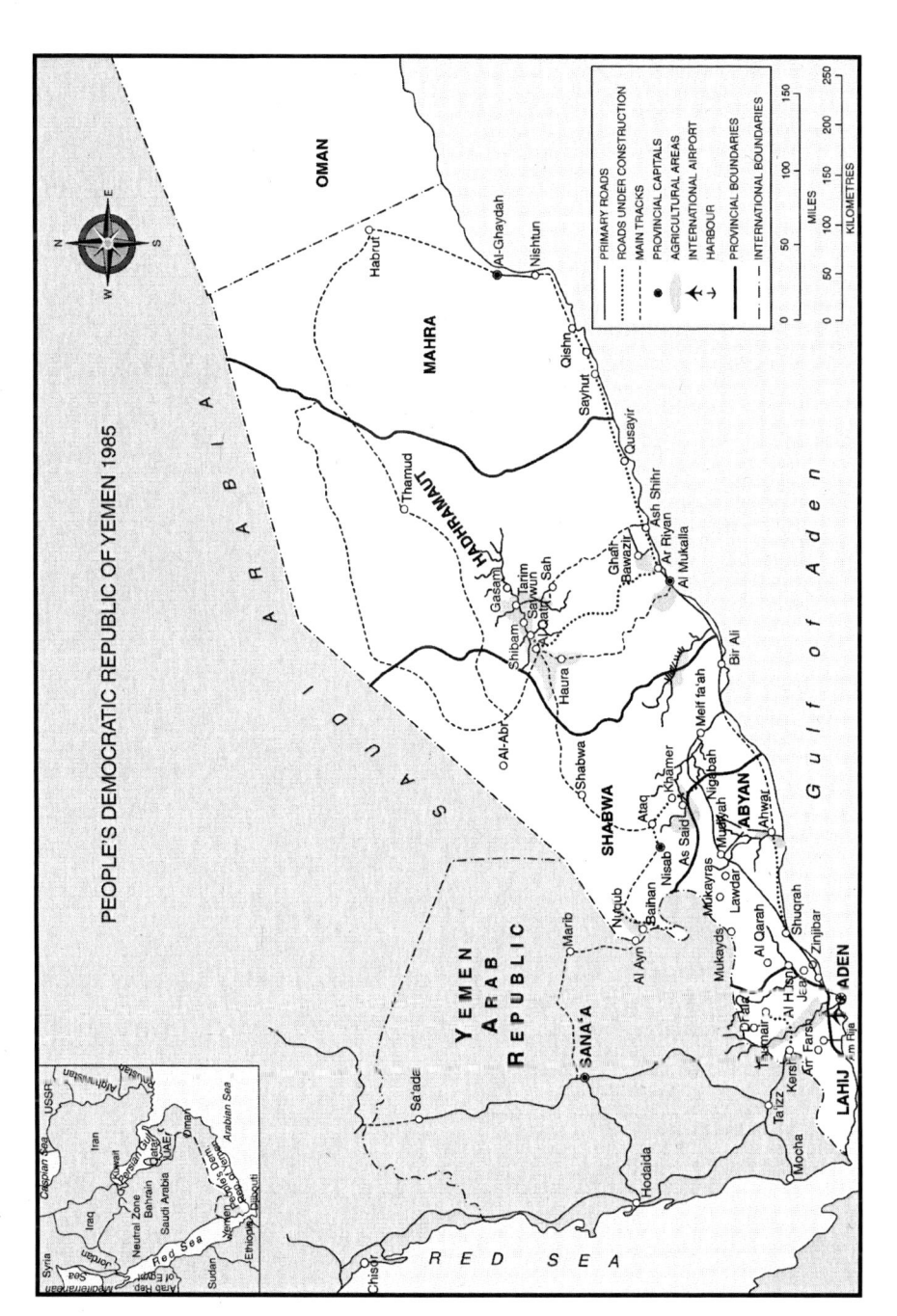

INTRODUCTION

It is an extraordinary story. The People's Democratic Republic of Yemen (PDRY) survived for less than twenty-three turbulent years as an independent state. The British had been in Aden since 1839, and had extended their control into the hinterland of sultanates, amirates and shaikhdoms. By the late 1950s, Aden was the second-largest port in the world, and in the early 1960s the British moved their main Middle East military base to Aden, stationing over 15,000 men there. The British hope was that the federation of sultanates would be granted independence but remain firmly tied to London, and continue to be a major base for British forces. Yet on 30 November 1967 the British abandoned South Arabia, and it was the National Liberation Front (NLF) that took power. How was it possible that the NLF, with only a few thousand members and led mostly by poorly educated people still in their twenties, could apparently oust a colonial power?

After a hesitant beginning, the new leaders, who had started political life as Arab Nationalists, turned to the ideas and experiences of Communist parties in the Soviet Union, China, Cuba and Vietnam. Within a few years they had set up the Arab world's only Marxist regime.

The new state could hardly have got off to a worse start. The NLF inherited the port of Aden, whose economy had been destroyed by the closure of the Suez Canal in June 1967. The removal of the British military base wiped out thousands of jobs. British subsidies ceased. The loss of these major sources of revenue was accompanied by an exodus of up to 200,000 people. Just over 1 per cent of the land was cultivable and there were few roads, schools or hospitals outside Aden. The British and many others gave the regime little chance of survival, thinking it might be overthrown by the army, or torn apart by the ideological differences within its leadership.

Unity was always seen by both Yemens to be inevitable. The leaders saw the North and South as two halves (*shatrayn*) of one country. The south had a greater land mass but its population was only a fifth of that of the north. The 1962 revolution had overthrown the centuries old Mutawakkalite

Imamate to create the Yemeni Arab Republic a regime that seemed to share many of the political ideas of the new government in the south. Yet the southern leaders did not opt for unity in 1967. Why did the PDRY remain independent for the next twenty-three years and why did it ultimately accept unity?

South Yemen in the early twenty-first century

The Arab spring, in 2011, opened up major fractures in the Yemeni regime that eventually led to the resignation of President Ali Abdullah Salih after thirty-two years in power, as part of a transition deal initially negotiated by the Gulf Co-operation Council (GCC), and is now being monitored by the UN Security Council. Yemen comes close to the bottom of indices measuring human development and the rule of law, while coming near the top of those assessing corruption. Too many Yemenis live in poverty and suffer from shortages of food, water, jobs, schools, hospitals and electricity. Revenues from oil and gas were misused by the previous regime to maintain itself in power and are now declining. There are few other resources. Al-Qa'ida in the Arabian Peninsula used the recent crisis to build an insurgency movement that was able to take over parts of the country. It has the will and capacity to lanuch attacks against the West. Al-Huthi forces control parts of the northwest. The transition process offers a way forward through an inclusive national dialogue. It faces many obstacles, and may not work.

The southern movement (which calls itself the Southern Mobility Movement) began in 2007 among former PDRY military and security personnel dismissed after the 1994 civil war, demanding the payment of proper pensions and benefits. It started as local movements in the provinces of Dhala and Lahij and spread quickly, becoming a magnet for people with other grievances: a lack of jobs, discrimination in favour of the north in the allocation of government resources and jobs, and the poor level of service-delivery and social protection compared with what they had enjoyed (or so they believed) in the PDRY. Some are asking for the restoration of the state that they say was stolen from them in 1994. They see a history of manoeuvres by the regime to marginalize and weaken southern leaders and to exploit southern resources (oil, gas and fisheries) for the benefit of the north. Not only did President Salih dismantle the PDRY state after 1994 with all its imagined benefits; he also allowed his northern henchmen to take over big landholdings in the south. They claim that the regime encouraged the re-emergence of tribalism and the spread into the south of Salafism and Wahhabism. Southerners speak of 'northern occupation'.

If the UN-sponsored transition deal fails, Yemen could fail as a state. The resolution of the southern issue will be crucial. Many South Yemenis reject the concept of unity which, they believe, was based on an illegimate agreement. They want to secede or be part of a federal Yemen. Others argue that the Yemeni leaders and the international community want to see Yemen's problems solved by a unified state. They include the current president and prime minister, who are both from the south, as well as leaders of the Yemeni Socialist Party, the ruling party of the PDRY, which in 2011 became part of a coalition government in Sana'a. The divisions among the southerners were inherited from the PDRY. Anyone interested in the future of Yemen will need to understand how the PDRY was formed and governed. Did the PDRY fail as a state? Or, did its leaders fail their people? What can those engaged in trying to build a new Yemen learn from the experience of the PDRY.

§

I have three aims in writing this book. First, I want to tell the story of the People's Democratic Republic of Yemen from its birth on 30 November 1967 as the People's Republic of South Yemen (PRSY – it became the PDRY on 1 November 1970) until its demise, which formally came with its entry into union with the Yemeni Arab Republic (YAR) on 22 May 1990, but in reality took place at the end of the three-month civil war on 7 July 1994. Second, I want to examine what drove the PDRY leaders in late 1989 to agree to union with the Yemen Arab Republic. Finally, I will consider the implications of the story of the PDRY for Yemen today, and the question of the restoration of an independent south.

In attempting to tell this story, I have divided the book into five sections. The first deals with the South Yemen taken over by the NLF in 1967. The period of British rule, especially the last twenty years, is well covered in numerous books, some of which are in the bibliography. I am summarising in a few thousand words an extensive literature by way of an introduction to subsequent events for readers with little knowledge of South Arabia. I have picked out those aspects that I think are important for understanding the PDRY's early years but some specialists may feel that I have left out too much or not given the right nuance to events. I have devoted a chapter to the formation of the NLF, which is well covered in Arabic literature but less so in English. I have also included in this first section a chapter on the first twenty months of independence, a period of turmoil as the new regime established itself and its more militant left wing pushed the pragmatic right out of power, in what became known as the Glorious Corrective Move. This period is well covered in the literature and in the FCO documents in the National Archives. The second section deals with the period of the presidency of Salim Rubayya Ali (popularly known by his NLF name of Salmin) from 1969 to 1978, which saw the party and government firmly established and their domestic and foreign policies defined. The third section discusses the turbulent presidencies of Abd al-Fattah Isma'il and Ali Nasir Muhammad. It is dominated by the manoeuvrings of the historical leaders, perhaps better referred to as historical rivals, in the lead-up to the bloody events of 13 January 1986. It looks at how Isma'il took the PDRY closer to Moscow and attempted to extend YSP influence into the YAR. Ali Nasir Muhammad was a more skilful politician, who tried to reform the economy and improve relations with neighbouring states and the West. However, his unwillingness to share power with other historical leaders undermined his achievements. I owe a debt of gratitude to scholars who wrote about these events in the 1970s and 1980s, especially to Fred Halliday, Helen Lackner, Tarek and Jacqueline Ismael, John Peterson and Joseph Kostiner. Throughout the book I have drawn extensively on Fred Halliday's *Revolution and Foreign Policy: The Case of South Yemen, 1967–1987* when discussing the PDRY's foreign relations.

The fourth section examines the bloody events of 13 January 1986 and their aftermath. The weakened regime, suffering a loss of legitimacy and direction, had to reform itself radically or find a solution in unity with the north. The section looks at the unity agreement and how it was agreed and implemented. I focus on what went wrong and what led to the disastrous civil war of 1994. This period is well covered in the literature and I have been able to draw especially on the writings of Sheila Carapico, Lisa Wedeen, Charles Dunbar, Robert Burrowes and Brian Whitaker. In the final section I ask whether the PDRY was a failed state, and what are the implications of its life and death for the future of Yemen.

In preparing this book, I have consulted the existing literature in English and Arabic, looked at the archival material that is accessible and examined contemporary accounts in articles, books and the media. The British government documents I quote have all been released to the National Archives. I set myself the task of drafting the book based on this written material before embarking on a series of interviews with former leaders of PDRY ministries, members of the upper reaches of the YSP, senior civil servants and some of the north Yemenis involved in the south. Memories of events can be inadvertently edited in the minds of those involved. Many of those I interviewed remain politically active within the Yemeni system and in opposition in exile. Their recollections of the same events do not always agree. It has been helpful to compare their accounts with the historical record and with each other. I say this with the greatest respect for those I have interviewed. Without exception they are deeply committed to Yemen and south Yemen, and have spoken to me frankly. Some see the PDRY as an unfinished experiment, and will talk of a utopian state where law and order existed, the rule of law prevailed and a modern administration was managed by wise and experienced figures. Others see a totalitarian state whose leaders destroyed the economy and the lives of many of its citizens before turning their guns on each other. Some see the PDRY as a failed state that had to be rescued by the north; others conclude that it was let down by its leaders and the regime they created, but believe that there should be room for a new south within Yemen – though they disagree on what form that should take: decentralized southern provinces, confederation, federation or secession.

Those I have interviewed, with few exceptions, agreed that I could say that I had consulted them. Most gave me the freedom to quote them, but I have used this freedom sparingly, and in some cases I have hidden their precise identity. I have done this because they are discussing events within living memory, and people who participated in some extremely violent incidents. I am conscious, through having talked to people from all sides in the PDRY conflicts, that these events deeply affected their lives and those of their families; the wounds have not always healed.

Finally, I have set out to tell the story of the PDRY as I interpret it. At times this departs from the analysis and conclusions of previous writers on PDRY, mostly because I have been able to add through interviews with some of the key south Yemeni leaders information and nuances that were not available to scholars writing fifteen or twenty years ago. I am conscious that for the period from 1989 to 1994, I am, as in the first chapter, summarizing complex events and detailed scholarship in order to tell the story. I have referred to the main writings of this period and I urge those who want to know more to read the works I have cited. I hope that all will see the value in trying to pull together, for the first time in English, the story of the PDRY.

PART A

FROM SOUTH ARABIA TO SOUTH YEMEN

I

SOUTH ARABIA IN 1967

Since the tenth century, imams based in the Zaydi highlands of the north expanded their rule into south and east Yemen when they were strong and retreated when weak, allowing local states to emerge until the next incursion from the north.[1] The PRSY/PDRY can be seen as the latest example of this phenomenon. It was two imperial powers, the Ottomans and the British, who established the line that divided Yemen in 1904 into its northern and southern parts[2] – a division that the imams and their republican successors never fully accepted despite the signing by an imam of a border agreement in 1934. The border cut through what Yemenis call the Central District – that is, the northern provinces of Bayda, Ibb and Ta'izz and part of the former southern provinces of Lahij and Abyan. This district was the main heartland of Sunni Islam of the Shafi'i School, to which south Yemenis belong. The imams of the Mutawakkalite kingdom of Yemen and the Yemeni tribal confederations of the northern highlands are mostly Shi'a, following the quietist doctrines of Zayd, a son of the fourth Shi'a imam, and known as the Zaydis.

When Captain Haines acquired Aden by force in 1839, he was acting for the East India Company and the British approach to running South Arabia was heavily influenced by its experiences in India, but without the detailed local knowledge of tribes and people they had gained during the Raj.[3] Aden was run from Bombay until 1932, and Delhi to 1937. British activity in the hinterland was limited to ensuring that no threat to Aden's security could develop there, and that internal trade routes were kept open to the north. Aden ('the eye of Yemen') was the country's main port.

It was only after the opening of the Suez Canal in 1869, and Ottoman manoeuvring among South Arabian tribes, that the British concluded they would have to adopt more forward defence arrangements for Aden. They needed to win the support of the tribal leaders, particularly of the Sultan of Lahij, whose fiefdom was richer and personal power greater than those of other rulers. In 1873, the Ottomans were asked to respect the independence of nine tribes.[4] The British signed agreements with these and other rulers under which the British had exclusive access to the tribal lands in exchange for protection from external attack. The signing of such treaties continued up to 1937, when protectorate status was granted to the whole area.

The British did not always have an understanding of tribal politics. As one official put it,

> Whereas a small family of half destitute goat keepers, the Atafi, were honoured with a full treaty with His Majesty's Government, large and influential fighting tribes such as the Qutaybi, of some three thousand warriors and through whose territory runs a main trade route, had been disregarded.[5]

The tribal leaders bargained for subsidies and stipends, and often arms and ammunition, which they used to persuade their often unruly 'followers' to accept their authority.

The Colonial Office took control of the protectorates in 1927 and Aden in 1937, and the defence of Aden was moved to the Air Ministry, which could use a squadron of aircraft to project the power of Aden to the frontiers with Yemen and, where necessary, into Yemen itself. A new military force, the Aden Protectorate Levies (APL) was raised to replace British Indian troops, who left in 1929. Many of the levies were recruited from the Awlaqi and Awdhali tribes, relatively distant from Aden as well as from the martial Yafi'i, which had provided the main source of troops in Hadhramaut and Hyderabad. The APL was run as a British army unit, and was distinct from the Government Guards – a gendarmerie that garrisoned the scattered forts along the frontier with Yemen and bolstered, when necessary, the tribal guards of the sultans and shaikhs.

During the 1930s, advisory treaties were signed with some rulers requiring them to introduce a more formal administration, set up state councils and improve the lot of the population. Rulers were allowed to recruit small armed forces. British Assistant Advisers were appointed and given delegated authority to secure the peace and ensure free movement along the main routes – a key part of the 1934 agreement with Yemen.

South Arabia in the mid twentieth century: three countries or one?

South Arabia was not a single political entity and did not have many of the attributes of a state. It was an amalgam of three political units held together by the British: Aden Colony, with a population of around 220,000 in 1960; the Western Aden Protectorate (WAP), with an estimated population of up to 600,000, and the Eastern Aden Protectorate, with perhaps 350,000, of which 230,000 were in the al-Qu'ayti and 66,000 in the al-Kathiri sultanates.[6] To understand later developments, it will be helpful to examine the differences between these entities.

Aden: a potential Dubai?

Aden boomed in the Second World War and in the years immediately following it to become the second port in the world, with a financial and support infrastructure equipped to supply the needs of the rapidly expanding population. The management of the port and the shipping business was in the hands of merchants and businessmen, many from British India. A relatively small number of British officials directed policy, while established Aden families played an increasing role in administration and the business sector. After the British abandoned their military base at Suez, they moved the headquarters of Middle East Command to Aden in 1958, and it soon had a garrison of 15,000 troops. Services and supplies to support these troops generated a large number of jobs: 11,640 out of a total labour force of 62,000 worked directly for the British military in 1961. The prospects looked good. Aden had the port, refinery and human skills to become a major city-state, perhaps anticipating Dubai by half a century.

Large numbers of migrants were drawn to Aden. The 1955 census showed that 26.7 per cent of the population were Adeni Arabs and 13.7 per cent were protectorate Arabs, while 34.8 per cent were north Yemenis. The Aden Legislative Council was partly elected under a system that deprived the large populations of Yemeni and protectorate Arab workers of a voice at a time of radical change in the Arab world.

Many critics of British policy acknowledge that it invested in the education of Aden's citizens and took an enlightened attitude to trade unionism and the evolution of local political movements. In 1963, the Aden Trade Union Congress (ATUC) had 22,000 members – one-third of Aden's registered workforce. The unions became increasingly militant and politicized under their largely north Yemeni leaders. Abdullah al-Asnaj from Ta'izz, the main leader of ATUC, remains active in Yemeni politics, albeit from exile in Jeddah.

The Western Aden Protectorate: tribes, amirs, sultans and 'anarchy'

In 1954, the British signed their last advisory treaty. By then Britain had concluded 31 major treaties and around 90 other agreements with entities in South Arabia. Even so, some parts in practice remained 'un-administered' in 1967 (that is, independent entities subject to tribal law, or, as the British sometimes called it, a state of 'anarchy'). There are some excellent accounts by British assistant advisers to show how the system worked right into the 1960s.[7] They bring out the great difficulty that the rulers could have in imposing their authority on the recalcitrant tribes they notionally ruled. Much would depend on the personality of the ruler and the resources at his disposal to buy and retain loyalty and tribes would switch allegiance from one ruler to another. In the 1950s, the imam's agents would compete with Aden for the loyalty of tribesmen, most of whom carried weapons. Progressive ideas were being introduced by the rulers at the behest of British political officers; but it was too little and too late, and the resources available were wholly inadequate. Assistant political officers were locally recruited, as were increasing numbers of agricultural officers, civil servants, clerks and drivers. The expansion of education and services led to the training and recruitment of Arab teachers, medical staff and skilled artisans. Several of these became ministers or senior officials in the PRSY/PDRY.

Migration and the development of education, experience of working in Aden, and the spread of the transistor radio all contributed to an awakening of political consciousness in many parts of the WAP. In the 1950s the tribal rebellions (such as that of the Rabizi in Upper Awlaqi sultanate in 1953) became more persistent and determined. There was an increase in violent incidents in the states bordering Yemen, and problems in the two most developed sultanates of Lahij and Fadhli as the sultans became less willing to listen to Aden and were deposed. Political movements such as the South Arabian League were stirring up rulers and the elites and there were signs of mutiny among the underpaid Aden Protectorate Levies. At this time, Britain reversed its forward policy in the protectorate: the Aden Protectorate Levies were brought back for retraining.

Appendix A gives a brief description of the main tribes of WAP, and Maps A and B show their locations in relation to the provinces or governorates of the PRSY/PDRY. NLF leaders often recruited within their own tribes, or tribes that were traditionally linked to their own. In PRSY/PDRY politics, the same leaders drew on this tribal support in conflicts with each other. Thus, some understanding of the location and size of the pre-1967 entities and tribes is helpful in understanding the political conflicts within the PRSY/PDRY.

The Eastern Protectorate – Hadhramaut and Mahra
Hadhramaut has always been distinct, and for much of the British period seemed a long way from Aden. Farmers in the Wadi Hadhramaut could extract up to three crops a year from its alluvial soils. To the north and

south were the Jawls – highland plateaus cut by wadis, which were the domain of nomadic tribes. To the east, Hadhramaut shaded into the lands of the Mahra province in the PDRY, under the often nominal control of the sultan of Qishn and Socotra, who lived on that island and who spoke a pre-Arabic, unwritten language.

The Hadhramaut had long supported an urban population living in multi-storey mud-brick buildings, notably in the cities of Shibam, Saiyun and Tarim. The Sayyid (*pl.* Saada) families, claiming descent from the family of the Prophet Muhammad, who had migrated into Yemen in previous centuries, had had an almost aristocratic status in the rigidly layered society of this region. The Saada (more often called Hashimi or Ashraf in the YAR) were found all over Yemen, but outside Hadhramaut their prestige was more limited and reflected their roles as men of learning and mediators in tribal disputes. Their high status in Hadhramaut carried into the PDRY, where several leading political figures were Saada. Even the left-wing Abd al-Fattah Isma'il came from a Sayyid family in north Yemen. There was an important religious centre at Tarim, and a much stronger sense of nationalism among the Saada. A high level of migration from the eighteenth century saw the establishment of Hadhrami communities in Indonesia, Singapore, India and East Africa, and later Saudi Arabia. Unlike other Yemeni migrants, the Hadhramis were often well educated people and made their mark – particularly in business – in their adopted homes. The Hadhrami community in Hyderabad, one of the most populous and wealthy of the Indian states, had a particular influence on the politics of Hadhramaut, to which many returned after making their fortunes. Another two features that were important later was the use of Yafi'i tribesmen as mercenaries, notably by the Nizam of Hyderabad, and the role played by Yafi'i and Awlaqi individuals in the politics of Hadhramaut. Estimates speak of 100,000 migrant Hadhramis (perhaps as much as a quarter of the population) who in the 1930s sent remittances of over £650,000 back home – perhaps a minimum of £32 million in today's prices.[8]

The al-Kathiri family, who were of Yafi'i origin, had conquered most of the region in the fifteenth century to establish a sultanate based in Saiyun, but it slowly collapsed and was challenged by the al-Qu'ayti, another Yafi'i family that had accumulated a large fortune in India in the nineteenth century. Fighting between the al-Kathiri and al-Qu'ayti reached a point that threatened to draw in the Ottomans from Yemen. The British intervened in the late 1880s when they helped the al-Qu'ayti to secure the coast and a protectorate agreement swiftly followed in 1888. For much of the twentieth century the British worked well with the al-Qu'ayti sultans, who had a relatively efficient administration. Just as the Sultan of Lahij was an important and usually trusted British ally in the West, so was the al-Qu'ayti sultan in the East.

The British left alone the much weaker al-Kathiri sultanate until 1918, when they persuaded the sultan to place himself under the nominal control of the al-Qu'ayti sultan and sign a Protectorate agreement. But the al-Kathiri, with little income of their own, continued to have difficulties in imposing their control, and had to contend with wealthy returning migrants with ambitions of their own. Both sultans faced acute problems in maintaining law and order within the Wadi Hadhramaut and the unsettled areas beyond, where life was bedevilled by tribal and clan disputes.

In 1936 a British political officer, Harold Ingrams, was sent to the area to assist the al-Qu'ayti and al-Kathiri rulers and their wealthy and highly influential adviser Sayyid Bubakr al-Kaff to persuade tribesmen to sign a series of truces to end the endemic warfare and chaos. Ingrams' Peace, as it was called, eventually spread to the whole Wadi and the surrounding tribal areas. This helped pave the way for the signing of an advisory treaty in 1937 with the al-Qu'ayti sultan, under which Ingrams was appointed as Britain's first Resident Adviser in Mukalla. The state's finances were put on a modern footing, while there were reforms to the education system and improvements in agriculture. The Resident Adviser created an important force under his direct control. This was the Hadhrami Bedouin Legion (HBL), modelled on the Arab Legion in Jordan, which helped the British to reach out into the remotest parts of the region. It had around 1,000 men in the mid 1960s.

Hadhramaut and Mukalla prospered: the British-encouraged development helped keep the peace and worked through existing local systems. Political parties emerged in Mukalla, but none challenged the status quo. Some were influenced by a movement (known as Irshadi) that had developed mainly within the new merchant classes in Southeast Asia, and challenged the predominance of the Saada. Underneath, however, Arab nationalist ideas were spreading and eroding the support base of the sultans. From the 1950s, Hadhrami merchants who had prospered in Saudi Arabia displaced the influence of those in the Far East.

International politics and events in north Yemen
Yemen in the mid twentieth century came under the influence of developments in a rapidly changing international political environment. The single most important of these was the rise of Gamal Nasser, who overthrew the

Egyptian monarch in 1952 and ruled Egypt until his death in 1970. He was determined to expel the British from the Middle East and his early success at Suez, the fall of the Iraqi regime and Egypt's union with Syria in 1958 won him enormous prestige. His command of the airwaves via the ubiquitous transistor radio gave his Arab nationalism and his calls for Arab unity the power to reach Aden and then the two protectorates.

On 26 September 1962, shortly after succeeding to the throne, Imam Badr was overthrown by a group of nationalist army officers led by Abdullah al-Sallal. The Egyptians rushed to support this shaky regime as resistance to it among major tribal forces threatened its survival. Within a few months some 15,000 Egyptian troops had arrived, and by the end of the following year there were over 30,000, rising to around 60,000 in 1965. The Saudis supported the tribal and other groups backing the imam – the 'royalists' – in a prolonged civil war. The Egyptians were able to dominate only limited areas around Sana'a, and the little progress they made elsewhere came at a high cost to Egypt's treasury and its men. However, Nasser was determined to throw the British out of Aden, and supported emerging nationalist groups in the south through propaganda, the provision of arms and money, and the training of fighters. This policy continued even after the British announced they were leaving – he wanted them humiliated. Yemen renewed its ambition to influence and then control the south, even if for much of the next few years it did so with an Egyptian accent.

The coup in Sana'a was greeted with jubilation by nationalists in the south, who saw it as the removal of an impediment to unity.

Towards federation

By the mid 1950s it was clear that Britain could no longer operate on the basis of its treaties with a series of scarcely viable entities. It needed a stable and coherent political unit that could cordon off Aden from the new forces in the Arab world. The idea of federation, first put forward to the rulers at a meeting in 1954, was constituted in 1959 from Bayhan, Fadhli, Awlaqi, Dhala, Lower Yafi'i and the Upper Awlaqi shaikhdom. Lahlj, under a new sultan, joined in 1959, while Aqrabi and Dathina followed in 1960, Hawshabi and Shu'ayb in 1963, and Alawi and Lower Awlaqi in 1965. The constitution set up a Supreme Council, consisting of the rulers, who divided the key ministerial posts between themselves and the security forces were reorganized and expanded with the merger of Government Guards and Tribal Guards to form the Federal National al Guards, which had 3,000 men by 1961. The Aden Protectorate Levies became the Federal Regular Army (FRA), with about 4,000 men, and a policy was initiated of 'Arabizing' its officer corps. Part of the Federal National Guard was later joined to the FRA, which by 1967 had around 10,000 men.

Aden joins the Federation
The British wanted Aden and the EAP to be included in the Federation but the al-Qu'ayti and al-Kathiri sultans had little enthusiasm, and had not agreed to it before both sultanates fell to the NLF in 1967. It took some manoeuvring to get Aden into the Federation in 1962. Britain offered a single defence treaty to the new Federation, and a promise of eventual independence; but there was widespread criticism of the move in Aden. The Federation was treated with disdain by the Arab League and the UN General Assembly, while the Arab nationalists set out to bring it down. Although being a member-state of the Federation, Aden remained a crown colony, in a Janus-like split identity that was impossible to sustain.

Meanwhile, the British were expanding their military base in Aden, making their previous promises of independence look decidedly unreal. Britain was gathering its allies in South Arabia into a Federation, but in doing so was stimulating Federation-wide opposition. It was in the middle of all this, in September 1962, that the revolution in north Yemen took place, bringing Britain's Egyptian *bête noire* to the borders of the new Federation that Nasser was determined to bring down. There were strikes, political demonstrations and growing violence as public opinion swung towards the nationalists. The next four years of turmoil and revolt showed the fragility of the Federation, and the emptiness of British policy in South Arabia.

Nationalist and opposition movements in Yemen in the 1960s
At the time that Aden joined the Federation, the main organized opposition groups were still mostly based in Aden.[9] The NLF was set up only in 1963, and was not seen as a major force in South Arabia until 1965. Unlike the other groups, it based much of its activity in WAP sultanates.

The South Arabian League (SAL) – formed in 1952 from the Union of Sons of the South, which had been set up two years earlier – did seek a South Arabia–wide membership. It attracted support in Aden, Lahij and Hadhramaut, but failed to make much impact elsewhere. Qahtan al-Sha'bi, the first leader of the NLF, had been a leading figure in SAL. In the 1960s it became a recipient of Saudi political and financial support, and re-emerged in Aden at the end of the 1980s. The United National Front split from SAL in the mid 1950s. It called for union between Aden and the WAP, as well as unity between the two Yemens after getting rid of the sultans. It aimed to recruit members among Adenis and workers from the WAP. It provided the first Federal prime minister, the able Hassan al-Bayumi, but faded away in the turbulent politics of the mid 1960s.

The most important group was the People's Socialist Party (PSP). This was founded in 1962 and was the political arm of the Aden Trade Union Congress. It was led by Abdullah al-Asnaj and Abd al-Qawi Makkawi, who was chief minister of Aden in 1965 for a few months. It drew most of its support from immigrant communities from Yemen and WAP. It called for free general elections based on universal suffrage, and wanted the Federal and Aden councils dissolved and the British base to be evacuated. In the first two years after its foundation, it dominated Aden politics. However, it failed to build up an organization of support outside Aden, and its pretension to speak for the whole of south Yemen – though taken seriously by the increasingly desperate British – was soon proved to be hollow. Unlike its main rival, the NLF, the PSP relied more on political protest than violence.

With Egyptian support, the PSP evolved into the Front for the Liberation of South Yemen (FLOSY), but it was never clear how involved FLOSY was in the terrorism that was increasingly used against the British and the Federation. It had set up the Popular Organization of Revolutionary Forces (PORF), recruited mainly from former NLF fighters, but it soon found itself fighting for FLOSY against the NLF for control of the streets of Aden. After 1967, FLOSY was the most significant opponent of the NLF from offices and bases in Saudi Arabia and Yemen in the 1970s and 1980s, and Abdullah al-Asnaj was a minister in several Yemen Arab Republic governments in this period.

The final days of South Arabia

The downfall of the Federation, and the departure of the British after 129 years in Aden, came quite quickly as the tide of events turned against them. There had been major changes in London as a Labour government replaced a Conservative one, and had to wrestle with the economic crisis that led to a devaluation of sterling in 1967. The financial and political costs of staying in South Arabia became too high. The start of the final phase came to be seen in retrospect by the NLF as 14 October 1963 (the day from which the NLF dates its revolution), when the Qutaybi tribes in Radfan protested at their mistreatment by the Amir of Dhala (whose authority they had rarely recognized), blocking the main route to the north and firing on troops seeking to set up a fort. This rapidly escalated into a major incident. It is not clear whether the NLF inspired the move or exploited it,[10] but it played into its hands and became something of a legend, known as the Radfan campaign fought by the 'Red Wolves of Yemen'. It was suppressed with some difficulty, using first regular British forces and then Special Forces, and went on to inspire revolts elsewhere. The NLF, which was able to draw on the backing provided in Yemen and by Egyptian Intelligence, believed that a direct violent struggle against the British and its South Arabian allies was the only means of achieving independence.

During 1964 there was an abortive Constitutional Conference held in London and after its failure the British government in November 1964 confirmed that it would evacuate Aden in 1968, retaining its military base and handing over power to the Federation. This was an open invitation to opposition groups to fight the Federation and each other for power.

Following an escalation of violence, Aden was placed under direct British rule. Abdullah al-Asnaj and other PSP leaders were jailed. The NLF attacked Special Branch officers, and later singled out middle-ranking officials for assassination, as well as Adenis and others associated with the British. Public opinion turned increasingly against the British and the Federal leaders. These events helped finally to persuade the British that they should abandon Aden with some order and dignity, hoping they could leave behind a relatively stable government that they might be prepared to support. This did not inspire much confidence among Britain's allies and associates, and the institutions of South Arabia quickly began to crumble. FLOSY and the NLF had to cooperate or fight each other and the now much stronger NLF chose the latter. The June War of 1967 saw the humiliation of the Egyptians by the Israelis, and ended Egypt's presence in north Yemen and its influence in the south. But the damage had already been done to the British structures, which collapsed within months.

The British withdrew from the old WAP in June 1967, and the NLF quickly took over the sultanates, amirates and shaikhdoms. In Hadhramaut, the NLF infiltrated the institutions of the sultanates and their armed forces, and managed to take over with little violence, helped by the absence of the two sultans, who were in Geneva for discussions with the UN. The situation in Aden became increasingly precarious as officers of the FRA and police moved towards the NLF, and the Federation was approaching breakdown.

FLOSY and the NLF now fought each other in Lahij and for control of the streets of Aden. By early November FLOSY had been decisively defeated, and the NLF signalled on 11 November that it was ready for talks with the British. These negotiations were held in Geneva from 21 to 29 November and on 30 November the last British forces left, and the country became the PRSY.

Civil war in north Yemen

Like the imams they succeeded, the republicans viewed the south as part of Yemen. The revolution of 26 September 1962 had been a momentous event, overthrowing an imamate that had existed more or less continuously since the ninth century. The coup immediately split the country; many in the Zaydi north opposed the revolution, and the Shafi'i south supported it – though, as always in Yemen, there were divisions within both communities. It quickly drew in volunteers from Yemenis in Aden and some of the protectorate tribes. The 60,000 Egyptian troops in the Sana'a district protected the regime and helped it keep the northern cities. Elsewhere the royalists, backed by the Saudis, were in control, with the British providing covert support.[11] The country remained divided and at war until a ceasefire was agreed between Nasser and King Faysal of Saudi Arabia in August 1965. Egypt's defeat in the 1967 June War led to the evacuation of its forces and paved the way for a more direct settlement of differences between Yemeni forces – now with many shades of opinion on both the republican and royalist sides. A bloodless coup saw the departure of al-Sallal in November 1967, and at the end of the year royalist forces besieged Sana'a for what became known as the 'seventy days'.

Many were surprised when the NLF opted for independence and did not immediately join itself to the north.[12] It had not had time to prepare itself to govern the south, and had no intention of rushing into unity. The NLF leaders wanted to impose their ideologies on the north and not become a province of a country that, in a famous phrase at the time, was 'rushing headlong into the thirteenth century'. But what was the NLF, and who were their leaders?

2

THE NATIONAL LIBERATION FRONT TAKES POWER

In the 1950s the Arab world was a ferment of ideologies and movements competing for adherents among peoples traumatized by the failure of Arab governments in 1948 to defeat Israel, and resentful of the influence of the West on their rulers. Arab nationalists wanted to destroy the old order and restore the Arab world to its past greatness. The region's ideologies were mostly secular. The Muslim Brotherhood had been in existence since the 1920s, but failed to identify with the nationalism of those years. The Cold War was at its height, as was the battle of ideas between West and East.

Nasserism, through the new transistor radio, reached the remotest parts of South Arabia. It found a ready audience in Aden among the tens of thousands of disenfranchised migrants from north Yemen and the protectorates. It resonated with those demanding an end to British rule and the overthrow of 'puppet' rulers in the protectorates. Nasserism shook the foundations of regimes in the 1950s, and there was widespread rejoicing when Syria and Egypt formed the United Arab Republic (UAR) in 1958, joining with Yemen to form the United Arab States in the same year. Nasserism was clearly against Western imperialism, but it was not clear what else it represented. Syria's secession from the UAR in 1961 was due to its suspicion that Nasserism could mean the creation of an Arab nation dominated by Egypt.

The Ba'ath Party, with its slogan of 'Nationalism, Unity and Socialism', established a foothold in both Yemens in the late 1950s through the Popular Vanguard Party (al-Tali'a), and made some headway in recruiting the students, teachers and intellectuals that formed its ranks elsewhere. Al-Tali'a was an Aden-based party, and failed to establish an effective presence in the protectorates, except briefly and weakly in Hadhramaut. It sometimes competed, and occasionally cooperated, with the PSP, as Abdullah al-Asnaj flirted with Ba'athism. Al-Tali'a was a minor force that eventually cooperated with the NLF, and became part of the Yemeni Socialist Party in 1978. The PDRY Ba'ath was closer to the Syrian party when divisions opened up between the Ba'ath regimes in Iraq and Syria in the 1960s and 1970s. The Ba'ath in the north was more often fighting the regime than cooperating with it, and in the 1970s it became identified with the Iraqi party.

Communism had some appeal because of its anti-Western associations. The south Yemeni version was the People's Democratic Union (PDU) led by Abdullah Abd al-Razzaq Ba Dhib, who became minister of education in PDRY. It emerged in the 1950s, operating initially through front organizations, and Ba Dhib was for a time a member of the South Arabian League. The PDU itself was set up in 1960, but its leaders concluded that it could never appeal to the masses in South Arabia and should thus cooperate with more populist movements to overthrow the colonial regime. Other emerging parties in the country kept the PDU at a distance but the NLF had great respect for Ba Dhib himself and PDU ideology had an important influence on some NLF leaders. The PDU, like al-Tali'a joined with the NLF in the 1970s to form what eventually became the Yemeni Socialist Party.

The ideas that inspired those founding the NLF came from the Movement of Arab Nationalists (MAN), which had been set up, in the wake of the 1948 defeat by Israel, by George Habbash, later leader of the Popular Front for the Liberation of Palestine (PFLP), Nayif Hawatmah, later leader of the Popular Democratic Front for the Liberation of Palestine (PDFLP), Muhsin Ibrahim, and others. In the early 1950s Arab unity was the overriding goal, but could only be achieved by destroying existing regimes to allow new vanguard parties to rebuild society. From the outset, MAN established a secretive cell structure and strong internal discipline, requiring members to obey orders from the leadership without question. It was a small, tight-knit organization with a focus on gaining power first in one Arab country and then the rest and its simple and disciplined approach had a powerful appeal to some students in the 1950s, mainly at universities in Beirut and Cairo. From the seeds planted there, it set up cells in several Arab countries, though at heart it remained mostly a Palestinian movement.

South and north Yemeni students studying in Cairo were attracted to MAN's credo. Faysal Abd al-Latif al-Sha'bi may have been the first southerner to join MAN in Cairo, in the mid 1950s. His fifth cousin – Qahtan al-Sha'bi, the first leader of the NLF – was broadcasting anti-British statements from Cairo Radio in the late 1950s. They helped set up the first MAN cell in the Shaikh Othman suburb of Aden in 1959, operating within the

Aden Cultural Club. Early members included Ali Ahmad al-Sallami, Taha Muqbil, Sayf al-Dhala'i, Abd al-Fattah Isma'il, Salim Zayn, Muhammad Ali Haytham and Ali Nasir Muhammad.[1] Today, Faysal al-Sha'bi is looked upon by his former colleagues as the most influential figure in the formation of MAN and the NLF.

The cells initially followed the advice of the central MAN leadership, who saw south Yemen as representing a 'golden opportunity' to establish its first regime.[2] MAN set up cells in the Aden refinery where Abd al-Fattah Isma'il was employed, and at Aden College, which by then was taking students from all over South Arabia. It used its recruits among protectorate Arabs in Aden to establish cells in their home areas. MAN's cells in the wider Arab region recruited Yemenis working in other Arab countries. There was an active branch in Kuwait, where Ali Antar and Ali Shaya Hadi were recruited.[3] By 1962 there was a substantial structure, though it remained secretive and underground. It recruited women, several of whom played a part in the fight for independence. Its mission was to get rid of the British and the rulers, and establish an independent regime under its control. MAN cells in north Yemen worked closely with those in the south, and agreed that the key to success in the south lay in first overthrowing the imam in the north, though that was ultimately achieved by Nasserist army officers.

MAN itself started to disintegrate in the 1960s as divisions emerged among its Palestinian founders that led to its splitting into the PFLP and the more left-wing PDFLP. The PDFLP leader Nayif Hawatmah believed that it was essential to change society from within as a prerequisite to Arab unity, and his followers used an increasingly Marxist language. These divisions spread to Yemen, though they were partially stifled in the focus on fighting for power. In the pre-independence period, the MAN leadership in the south was closer to Habbash, and that in the north to Hawatmah but following the triumph of the left wing within the NLF after independence, Hawatmah personally took a great interest in the independence struggle in south Yemen, and became a mentor to the NLF before and after independence. Habbash also maintained close personal contacts with the NLF leaders.

It was the revolution of 26 September 1962 in north Yemen that gave MAN the opportunity for which it had been waiting. Both MAN and the Egyptians had a common interest in throwing the British out of the south and the new YAR regime shared the long-held view of the northern elite, whether royalist or republican, that the south was a part of Yemen and, thus should be liberated.

MAN now had a potential base from which to operate, and the support of Egyptian forces and intelligence in arming and training its fighters. The armed struggle in the south could start.[4] But first MAN would need to persuade a number of small organizations, some MAN-inspired and others not, to form a united group. Qahtan and Faysal Abd al-Latif arrived in the north in 1962, and Qahtan was soon appointed an adviser on south Yemeni affairs to the new regime and its Egyptian allies. In November 1962 the Egyptians announced the formation of a national liberation army to free the south, headed by Qahtan.[5]

The formation of the NLF

The first steps in setting up the NLF were taken in March 1963, with the creation of the Front for the Liberation of Occupied South Yemen at a large conference in Sana'a.[6] The foundation of this organization was not announced until May 1963, a few months after Aden had joined the Federation. An eleven-man politburo was set up that included Qahtan al-Sha'bi.[7] A national charter was agreed, built around MAN ideology and calling for a fight against colonialists and the Federation. It stressed the goal of Yemeni unity, and saw the creation of a nationalist regime in the south as providing a base for national struggles elsewhere in the Arab world. In August 1963, at a second and better-organized conference, the name of the organization was changed to the National Front for the Liberation of Occupied South Yemen – the NLF. There was a twelve-person leadership, of which six members were said to be from MAN and six from 'tribes'. The most prominent names were Qahtan al-Sha'bi, Faysal Abd al-Latif al-Sha'bi, Abd al-Fattah Isma'il, Sayf al-Dhala'i, Ali Salami, Salim Zayn and Taha Muqbil.

A number of different groups, mostly dominated by MAN, became part of the NLF either at that time or shortly afterwards. Little is known about them, but they seem to have been involved in some small-scale anti-British and anti-Federation activities after the September 1962 revolution. They included:

1) The Yafi'i Front for Reconciliation, probably a MAN organization based on Yafi'i working in Aden, which tried to persuade the fractious Yafi'i tribes to cooperate with each other in the fight for freedom.
2) The Patriotic (Nationalist) Front, which was made up of MAN and PSP members. The PSP enjoyed some support among north Yemeni ministers at the time. It was led by Abd al-Qadir al-Amin.

3) The Formation of the Tribes. This was the name given to a group fighting in Radfan.
4) The Nasserist Front.[8]
5) The Revolutionary Organization of Occupied South Yemen.
6) The Secret Organization of Free Officers and Soldiers – said to have been made up of Yemenis who had fought in the Saudi armed forces.[9]
7) The Aden Organization of the Revolutionary Vanguard.
8) The Mahra Youth Organization, which was apparently one of the first steps in bringing that distant province firmly into the fold.
9) The Revolutionary Organization of the Youth of Occupied South Yemen.

Salim Salih Muhammad, who eventually became Deputy Secretary of the YSP, says that he and other prominent Yafi'i including Muhammad Salih Muti'a and Fadhl Muhsin Abdullah belonged to the 'Free Revolutionary Movement of Occupied South Yemen Liberals'. He also remembers that there was a Hadhramaut National Front.[10] There was also a Yafi'i Reform club which evolved from organizations originally founded in the diaspora.[11]

Membership was open to anyone believing in the armed struggle. Talks were held with the Ba'ath and the PSP, but although they prepared to cooperate with the NLF, they wanted to remain independent. An attempt to unite with the PSP in 1964 came to nothing, because the PSP wanted half the seats in the leadership.[12]

The NLF adopted the cell structure and organization of MAN, as well as its internal discipline. There was little discussion of ideology at this early stage; liberation had to come first through armed struggle. The NLF leaders believed that fighting was a means of improving the solidarity of a downtrodden people. A few also saw it as exploiting the tribes' natural aversion to outsiders.[13]

The NLF started to plan its campaign almost immediately and the Yemeni government allowed it to open an office in Ta'izz to set up camps and to broadcast to the south. The Egyptians may have preferred the more Nasserist PSP, but they appreciated that the NLF was a viable guerrilla organization, and provided money, arms and training as part of Egypt's wider struggle with the British, who were giving covert support to its enemies in the north. Cairo's backing was a major factor in enabling the NLF to achieve its objectives in such a short time.

14 October 1963: the revolution begins

The NLF dated the start of its campaign for liberation to 14 October 1963, and Yemenis today still celebrate the revolutions of 26 September 1962 and 14 October 1963. This is the day that the disaffected Qutaybi tribe launched what the British called the Radfan campaign. The Qutaybi had obtained arms from Yemen, and had a charismatic leader called Rajih Labuzah. Other tribes joined the battle in the very difficult terrain of Radfan, and it took a major British operation lasting several months to crush it.[14] Ali Antar played a leading role in the rebellion after the death of Labuzah, and was certainly active in Radfan before it started. The British followed up their military success with an energetic attempt to address problems in the region, but this proved to be a first step in losing the war.

The NLF's fighting abilities developed quickly, first in the Federation (there were soon attacks in Lower Yafi'i sultanate, Dathina, Awdhali and others parts of Dhala and Lahij) and in Aden, from August 1964. Operatives received training in camps in Yemen mostly from Egyptian intelligence and were organized into small squads that were often tribally based, and were supplied with intelligence on targets in the early stages by the Egyptians. From the outset, the NLF appreciated the need to persuade tribes to desist from pursuing local vendettas and turn their aggression against their rulers and the British. PDRY leaders later spoke of their ideological conquest of peoples' minds, but at the time many of the participants were fighting for material and often local interests as the NLF proved skilful at exploiting local and sometimes personal grievances. NLF cells were set up in most parts of WAP, giving the organization a good understanding of the politics of the various individual sultanates and ammunition to exploit local grievances to promote their cause and it also proved adept at solving local tribal disputes.

Support for the NLF developed rapidly in Aden, with the majority of its members and much of its leadership in their twenties. In parallel with its fighting forces, the NLF expanded its recruitment in Aden and elsewhere of cadres that were engaged in political and propaganda work. Their mission was to build up the NLF's cell structures, penetrate organizations such as the ATUC and appeal to students and workers who might otherwise be attracted to the PSP.[15] The NLF fighters in Aden were trained in urban terror tactics, and many of the leaders not only organized terrorist groups but took part in operations themselves. The way that the NLF virtually eliminated the leadership of the Aden Special Branch by assassinating its senior officers showed its ruthlessness, as well as its effectiveness. Violence was an everyday tactic, and it was not surprising that some of those involved who later became senior figures in the PRSY and PDRY started to use such methods against south Yemeni opponents, and then each other.

Despite this, it took the British some time to appreciate the nature of the threat posed by the NLF. It was not banned until June 1965, and even after then there was much uncertainty about its true strength and abilities. A British government paper written in 1977 tried to answer the question of how the NLF had taken power:

> The answer lies in the fact that the NLF alone had firm roots in the tribal hinterland. Also its aims were far more radical than those of other nationalist groups. The early leaders of the NLF planned not simply to bring about the withdrawal of the British presence but to break down the entire tribal structure of the protectorates, destroy the Sultan system on which the South Arabian Federation was being constructed and create a classless, disciplined society out of the ashes. Their ideas did not originate at the LSE, nor were they trained by other Middle Eastern radical groups. Their thinking was very direct and unsophisticated and reflected their extreme youth and ignorance of the outside world. What they lacked in sophistication they made up for in ruthlessness and willingness to fight long, hard and if necessary dirty.[16]

As the NLF developed, so its relationship with the Egyptians changed. It opened an office in Cairo in August 1964 to deal with the Egyptian government, the Arab League and other Arab governments, who reacted positively to its call for financial aid and support. When, in November 1965, Nasser and King Faysal agreed a ceasefire in north Yemen, the NLF saw this as a betrayal of the nationalist cause. From then on, the NLF leaders began to distinguish between the Egyptian president, whom they professed to admire, and the different agenda of the Egyptian army and intelligence organizations. Abdullah al-Asnaj believed that the Egyptians preferred FLOSY, and ideally wanted a single united movement. But they continued to back both FLOSY and the NLF, assuming that if one did not win, then the other would.[17]

Early organizational and operational problems
In 1965 there were the first signs of differences within the leadership that were to come to a head in the PRSY. These are usually described as the external (later known as the 'right') and internal (sometimes called

'secondary' or the 'left') leaderships, which were affected by their respective roles and by the divisions that had by then broken out in MAN all over the Arab world. The right was based partly in Cairo, where it had to deal directly with the Egyptian government and its various arms, as well as with the Arab League and other Arab governments. It understood that its Arab friends wanted both unity within the liberation movement in south Yemen and a close marriage between the military and political struggles.

Qahtan al-Sha'bi, who was then in his mid forties and nearly 20 years older than the internal leaders, already had a significant profile in South Arabian politics and had been an early member of the South Arabian League. Closely allied to him was the able and popular Faysal Abd al-Latif al-Sha'bi, who had been secretary to the president of the Board of Trade in Aden. They were from a family of Saada in the Subayhi district in Lahij. Qahtan was from a more paternalistic age than the younger cadres in the country, and both Faysal and he understood the international environment in which the NLF had to operate, and learned from watching other regimes that effective government required a degree of pragmatism.

The most influential figure on the left-wing leadership was Abd al-Fattah Isma'il, the north Yemeni leader of the fighters in Aden. He and his colleagues argued that the NLF must develop economic and social policies that would attract mass support. They were moving in a Marxist direction and were influenced by the ideas and philosophies of other successful liberation movements, and, unlike Qahtan and his cousin, they had no interest in any cooperation with the sultans or traditional elites. They assessed their relationship with the Egyptians and other Arabs according to what they could do to support the fight for independence and power.

These divisions between the right and the left leaderships were not always clear-cut. Some on the right, for example, found Qahtan too authoritarian. Ali Nasir Muhammed, one of the three men to dominate south Yemeni politics, and Mohammad al-Haytham, who became prime minister in 1969, switched allegiance from Qahtan because of his leadership style. The north Yemeni branch of MAN split, with the majority supporting the left, thus causing difficulties in relations with Qahtan and his friends. Ordinary NLF combatants such as Muhammad Ali Ahmad (who became a leading figure in PDRY politics in the 1980s) recalled that he only thought about liberation and nationalism; Marxism meant nothing to him or his colleagues in Abyan.[18]

The First National Congress and the National Charter

By mid 1965 there were pressures within the NLF for it to define what it would do when it achieved power; there was also a need for it to look at its own organization. Several structures had developed to meet specific requirements, but there was a lack of coordination between them. The NLF had to find the right balance between the political need for tight discipline and the operational one of allowing some freedom to local groups to mount their own actions against the British and the Federal government.

The first National Congress was held in June in Jiblah, in north Yemen, to resolve some of these issues. It was the only significant Congress in the area of policy development before independence: the second and third Congresses, held in 1966, dealt with the NLF's relationship with the PSP.

It issued a National Charter, which began by affirming that it was the sole representative of the south Yemenis, and that the armed struggle was the only route to victory. The NLF was a front organization that others could join only if they left their ideology behind them. It dismissed some of the ATUC and PSP leaders as being too affected by their bourgeois origins to be close to the people. The NLF wanted to transform society by mobilizing peasants, soldiers, students and intellectuals. Yemeni unity was essential, and represented a step towards Arab unity. It spoke of the backwardness of the sultanates – caused by their exploitation of the people and colonial neglect and discussed the need to raise the economic and social level of the tribal areas. Its economic programme avoided too much Marxist doctrine, and left a place for the private sector, albeit small. But it talked of the nationalization of assets, the ending of the free-port status of Aden, and extensive land reform. It called for the modernization of agriculture and improvements to the lives of people dependent on it. There would be free education and health for all. Its ideas for social transformation included a new role for women, which the NLF later put into practice in government. Islam hardly got a mention.

The Charter was a radical document, but did not yet bear the hallmarks of Marxist ideology that emerged at later Congresses.[19] It was a compromise necessitated by the overriding objective of winning the struggle against the British and their allies, and destroying the Federation. The external leadership had made concessions to the internal leadership in the language and content of the Charter, but both could support it.

The congress set up a National Council with 42 members to act as the NLF's principal policy-making body. An Executive Committee was elected, led by the secretary general of the NLF and the heads of 'bureaus' covering political, information, financial and organizational issues. The

NLF operated within a number of regions (called 'fronts'), which often had their own fighting, political and propaganda bureaus, depending on their size. There was also a separate command of fighters (Fida'iyyun) mostly operating in Aden, led by Abd al-Fattah Isma'il but at times by Ali Salih Ubad (party alias 'Muqbil'), Sultan Ahmad Umar ('Faris') and Abdullah al-Khamiri, who were all later prominent in PDRY politics. A Liberation Army had been formed with about 500 fighters, which included the various fighting units outside Aden and a central reserve that was available to support local groups in organizing large operations. As the campaign developed, the role of the Liberation Army expanded. Ali Antar, with his experience of Radfan, was the first commander, and many of its members were recruited from the Dhala region. The NLF also set up Revolutionary Committees to prevent inter-tribal disputes and provide government, law and order in what the NLF called 'liberated areas'. By 1967 these had become Popular Committees, which took over the running of the sultanates after the old regimes had been overthrown. A People's Guard was recruited from the most dedicated of the NLF members to provide security and, where necessary, to eradicate the NLF's enemies.

The NLF, FLOSY and Egypt

In November 1965, six unions in Aden – oil workers, teachers, port workers, bank staff, construction workers and civil aviation employees – broke away from ATUC and declared for the NLF. Abd al-Fattah Isma'il was working at the BP Refinery and the president of his union was Mahmud Ushaysh, a leading figure in the NLF. The defection of these unions was important in weakening the PSP, and in giving the NLF a political as well as terrorist front in Aden. The PDU was influential in helping to bring about the secession of the six and the PDU's newspaper became one of the NLF's main mouthpieces.

With its growing success and clear influence outside Aden, the NLF came under increasing pressure from the Egyptians and the Arab League to unite with the PSP and its offshoot the Organization for the Liberation of the Occupied South (OLOS) to form FLOSY. The Egyptians knew that the PSP and its allies were strong in Aden but weak in the Federation, and were better at political work than fighting the British. Egyptian priorities in Yemen were changing as they were beginning to look for a way out. A victory for the revolution in the south would allow the Egyptians to withdraw from the stalemate in the north with dignity although they would stay until the British had gone.

The Egyptians wanted to unite the various liberation movements in the south. Some in the north Yemeni regime were becoming worried about the NLF's long-term aims and its links with MAN in the north and preferred the PSP. Both Cairo and Sana'a were aware of the radicalization of the internal leadership of the NLF, and wanted to isolate it before it became too important. Cairo concluded that without a merger between the PSP/OLOS and the NLF, they could end up fighting each other for power as the British withdrew, which would only be to the benefit of the leaders of the Federation.

The Egyptians manoeuvred a very reluctant NLF into an agreement signed in January 1966 by Ali al-Sallami, Salim Zayn and Taha Muqbil (all from the external right wing leadership) to set up FLOSY, a marriage between the NLF and the PSP/OLOS. It was promptly disowned by the internal leadership, and even Qahtan, who was acutely aware of the Arab pressure for unity among the south Yemen movements, objected, calling it a 'forced merger'. It required the intervention of the MAN leaders, who travelled to Ta'izz at Egyptian instigation to persuade the NLF leaders that it was in their wider interests to accept it. The NLF in Aden was vehemently opposed.

Some in the NLF leadership tried to make FLOSY work and there were attempts to get FLOSY to participate more actively in operations against the British.[20] Meanwhile, the internal leadership increased operations in the sultanates and Aden, and launched a campaign to penetrate and convert the recently established Federal Armed Forces, Federal Guards and the police, calculating that it would need their support when, rather than if, it would have to fight FLOSY. There was soon evidence that the NLF was successful and support for the NLF spread rapidly in Aden, with a greater focus on political work. Political education classes started in Aden, in which Abdullah al-Khamiri, a future minister of culture and important NLF theoretician, played an important role. The NLF had started to believe at that stage that it could take power by the end of 1967.

The second NLF Conference took place in June 1966, also at Jiblah, where it endorsed the 'forced merger' but suspended from the Executive Committee those who had signed the agreement. Major divisions emerged between the right and left leaderships, the latter showing an increasing preference for Marxist-style language. It elected a new governing body – the General Leadership – that included Abd al-Fattah Isma'il, Mahmud Ushaysh (who was known as 'S' – his name was not announced at the time), Ahmad Salih al-Sha'ir, Ali Salim al-Bidh, Sayf al-Dhala'i, Muhammad Ahmad al-Bishi, Ali Antar, Faysal al-Attas, Ali Salih Ubad

('Muqbil'), Salim Rubayya Ali ('Salmin'), Muhammad Ali Haytham and Abd al-Malik Isma'il.[21] Most of these new leaders were much more radical in outlook than Qahtan or Faysal Abd al-Latif. Like others on the left in the mid 1960s, the NLF radicals had been reading the works of Fanon, Debray and Guevara, and were admirers of China, Cuba and Vietnam. Fred Halliday points out that NLF leaders holed up in Aden had time to read such tomes.[22] These influences were reflected in the 'the unbridled, narrow-minded doctrinarism, juggling revolutionary phrases' that described many NLF documents of the period.[23]

The leaders agreed that they should prevent the divisions in their ranks from affecting NLF military operations but they were conscious of a growing restiveness in cells in Aden while some of the units operating outside Aden were taking on a strongly local character, and were not always responsive to the leadership's orders.[24] The leaders needed to persuade all cells to focus on liberation and put aside any talk of division. There were also moves to strengthen groups within the NLF that might be needed in any future confrontation with FLOSY.

With the forced merger, the Egyptians stopped supplying arms directly to the NLF. The NLF made preparations for what it called 'self-sustained' operations, which meant using its cells and fighting groups to raise cash by whatever means were necessary.

The end of the forced merger

The merger started to fall apart soon after the Jiblah conference. Opponents of the merger mobilized protests over the arrangements for the first meeting of the FLOSY National Council. One interesting letter of protest (sent to the Egyptian president) was signed by the heads of the various NLF battlefronts.[25] The NLF stepped up its operations in Aden, killing, among others, the British Speaker of the Aden legislative Council. British figures show the increasing number of incidents in Aden: 36 in 1964; 286 in 1965; 510 in 1966 and 2,999 in the first ten months of 1967.[26]

The main weakness of the merger was that the PSP/OLOS and its associates lacked both the NLF's organization outside Aden and its ability to mount major military and terrorist attacks (though the PSP did organize terrorist attacks in Aden and Lahij). PORF was set up to improve OLOS's capacity using mostly former NLF fighters, but it was ineffective and again restricted to Aden. It appears to have been a device of the Egyptians to create a fighting organization that would be more responsive to Egyptian interests than the NLF, which was now out of its control.

The 'coup of 14 October' was a series of protests against the forced merger, and was organized by some Adeni leaders of the NLF.[27] This led to the Third NLF Congress at Humar in north Yemen, in November 1966. The majority wanted the end of the forced merger, but there were many delegates that thought priority should be given to national unity at a time when the British had signalled they would abandon the Federation. These included significant figures such as the right-wing Muhammad Ali Haytham and firebrand leftist Ali Salim al-Bidh. It was the commanders of fighters on the ground in Dhala, Radfan and Shu'ayb who demanded the end of the merger, and carried the day and the NLF announced its withdrawal on 12 December 1966.

There were changes to the Executive Committee which suggested that the power of the left was growing. However, many on the left fully understood that they would need the help of right-wing figures such as the two Sha'bis and Muhammad Ali Haytham to help win over the Federal Armed Forces and keep the NLF united at a time when victory seemed within its grasp. The left could bide its time.

The endgame

With its withdrawal from FLOSY, the NLF stepped up its campaign on all fronts. It recruited many new members and raised cash through robberies and intimidation in Aden. It no longer needed the Egyptians as its terror attacks and political demonstrations increased. Some of its NLF leaders abandoned their secrecy and started appearing in the media outside South Arabia. The movement rapidly penetrated the junior officers and other ranks in the FRA, exploiting tribal differences within the officer corps in which the Awlaqi were over-represented. One British observer noted that the army officers were essentially 'mercenaries' working for the British, adding that 'Lieutenant Colonels were big boys in the army but they were still nobody in their tribal villages and thus had a direct interest, apart from ideology, in getting onto the right side'.[28] The NLF leadership did not trust the army, but the priority in 1967 was to win enough support within its senior ranks to ensure that it would not join the fight against the NLF either for the Federation or for FLOSY.

FLOSY attempted to build up support outside Aden, and had some success in the Subayhi area of Lahij and in the Awlaqi tribal region, but it could not match the NLF's well-established organization. There was fighting between the two organizations in Aden in January, June, September and November. Strikes, protests and demonstrations were virtually daily occurrences, and the number of attacks on the British and their allies increased.

When Humphrey Trevelyan arrived in Aden in May 1967 to organize the British exit, he first saw FLOSY as the party to deal with in his hope of forming a broad-based government. Egypt indicated that it would support FLOSY. Defeat in the June 1967 war with Israel took Egypt out of the equation; but Egyptian claims that the British had supported Israel were widely believed, and made the people of South Arabia much more hostile to the British and in favour of those fighting against them.

Shortly afterwards, as the British pulled out of the hinterland, the NLF overthrew the sultans and shaikhs – sometimes with comparative ease, at other times only after heavy fighting. Dhala and Shu'ayb fell in June. In August, Maflahi, Lahij, Dathina, Awdhali and Abyan were taken over, isolating those areas further to the north. By the end of September the NLF controlled the Bayhan, Wahidi and Awlaqi sultanates. They set up administrations and Peoples' Committees to maintain law and order. There was a de facto NLF 'government' in Abyan.[29] The NLF also took over, through different means, organizations such as the ATUC and soon took virtual control of parts of Aden. In the East, the al-Qu'ayti sultanate succumbed in September, and al-Kathiri in early October. Mahra followed in October, and in the last few days before independence the Awlaqi shaikhdom was finally taken over. By 30 November only Socotra was left, and the NLF landed on the island on that day.[30]

FLOSY had meanwhile been greatly weakened by the Egyptian withdrawal. A conference organized in Cairo in October 1967 to try to heal the rift between FLOSY and the NLF failed. The NLF was just too strong, and was not interested in sharing power in the imminent new regime. On 2 November the British announced that they would leave at the end of the month; the final battles in the war between FLOSY and NLF started in earnest, and within a few days FLOSY had been decisively beaten in Lahij, and then Aden. The FRA declared its support for the NLF on 7 November, its FLOSY officers (mostly Awlaqi) having returned to their home states. On 8 November the NLF stated that it was in full control of the country, and two days later it started acting as a sort of provisional government, issuing its Official Gazette to lay down new laws. A final attempt by a muddled UN team and Arab countries to get FLOSY back in on the act was doomed before it started. The British government announced on 13 November that it would negotiate with the NLF.

Divisions had re-emerged within the NLF in the two months before its final triumph – a portent of what would happen later. The left was pressing for a new NLF Congress to be held before independence. Qahtan rejected this, alienating Abd al-Fattah Isma'il, Khamiri, Ali Salim al-Bidh and others on the left.

The NLF in the Eastern Protectorate

Hadhramaut remained calm until early 1966 – that is, about the time that the UK had said it would not offer a defence agreement to a South Arabian state. The al-Qu'ayti, al-Kathiri and Mahri sultans did not join the Federation. The Commander of the Hadhrami Bedouin Legion was killed in July 1966, apparently by one of his own men. Guerrilla operations by groups linked to the NLF followed, but the attacks did not become serious until May 1967, and the British pulled their staff out at the end of August when the adjoining WAP states started falling to the NLF. At the time the three sultans were in Geneva for meetings with a UN delegation and when they managed to get back to Mukalla by sea, on 17 September 1967, they were turned away by the NLF. (Only the elderly and infirm Mahri sultan was allowed safe passage.)

The MAN developed an organization in Hadhramaut, but it had to compete much more fiercely with the Ba'ath and others. The Hadhramaut was better administered, and had more institutions and a lighter British presence than elsewhere. There were rudimentary political institutions, and there was a greater possibility to organize political groups among a better-educated population. Some political parties were licensed by the authorities in the al-Qu'ayti sultanate. MAN, as elsewhere, generated a number of movements, but it seems to have taken until the mid 1960s for the NLF in Wadi Hadhramaut and Mukalla to start a rapid expansion of its membership and activities. Ali Salim al-Bidh (a Sayyid, like so many of the NLF leaders in Hadhramaut) was a leading figure in the People's Democratic Front (PDF), which emerged from the Arab Socialist Party when it dissolved after being unable to agree on whether or not to support the armed struggle. The PDF leaders and their allies were from the most radical section of the NLF,[31] and set up an administration that, even before the PDRY became independent, implemented some of the ideas that had been discussed much earlier by elements of the internal leadership of the NLF. Land was appropriated and distributed to peasants. There were some small-scale nationalizations. The HBL was replaced by a People's Guard, though the HBL continued to exist until brought into the PRSY armed forces in 1969.

Mahra was also a special case, in that the British presence was light to the point of near absence. It did not include a permanent British adviser until 1963. It fell as soon it was pushed by the NLF. Ali Salim al-Bidh played an important part in the creation of the NLF in Mahra, together with the Mahri Muhammad Salim Akkush.[32]

The NLF started its activity quite late in the EAP. As a result, there were fewer NLF cells and members in Hadhramaut and Mahra than in the WAP. One consequence of this was that these provinces had less influence in the NLF in the early years of an independent south Yemen.

Independence negotiations

The NLF delegation to Geneva to the negotiations which started on 22 November 1967 consisted of Qahtan, Faysal Abd al-Latif, Sayf al-Dhala'i (by then chairman of the NLF's Political Committee), Muhammad Ahmad al-Bishi, Abd al-Fattah Isma'il, Khalid Muhammad Abd al-Aziz, Abdullah Salih al-Awlaqi and nine advisers, including a major from the HBL. The British found that the NLF had prepared itself professionally, and conducted the negotiations in a surprisingly cordial atmosphere. Qahtan and Sayf al-Dhala'i did most of the talking, but treated Abd al-Fattah Isma'il, who said little, with great respect. They were impressed by Faysal al-Sha'bi and the delegation's military advisers, and surprised to find several people whom they had thought were loyal to them in the NLF's delegation. It was clear that both sides wanted the agreement concluded as soon as possible, with the deadline of 30 November helping to concentrate their minds.

There was a major disagreement over the future status of the Kuria Muria Islands, which the British had returned to, in their view, their rightful owner, the Sultan of Oman, but which the NLF regarded as Yemeni. The NLF not only expected the British to honour a promise of aid made to the Federal government, but to double the amount. The British, facing financial problems at home and a public and political distaste for helping a group that had been killing British citizens, was in no mood to agree. The British promised £12 million in aid for the first six months, after which the two sides would negotiate a further aid package. But there was a string attached: the new regime would pay the pensions of civil servants working for the Federation. Diplomatic relations were to be established. The NLF promised not to interfere with the British withdrawal and to protect any foreigners who decided to remain behind, as well as those the British lacked the means to evacuate. It agreed that a small British military advisory team would stay on. FLOSY fighters in British custody were flown out.

Qahtan al-Sha'bi flew into Aden on 30 November in an aircraft that avoided a stop in Egypt. In the words of Trevelyan, 'The People's Republic of Yemen was born, without friends, with only a promise of temporary aid and with indigenous resources to meet no more than a third of the previous level of expenditure.'

The NLF had won the battle to control an independent South Arabia only four and half years after its foundation. The British were leaving a country where they had been present for 129 years, but, in the words of Trevelyan had done 'little permanent good'.[33] The NLF had caught the tide of history and events: the revolution in Yemen, the practical support from Egypt, the mood of nationalism sweeping the Arab world, and Britain's declining ability or will to maintain a costly presence. The British had always regarded Aden as the chief prize, albeit for different reasons at different times. For most of the British period, enough was done to prevent any threat to Aden emerging from the hinterland or Yemen. But it was the British failure to invest in modernizing in the hinterland that gave the NLF the opportunity to turn what had been Aden's protection into its Achilles' heel.

3

FROM PRSY TO PDRY VIA THE GLORIOUS CORRECTIVE MOVE

Independence was proclaimed on 30 November 1967 by the General Command of the Political Organization of the National Front – or the National Front (NF), as it would call itself from now on. The NF took over a state that had barely existed and an economy that had collapsed; there was no central government or constitution. When the British and the sultans departed, many civil servants, businessmen and others left, as did large numbers of FLOSY supporters. The treasury was empty and the British subsidies had ceased. The closure of the Suez Canal in June had cut the number of ships using Aden by 75 per cent, while the British military base, which had an important source been of direct and indirect employment, had gone. Those banks and businesses that were left had lost most of their staff. Up to 200,000 people left Aden; 20,000 had lost their jobs as a result of the closure of the base. There were few resources outside Aden, Lahij and Abyan. As one observer said, 'it is wrong to think of [this] as an undeveloped territory since the indications are that there is very little to develop'.[1] GNP fell by 15 per cent in 1968, and again in 1969.

The NF was composed of 3,000 to 4,000 people and had existed for only four and a half years. Few of its leaders, who, apart from Qahtan, were in their late twenties and early thirties, had received a higher education and none had experience of government. 'They placed too much trust in the Marxist–Leninist formulae they had espoused in the last stages of the struggle when this meant no more than a critique of Nasserism.'[2] They were intent on building a new society, and did not suffer from any lack of confidence in their capacity to govern.

The new country faced a number of other difficulties internally and internationally. First, the often bitter divisions within the NF between the right and the left had not been resolved. A PDRY government paper published after the bloody events of January 1986 acknowledged the problems:

'Independence brought the class struggle into even greater focus. The NLF was split into a "right" stream satisfied with political independence and not at all inclined to change anything in the country, and a "radical left" that wanted to push ahead with social and economic transformation, serving the broad toiling masses rather than the privileged few.'[3]

Second, the civil service, army and police had been expanded in the last years of British rule. Though many in these organizations were sympathetic to the NF, the army in particular was clearly a potential threat. Abdullah al-Asnaj has said that the deciding factor in the struggle between FLOSY and the NLF[4] had been the army's support for the latter. However, it was far from certain whether or not the army would respond to NF directives. The army leadership viewed the Liberation Army and People's Guards, created by the NF, with suspicion. NF leaders feared the possibility of a military coup and the British ambassador predicted there would be one.

Third, FLOSY and SAL had not given up the struggle. There was an incident attributed to FLOSY in the first few days of independence at Mansurah, near Aden. Some groups were talking to the Saudi government about support, conditions in the YAR were chaotic, and the NF's clear support for the Dhufari rebels was unlikely to appease the Omani government, dependent on British support. The first attacks from across the Yemeni and Saudi borders came within three months of independence.

Fourth, the struggle in the YAR continued. The royalists seized the opportunity of the Egyptian withdrawal to attack and Sana'a was under siege from December for what became a legendary 'seventy days'. Aden sent fighters to help lift the siege, working with the north Yemeni MAN, but the royalists were able to continue fighting the republican regime for several more months. The republican movement split, and there was bitter fighting between rival factions in the summer of 1968. It was the right wing that eventually won in the north, leading to difficulties in its relations with the south, which had supported the left. FLOSY had a substantial presence in Ta'izz and Sana'a, which the Yemeni regime could use when convenient to put pressure on the south.

Fifth, Arab regimes gave PRSY a frosty reception. They had backed FLOSY, and had been disappointed at the NF's rejection of Arab League and Egyptian efforts to merge the two organizations. Saudi Arabia was hostile, and some in the PRSY feared that Saudi Arabia aimed at detaching Hadhramaut from the rest of the country.[5] The PRSY's borders with Saudi Arabia and Oman had not been agreed. Disobliging comments by NF leaders on the inadequacies of the Arab socialist regimes, the PRSY's potential friends, did not help.

Sixth, Britain had offered £12 million up to the end of May, pending negotiations on assistance after that date. The British did not offer cash, but the South Yemenis were told that a third or more of the £12 million would be for capital items already ordered or in the pipeline'. In fact these items came to much more than a third, so that the PDRY ended up with very little money. By the time negotiations took place for aid, after May 1968, there was almost no interest in London – following a traumatic devaluation of sterling – in extending aid to a government that had fought it bitterly for independence. The British were uncertain as to whether the regime would survive.[6]

Finally, the Soviet Union and China (then at odds with each other) failed to rush to Aden to welcome the new country. They recognized the PRSY more quickly than some Arab regimes, but were suspicious of the NF's ideology. The prospects for the regime's survival seemed poor.

NF organization and government

The first priority was to establish government. The NF would be the sole governing power, and its General Command, then consisting of 29 members, would act as the supreme legislative body, pending the writing of a constitution, would deal with relations between the NF and the army and police, and would outline policy. Qahtan al-Sha'bi was made president for a two-year period, and he appointed the first government, with himself as prime minister and Commander in Chief with Faysal al-Sha'bi as secretary general of the NF. Qahtan at the time was internationally known, and had a higher level of education than many others in the leadership but the left saw Qahtan as a temporary figurehead and Qahtan regarded himself as executive president.

The NF aspired to create an ideological vanguard party capable of dealing with the many complicated problems, and leading the masses. Leaders in the first few weeks used careful language that both the right and the left could accept, as long as it was not further defined. Though no other political organization would be allowed, the NF leaders wanted to work with the communists and Ba'athists to help stabilize the regime.

Qahtan announced the formation of his government, whose key members were Sayf al Dhala'i (foreign affairs), Ali Salim al-Bidh (defence), Muhammad Ali Haytham (interior), Mahmud Abdullah Ushaysh (finance), Faysal al-Sha'bi (economy, trade and planning) and Abd al-Fattah Isma'il (culture, national guidance and Yemeni unity).[7] Most of its members were drawn from the right. There were only three from the left: Abd al-Fattah Isma'il, Ali Salim al-Bidh and Mahmud Ushaysh, the former leader of the oil workers' union and a qualified accountant.

Haytham and Faysal al-Shaʻbi were the most impressive figures, and were from the right, but Haytham enjoyed the respect of the left. Sayf al-Dhalaʻi had impressed British negotiators at Geneva with his good sense, moderate views and openness. The minister of education was a well-known intellectual, while Faysal bin Shamlan (public works) was also clearly a man of ability, who stood against President Ali Abdullah Salih in the 2006 Yemeni presidential elections.

However, within the NF General Command, which had the real power, those on the left outnumbered the right, and they were waiting for the opportunity to force their policies on the regime. They understood that it was tactically appropriate to appoint ministers who could reassure the army and police, as well as the general public and those businessmen and civil servants who had remained. The appointment of al-Bidh, then on the extreme left, as defence minister was balanced by the much more acceptable Haytham at interior. In these early days, with so many problems and threats, there was a vital need to work together. Qahtan was well known in the Arab world, while Sayf al-Dhalaʻi was probably the best foreign minister available.

The civil service remained intact, despite losing a large number of senior staff. Abdullah al-Asnaj claims that he told his old friend Faysal al-Shaʻbi at a secret meeting in Beirut in November 1967 that, whatever the NF did, it should retain the civil service, which worked well.[8] Qahtan and Faysal recognized the merits of this part of their inheritance, and there was an early decision to apply the Federal and Aden administrative systems to the whole country. This proved to be one of the best decisions made in the early days.

Policy statements spoke of the land reform and nationalizations outlined in the first NLF Congress, but nothing could be done until urgent action had been taken to deal with the dire financial situation. Cuts in wages and new taxes were imposed. On 11 December 1967, the sultans and 'feudal figures' and other 'stooges of the British were stripped of power and rank, and their property was confiscated. Six days later, the PRSY was divided into six provinces named First to Sixth, and each was subdivided into numbered regions and then districts.

This was part of a wider attempt to minimize the influence of tribalism. Tribal and traditional names were thus abolished, and the boundaries of the provinces intentionally ignored those of previous sultanates or tribes.[9] In March, all tribal disputes were suspended and a truce was imposed, with dire punishments for anyone infringing the new rules. Disputes in future would be dealt with by the government. This was vigorously followed up.

In many parts of the country, the NF replaced whatever previous administration had existed and initially ensured that its orders were obeyed by the traditional use of patronage (jobs in the government) and force. Some of the so-called 'wild tribal areas', such as the Upper Yafi'i sultanate were left alone in the early days of the PDRY. Trials of people associated with the previous regime were conducted by a new Security Court under the leftwing intellectual Abdullah al-Khamiri and on 19 March 1968 it issued long sentences against many of them.

There were only passing references to Islam. The NF leaders drew on secular ideologies; religion, it seemed, was not important to them, or was associated with feudalism, tribalism and the backward states of the old South Arabia.

The attitude of the armed forces

The armed forces remained relatively cohesive, and posed a potential threat. The majority of army officers had come out in favour of the NF in November, but the top military leadership did not seem to know much about the NF and its leaders at independence. It was prepared to deal with Qahtan, but a deep mutual suspicion soon developed between the military leadership and the left. Ali Salim al-Bidh made little secret of his ambition to purge the army and turn it into a revolutionary fighting force and he quickly sacked some senior officers and expelled the remaining British advisers. Qahtan and the right cultivated the military leadership to forestall a potential coup, and perhaps ensure that the army would support them if they decided to move against the left.

It was a difficult and often tense relationship. The army objected to the cuts in salaries and allowances that were imposed on it. The senior officers prevented an attempt in January 1968 to give the NF greater control over the army, demanding that all communications between the army and the NF pass through the army command, and not directly to NF members inside the armed forces. They wanted the army as a whole to become a de facto branch of the NF, and participate in party conferences under the top military leadership. They called for the disbanding of the NF's Liberation Army and the People's Guard.[10]

Divisions within the NF

The divisions within the NF were more complicated than a simple division between right and left. Vitaly Naumkin,[11] a Russian scholar who knew the NF leaders well in the late 1960s, saw four main left-wing factions:

1) A Marxist radical core led by Abd al-Fattah Isma'il, who saw the NF as an instrument for revolutionary socialist change and wanted to build up the party and its organization as quickly as possible. Many of those involved were, like Abd al-Fattah, Adenis from northern Yemen with no tribal or family base within the PRSY. They were close to the Marxists of the PDU.
2) A neo-Trotskyite group close to the extreme left of MAN and led by Ali Salih Ubad ('Muqbil'), who came from a landowning family in Abyan. It called for the destruction of all remnants of the previous system.
3) A very loose grouping of leaders of the NLF in the field. These were people like Salim Rubayya Ali ('Salmin', who had commanded NLF forces fighting FLOSY in Aden in 1967), Ali Antar and Ali Nasir Muhammad. They had no interest in ideology, and asserted that decision-making should be left to field commanders with deep roots in the PRSY. They drew their closest support from tribes or regional interests in their homelands.
4) 'Conservative' figures from tribal regions that supported the left more out of personal antipathy towards Qahtan than any ideological conviction. Their numbers grew as Qahtan became more irascible.

At lower levels of the NF, people followed leading figures from their tribe, or even from the previous sultanates or amirates from which they came.[12] These leaders had a personal following and prestige unrelated to their ideological position. They provided the same type of patronage to their supporters found elsewhere in the Arab world, as well as in the Yemen of the twenty-first century.

Right and left in PRSY at this time need to be understood in the context of divisions within MAN. Most other regimes, including those of the socialists in Iraq and Syria, would have regarded Qahtan and his associates as being from the extreme left, and people like Abd al-Fattah Isma'il as being from the outermost bastions of Marxism. The main differences between them in the early days were less about ideology than the respective roles of the party and government. The pragmatic Qahtan saw himself as taking over the ministries, armed forces and police of the previous regime and using them, albeit purged and reformed, to run the state using the people and resources to hand. This was not a time to allow the left to apply their untried ideas to a society facing so many difficulties. There was only one leader, and that was him. His supporters on the right found his personal style grating, and resented his belief that he was indispensable to the survival of the PRSY. A leading right-wing figure at the time said that the influence of the left increased as a result of a visit by Nayif Hawatmah. He urged the NLF to adopt a more radical ideology than that advocated by Qahtan and Faysal al-Sha'bi.[13] Others have confirmed that in the period 1967–69 Hawatmah used his influence to persuade the NF to move to the left.

Hadhramaut had been taken over before independence by a group of the extreme left who came close to seceding to set up a Maoist regime. With some encouragement from al-Bidh, its governor Faysal al-Attas (then on the furthest reaches of the left) virtually ignored directives from Aden as he thoroughly purged the local civil administration and the military and made moves to set up village soviets and to destroy some mosques. Some bellicose statements were issued about the PRSY's neighbours. Events in Hadhramaut created an impression of chaos within the PRSY, and of an extremism that was unwelcome not only on the right but to some on the left. On the other hand, Hadhramaut was one part of the PRSY that had had a functioning administration, and there were many educated Hadhramis who were brought in to replace some of the civil servants and others who had left Aden.

The Fourth National Congress

There was clearly an urgent need for the NF to decide how it would organize itself, define the respective roles of party and government, and produce a set of policies to deal with the multitude of problems. These issues were tackled by the Fourth Congress, which took place at Zingibar on 2–8 March 1968, and was attended by 167 delegates. Qahtan and Faysal strove to delay the Congress, as they knew that the left would have a majority of the delegates and use this to push through their agenda. When that failed, they tried in vain to exclude some of the most militant of the left from committees preparing policy statements.

The distribution of delegates was interesting: Abyan had 45 delegates and Lahij 32, compared with 25 for Aden, 13 for Hadhramaut and seven each for Shabwa and Mahra.[14] Most of those from Lahij came from Dhala, Shu'ayb, Hawshabi and Halmayn.[15] The army, against protests from the left, had eight places: two were from the left, two were not members of the NLF, and the rest were either from the right or were neutral. The left were in the majority, and were better organized than Qahtan and his supporters.

The left tabled a document under the title National Democratic Liberation, which had been drawn up by Abdullah al-Khamiri, Ali Salih Ubad, the north Yemeni Sultan Ahmad Umar and Abdullah al-Ashtal. Nayif Hawatmah took an active part in discussions leading to its drafting. Though significant parts of this programme were not approved, it showed the degree of radicalization taking place within the NF: the government should be placed under the supervision of the NF, which should rid itself of the opportunism, tribalism and individualism that had infected the movement; there would be a new Supreme People's Council elected through a system of locally elected popular councils; a collective leadership should replace presidential power; society had to be transformed through nationalization, agrarian reform, purges of the government and the disbanding of the army and police. The document called for a people's militia to protect the NF.[16] The response of the right was feeble. A paper drawn up by Abd al-Malik Isma'il was mostly a comment on the left's documents and did not present a competing programme, only a demand for a strong presidency.

The left was able to push through much of its programme despite an attempt by Qahtan to steal a march by announcing an agrarian reform law. The left had taken control of the group organizing elections for an expanded General Command of 41 members. Politicians from the left won the most votes in these elections: Abd al-Fattah Isma'il, Ali Antar, Abdullah al-Khamiri, Salih Muslih Qasim, Abd al-Aziz Abd al-Wali, Muhammad Salih Muti'a, Ali Salim al-Bidh, Salim Rubayya Ali (Salmin), Muhammad Sa'id Abdullah (party name 'Muhsin') and 'Muqbil'. Qahtan came in only sixteenth place, Sayf al-Dhala'i came ninth, and Faysal al-Sha'bi tenth.

The Congress produced a political statement that set out the policy principles sought by the left, but the right insisted that the statement should not specify how the principles would be implemented, leaving this to the leadership. It defined the NF as a 'revolutionary organization which represents the interests of the workers, peasants, soldiers and intellectuals and adopts scientific socialism as its method of analysis and practice'. Among the objectives decided upon were the following:

1) Restructuring of the NF as a vanguard party based on 'scientific socialism'.
2) Opening up the NF to other revolutionary parties – meaning the PDU and the Ba'ath (al-Tali'a).
3) The setting up of Popular Councils in all regions.

4) Large-scale agrarian reform
5) Conversion of the economy to one based on production, not services, with a large new public sector and extensive nationalization.
6) Purging of the military and civilian organizations.
7) Strengthening of the Popular Guard and the creation of a People's Militia, consisting of between 100,000 and 150,000 members drawn from 'workers, students and peasants'.
8) The eradication of illiteracy.
9) Cooperation with the international socialist system, and drawing on the experiences of socialist states.
10) Provision of support to the revolution in north Yemen and the liberation of the Arabian Peninsula and Gulf.

There were few in the Arab world – even 1968, that year of revolution – who proposed such a programme and had the power and means to implement it. While the right favoured pragmatic policies to deal with the inherited problems of the PRSY, the left wanted to create a new reality based on revolutionary socialism. Qahtan soon made it clear that he had no intention of implementing this programme. The first meeting of the NF General Command on 15 March brought the dispute between the right and the left clearly into the open. The left wanted Abd al-Fattah Isma'il appointed prime minister and given powers that would undermine the position of Qahtan, who strongly rejected this.

The events of 20 March

The army and police commands were deeply disturbed by the decisions of the Congress. On 20 March the army launched a de facto coup, not to overthrow the regime but to persuade it to change direction. Army units occupied the radio station in Aden, which announced that the moves had been made to save the country from communism. Many on the left were arrested, including Abd al-Fattah Isma'il (who was injured in the process), al-Bidh and other members of the General Command. Borders were closed and movements restricted. The army surrounded the house of Qahtan, demanding a change of government and policies. Some accounts say that he was beaten up by the army when he tried to face them down. Qahtan may have had some sympathy with those launching the coup, but he could see the longer-term dangers for his own position if he gave in to the army's demands without resistance. The PRSY government later claimed that Qahtan had instigated the coup, while other observers thought that Qahtan knew what was coming from the army and did nothing to stop it. People close to him say he was appalled at the army's action.[17]

There were major demonstrations against these moves in Aden and other towns. Some of those arrested managed to escape, including the army's *bêtes noires* Ali Salim al-Bidh, Salmin and Salih Muslih. Outside Aden, elements of the Liberation Army arrested regular army officers. Trouble spread into the army itself, and some soldiers declared their loyalty to the left.

Qahtan and the army leaders understood within a few days that they would need to negotiate or face the possibility of civil war. Qahtan persuaded the military leaders, who were clearly surprised that he had not welcomed their action, to stand down in exchange for no action being taken against them. He described the military move as a 'sincere' error caused by the extremism of the left. He got the NF to grant him special emergency powers, had both Isma'il and al-Bidh removed from their ministerial positions, and gave Faysal al-Sha'bi the task of reorganizing the NF. After a meeting of the NF General Command, Qahtan promised that the army would be purged, and that he would implement the decisions of the Fourth Congress, but he clearly had no intention of doing either, though he did issue the decree on land reform on 25 March. In April he sanctioned the arrest of two of the important intellectuals leading the extreme left in Hadhramaut and had them incarcerated in Aden.[18] The outcome of 20 March was to strengthen the position of Qahtan as defender of the army against the left, and defender of the left against reaction from the right. Isma'il left the PRSY for the Soviet Union for extended medical treatment. A limited purge of the military followed, but the organizers of the coup remained in their posts.

The left had been caught by surprise. The leading figures concluded that they should cooperate with Qahtan in the short term and rebuild their strength in the party, government and armed forces until they were in a position to oust him.

The events of 14 May

Others on the left, however, were determined to challenge Qahtan, and on 14 May there was a rebellion by the left in Abyan at Ja'ar and Zingibar, which was supposed to have been coordinated with moves by the extreme left, who remained in control in Hadhramaut; but difficulties in communication prevented this. There were also plans to launch an uprising in or near Aden. The instigators included the most important leaders of the left: Salmin, Ali Antar and Muqbil. Fourteen members of the General Command issued a statement in support of the rebellion.

Qahtan was ready, and did not hesitate to use the army to crush the rebellion, and to extinguish the already weakened Maoist 'administration' in Hadhramaut. He denounced it as a plot by a few opportunists who were bent on gaining personal privilege, and who had contempt for the NF and its constitution. He heaped blame on the left for a string of failures, including the breakdown on 12 May of negotiations with the British over future aid. The rebels had miscalculated, overestimating their strength, and failed in their organization and coordination. They expected a public uprising and a mutiny within the army; but the army remained loyal and defeated the rebels, killing some of their leaders and forcing others to flee into north Yemen though a few remained to fight in remote parts of the country. A new government was appointed in which the right had a clear majority.

The right appeared to be in the ascendant but the left, though weakened, was entrenched within the NF organization, and it would have been impossible to run the regime without their cooperation. The left concluded that it would need to act more subtly and employ better tactics.[19] It would need to penetrate the armed forces and police. It learned from what happened in May 1968, and applied the lessons a year later. Qahtan, in the words of Abd al-Fattah Isma'il, 'learned nothing'.[20] Events on the borders helped the left just when it seemed to be at its weakest.

The external threat

The sultans and FLOSY were determined to bring down the NF and were given bases, training and support by Saudi Arabia and by anti-MAN forces in Yemen after the end of the siege of Sana'a in February 1968. The first clashes took place in early 1968, when the Sharif of Bayhan, who had been appointed Commander of the FRA in mid 1967, attempted to retake the former state. He was repulsed, but by the middle of that year other groups were launching attacks at what they believed to a weak but potentially dangerous regime in Aden. There was a rebellion by some Awlaqi clans in Shabwa led by ex-officers forced to leave the army just before independence because of their sympathy for FLOSY. The Awlaqi commander of the PRSY security forces, Colonel Salih Sabaa, crossed into Yemen with 200 men rather than face his fellow Awlaqi in battle. A group of armed rebels seized part of Abyan and tribes in Lahij rebelled. A reorganized FLOSY and SAL launched attacks across the borders of Yemen and Saudi Arabia, respectively. There were threats from Saudi Arabia against Hadhramaut and from Oman by British forces fighting the PRSY-backed Dhufari rebels.

Despite the support of neighbouring regimes, these moves were poorly organized and coordinated, a characteristic of the much larger incursions made over the next two to three years. None of these attacks seriously threatened the regime, but they showed the NF leaders, on both the right and the left, that unless they worked together the regime could fall.

The return of the left

One of the 14 May rebels, Salmin, intervened on the side of the regime in the Awlaqi area, persuading even Qahtan that he needed people like Salmin and other former leaders of the Liberation Army to counter threats to the regime. These leaders had recruited people from their tribes to fight the British, and had the ability to mobilize support in those areas being attacked from over the PRSY's borders. Abd al-Fattah Isma'il, who was then in Moscow, advised the left that it should work with Qahtan to undermine him from within.

Qahtan's increasingly autocratic style weakened his popularity among the General Command and the government, and there was a marked rise in tension from late 1968. Qahtan, perhaps aware of the gap in age and experience between himself and the other leaders, thought he knew best and came to regard himself as indispensable. He failed to appreciate that his younger colleagues believed that their role in fighting the British and the NLF's enemies before 1967 gave them the right to say how the state should be run. Qahtan lacked the patience and political skills to exploit the divisions within the left, or at least to ensure that moderate people such as Muhammad Ali Haytham and Muhammad Salih Awlaqi, who had networks of support in the army and in their home regions of Dathina and Shabwa, worked with him and not his opponents.

He managed to upset some of those who had supported him in March and May 1968, and they put out feelers to the reviving left wing. The formal rehabilitation of the left took place in October 1968, after Abd al-Fattah Isma'il returned from Moscow and negotiated an understanding with Faysal al-Sha'bi that would allow the left back into the leadership of the NF though not yet to positions in government. The two men also agreed on a political way forward, entitled 'Programme for Completion of the Stage of National Democratic Liberation'. It called for unity and changes in the party structure. Collective leadership was essential in dealing with the threat from external forces, and to prevent tribal conflict. It reaffirmed the need to purify the armed forces and create a revolutionary consciousness. This implied that both the right and left had concluded that, unless the army was made subservient to the NF, it would remain a potential threat to all of them, not just to the left.

The main thrust of the programme was economic: a year after independence the rate of economic decline seemed to be accelerating. The hoped-for British assistance had not materialized, and the outside world was not rushing to assist a regime that looked weak and had the knack of antagonizing its neighbours and friends in the Arab world. The Russians were intrigued by the emergence of the left, but regarded what was going on only as an 'interesting experiment'.[21] There was some Soviet military support, and after January 1969 some economic assistance, but far short of what the PRSY needed. Ministers realized that they would need to moderate their language if they were to attract external support, and the cooperation of what remained of the industrial and trading community. Some limited pragmatism was expressed in words, but not actions.

The left, as Abd al-Fattah Isma'il had concluded, should co-operate with Faysal and Qahtan to build up support within PRSY institutions, particularly the armed forces. He and his colleagues had mostly given up the senior colonels as a lost cause, but worked away at the lower levels. Among the junior ranks a significant number of Dathinis and Awdhalis appear to have listened to NF leaders from their region: the left-wing but pragmatic Ali Nasir Muhammad and the centrist Muhammad Ali Haytham. Ali Antar and Salih Muslih talked to those from Dhala.[22]

The downfall of Qahtan

There were several clashes in early 1969 between Qahtan, ministers and members of the NF General Command as Qahtan's autocratic style was starting to lose him support from all sides. He had come to regard himself as indispensable, and used the weapon of resignation to face down opposition on several occasions. His opponents within the General Command worked to undermine him, and he was forced to give up the post of prime minister on 6 April 1969 in a cabinet reshuffle that saw some of his supporters leave. He was only partly appeased by the appointment of Faysal al-Sha'bi as prime minister. Faysal's colleagues say that Faysal had by then been persuaded by Isma'il that Qahtan would have to step down.[23]

Qahtan fell out a few weeks later with Haytham, a man who shared many of his political views and his pragmatic approach and had been a key figure in binding the army to the NF. He was a respected personality from Dathina, the home of many officers, and had worked in the mid 1960s to bring them on to the side of the NF. Since his appointment as minister of interior a year earlier, he had grown in strength and appeared to see himself as a potential prime minister building up his relationship with the left as well as with Qahtan, who had become wary of Haytham's ambitions. Not surprisingly Qahtan resented attempts by Haytham to build up his support in the armed forces and relations between them came close to breaking point more than once. In a fit of pique over a trivial incident, an overconfident Qahtan dismissed Haytham on 15 June 1969. It was a fatal mistake, and provided the opportunity the left had been waiting for. They could now move against Qahtan with the support of Haytham and Muhammad Salih Awlaqi, the defence minister and a pragmatist in the Haytham mould.

A meeting of the NF General Command was called, at which the left insisted that Haytham be reinstated. Qahtan, with the support of Faysal, argued that he was exercising his right as president and head of the executive in dismissing Haytham. He and Faysal clearly believed that they could face down the left but found that the majority in the General Command criticized them for departing from the principle of collective responsibility and accused Qahtan of seeking to become a dictator. Qahtan and Faysal offered to resign, believing that their opponents were too divided or too weak to accept it. However, there was now a majority against them. The game was up and their resignations were accepted on 22 June. The left despatched a handful of troops to secure the radio station which broadcast news of their resignation from all posts.[24] Qahtan was said to have walked directly from the General Command meeting to house arrest, where he remained until he died of a heart attack in 1981. Faysal was arrested soon afterwards.

Some observers, noted the British ambassador, were surprised at the lack of action by the military in support of Qahtan.[25] Isma'il later said that units of the army outside Aden started to move on the capital, but were stopped when left-wing elements intercepted them to persuade ordinary soldiers to support the NF General Command.[26] Some senior officers left their units and crossed into north Yemen, suggesting that they could see the position was lost. NF commentators later attributed this to the success of the campaign to infiltrate the armed forces. Haytham (and Awlaqi) had the confidence of many senior officers, and it may be that his siding with the left was enough to reassure them. Writing in 1976, Abd al-Fattah Isma'il believed that Qahtan thought the army would back him, but failed to understand the changes that had taken place in it. Some on the right blamed Haytham, accusing him of disloyalty and naivety.

The 'Glorious Corrective Move' of 22 June 1969

These events and the subsequent changes within the NF were trumpeted by the victors as the 'Glorious Corrective Move'. It was the most decisive event in the early history of independent south Yemen and brought to power the leaders who would dominate the country for the next 17 years and shape its policies. It marked the emergence of the PRSY as a truly revolutionary state. The process of setting up the institutions, appointing the main personalities and defining the policies was not fully completed until the third anniversary of independence, in November 1970, when the name PRSY was dropped.

The NF leadership issued a statement condemning the individualist actions of Qahtan and Faysal, and stating that the revolution must make use of the popular authority of the NF as the only democratic authority that was able to protect the people from such individualism. It talked of strengthening relations with the Soviet Union and other socialist countries, while also working for better relations with Arab countries. It pledged support for left-wing groups in the YAR, and for the Popular Front for the Liberation of the Occupied Arab Gulf (PFLOAG) in Oman, as well as revolutionary groups in the Arabian Peninsula. This was rapidly followed up by a series of measures to consolidate the position of the left and initiate its policies.

Abd al-Fattah Isma'il became secretary general of the NF, working closely with a leadership group that included Salmin, Ali Antar, Muhammad Salih Awlaqi and Mahmud Ushaysh. The country was to be run formally by a Presidential Council of five: Salmin as chairman, and therefore head of state; Abd al-Fattah Isma'il, Muhammad Ali Haytham, Muhammad Salih Awlaqi and Ali Antar. The alliance between pragmatists such as Haytham and Awlaqi and the ascendant left could not last long. The size of the presidential council was reduced to three in November, with Antar and Awlaqi leaving on the grounds that council members should be ex officio – president, prime minister and secretary general of the NF. Haytham stayed on as a member and prime minister until August 1971, when he was replaced by Ali Nasir Muhammad, who like Haytham was from Dathina, but was closer to the left. The left were in control, and the pragmatic Haytham, who appears to have had hopes of becoming head of state instead of Salmin, could no longer work with them (particularly Salmin) and went into exile, later becoming one of the leaders of an opposition group trying to overthrow the regime, and the target of assassination attempts. He returned to government as a minister in the unity cabinet of 1993, and died a few weeks later. Many now look back to him (and Faysal al-Sha'bi) as the most able of the early leaders, and a man who might have taken the country in a more moderate direction if he had survived in power

There were mass expulsions of the right, and further desertions from the army and police. A number of these moved to the YAR, and from there to Saudi Arabia, and joined the sultans and former NLF members now fighting the regime. By the end of 1969 there had been a thorough purge of the army including officers associated with Haytham.

In March 1970 there were large-scale arrests of people associated with the right, and there were claims that a plot aimed at restoring Qahtan had been uncovered. The plotters were sentenced in October 1970, following a trial by the Supreme People's Court under the control of Abdullah al-Khamiri. Five received death sentences, including Ali Salim al-Kindi, a former governor of the Hadhramaut and Abdullah Salim Maysari, a brigade commander. Thirteen others, mostly military and security officers from Abyan, were given prison sentences. It seems that they were planning to install Faysal al-Sha'bi as president (Qahtan was rumoured to be ill). This may explain why Faysal was shot 'whilst attempting to escape' on 2 April 1970, shortly after the main arrests were announced. With his murder (as former PDRY leaders now call it), the right was finished.

The achievements of the Qahtan period

In January 1970 the British ambassador commenting on the events of 1969 said,

> Potential mutineers, whether military, mercantile, tribal or religious appear disorganized and leaderless. The present (NF) leadership is in my view more likely to collapse by internal fission, caused or aggravated by personality clashes and a deepening economic crisis, but so far as I can see any successor grouping will only be more practical, rather than less committed to the Communists.[27]

These were prescient words. The regime was here to stay, but the tensions within the leadership would continue to devour the people that had fought for independence. This contrasts with the comments made by the ambassador's predecessor a year earlier. He began his Annual Review with the comment, 'Well, at any rate they are still here' and finished by suggesting it was improbable that they would be there by the end of 1969.

It was almost inevitable, given the enormous problems the country faced at independence and the nature of the NF, set up less than five years before independence, that it would take many months for the regime to stabilize. The corrective move brought a greater degree of unity to the leadership, and thus to the direction of policy and there would now be a chance to implement some of these ideas. Qahtan had reorganized the finances, forcing the government to trim its plans according to the budget. He had not implemented the calls from the left (or the decisions of the Fourth Congress) to nationalize what remained of the economy, and had rejected the more radical agrarian reform that the left wanted. Political instability both deterred investment and encouraged further emigration. The system of local administration had been reorganized to get rid of the tribal past and reduce the influence both of the former leaders and of Islamic clerics. Though the opposition groups operating from beyond Yemen's borders had been beaten back, they had not been destroyed, and were re-organizing.

There was little Qahtan could do to control events in the YAR. The Yemeni leaders had been too preoccupied with their own civil war to translate their objections to the setting up of an independent regime in the south into moves to undermine it. Both regimes proclaimed their commitment to unity, and set up ministries for unity affairs. The YAR leaders had talked to NLF leaders about unity even before independence. Mohsen Alaini, for example, says that he asked Qahtan and Isma'il – while they were on their way to Geneva to sign the agreement with the British just before independence – why they wanted to set up a state in the south, arguing 'we could face the Sultans of the South and the Royalists of the North and together build a modern unified state'.[28] Other Yemeni leaders understood that unity was impossible until the civil war had ended and the north had been stabilized.[29]

The PRSY continued to support the Revolutionary Democratic Party, which was led by MAN members intimately connected with the left wing of the NF and which later became part of the northern branch of the Yemeni Socialist Party. It was this group that fought the right for control of the republican regime in Sana'a, and lost. Qahtan and the Yemeni leaders criticized each other, but had more pressing problems at home and little interest at that stage in settling any differences in battle.

Relations with the rest of the Arab world did not improve much during Qahtan's period. Saudi Arabia, Oman and the rest of the Gulf states, still under British influence, were hostile. The Aden government made little secret of its support for Dhufari rebels. The NF rejected the Nasserist version of Arab unity, socialism and nationalism. Aden was at that stage distant from the Ba'ath regimes in Baghdad and Damascus. It worked for good relations with Egypt and acknowledged the role of Nasser, but the relationship lacked substance because of Cairo's support for FLOSY and the NLF's ideological links to MAN.

The Soviet Union sent a delegation to open diplomatic relations in December 1967, and al-Bidh led a military delegation to Moscow in February 1968. Moscow-watchers judged that the Russian reaction to the PRSY was tentative, welcoming its neutralism but uncertain about its ideological soundness or direction. Moscow had backed FLOSY before independence, and appeared to have had no direct links with the NLF. The Soviets – like the British – may have questioned whether the regime would stay in power. However, in the summer of 1968 three Soviet warships visited Aden and a military delegation arrived, leading to an agreement that brought deliveries of aircraft and weapons the following January. That same month Qahtan took a large delegation to Moscow. He was received with great pomp, but there were indications that the regime did not fully approve of Qahtan, possibly because he was then excluding the left from government.[30] On the other hand, one leading Russian diplomat at the time found Qahtan much more sensible than people like Isma'il, judging that he was 'less prone to being swayed by dogma'.[31] Though the military support was clearly useful, the USSR did not meet the PRSY's economic expectations. There was no budgetary aid, only loans for specific projects. The Russians agreed to support a fish cannery and modernize the fishing industry. The Soviet navy was granted access to Aden port, and anchorages off Socotra.

Relations with China – then embroiled in the Cultural Revolution, and competition with Moscow – got off to a slower and even more cautious start. Beijing recognized the PRSY on 31 January 1968, and a PRSY delegation arrived in China the following September, led by Sayf al-Dhala'i, Faysal Abd al-Latif al-Sha'bi and Ali Antar. There followed agreements that provided Chinese long-term loans for economic development and the supply of weapons. But throughout these discussions the Chinese constantly warned about the danger of straying into 'infantile leftism', and spoke of the need to be practical.[32]

In the early months Qahtan tried to keep lines open to the West. The US, Germany and France established diplomatic relations, and there was a hope that Britain would provide economic aid. Relations, however, became strained as the PRSY developed its contacts with Russia and China. Neither the US nor West German embassies survived beyond the end of 1969 (the US military attaché was expelled during the March 1968 events, but the embassy clung on). Britain drastically cut the size of its mission, and there were questions in London about whether there was any point in staying.

Qahtan was stigmatized as a 'right-wing opportunist' for most of the life of the PDRY, and was only rehabilitated in the run-up to unity in 1990. He had spent far too long outside the country, having been a virtual prisoner in Cairo during the independence struggle, and had not had the opportunity (and lacked the skills) to develop an effective organization. There was throughout the life of the NLF a gap between the right-wing leadership in Cairo and the internal command, made up of fighters and organizers on the ground, who, isolated from the international leadership, turned to the far left for inspiration. Qahtan's pragmatic policy of trying to work with what he inherited was arguably the most sensible course for a new state facing so many difficulties. But he was unable to persuade the left of this, or to exert sufficient influence on the army and police to build his personal power and force the left into accepting his policies. The left was better organized and stronger, and Qahtan overestimated his own importance to the NF and failed to rally potential allies, such as Haytham, to his cause.

Revolutions devour their children, and Qahtan, Faysal and others were the first to be consumed. They were not to be the last. Throughout its life, the NF rejected the attempts of individuals to impose their leadership on the organization. Qahtan was merely the first of those who fell at the hands of a collective leadership.

PART B

THE SALMIN YEARS

4

STRUCTURES AND LEADERSHIP IN THE EARLY 1970S

The left wing had clearly triumphed after the Glorious Corrective Move, and its control was further tightened when Muhammad Ali Haytham was forced in August 1971 to resign and leave the country. However, the left was not a cohesive, organized group, but a collection of powerful personalities that had worked together to fight for independence, and then to overthrow Qahtan and the right. At the heart of the personality and factional disputes of the 1970s were the so-called 'historical leaders' whose prestige derived from their role as heroes of the liberation struggle and founding figures of the movement.[1] They became powerful patrons to their supporters, who were mostly drawn from their home areas in the case of those born in the south.

The Presidency Council

The three men who dominated PDRY politics in the 1970s were members of the Presidency Council.

Salim Rubayya Ali (popularly known as Salmin), chairman of the Presidency Council, was a first among equals. He had a great deal of influence in the army and the militias, and a strong base in southern Abyan, the Fadhli tribal area. Salmin had the reputation of being the most extreme of the top PDRY leaders, but his colleagues and foreigners who dealt with him found that he was a practical man of politics.[2] In the early 1970s he appeared to pick up ideas for a time, only to drop them.[3] Salmin was often labelled a Maoist. He had been impressed on a visit to China in the later stages of the Cultural Revolution, and wanted to apply some of its ideas to the PDRY – notably that of uprisings by peasants to seize land, and by workers to take over factories. He looked at how Maoism could be applied, not at its ideology. Salmin was a man who seemed to draw inspiration from the people and one who liked to deal directly with peasants, workers and tribesmen, and he abhorred bureaucracy. Ali Nasir Muhammad described how Salmin would often miss vital meetings of the party or with foreign visitors. Salmin kept his own diary, and would dash to meetings outside Aden or to tackle a problem in the provinces without telling his colleagues.[4] His erratic behaviour would sometimes drive his colleagues to despair. But, at least in the early 1970s, he was the most popular of the PDRY leaders.

Abd al-Fattah Isma'il, secretary general of the NF, was a very different personality. He was the leading intellectual of the NF, and perhaps the only one of the top leaders with a firm understanding of Marxism. The rest, according to one former colleague, 'just did their month at a Soviet or an Adeni party school'.[5] He lacked Salmin's charisma, though he inspired those around him with his ideas and the clarity of his thinking. His writings and speeches were usually too wrapped in ideological jargon to be comprehensible to all but disciples of Marxism. A leading north Yemeni politician, Yahya al-Mutawakkil, described him as a dreamer, not a practical man of politics, an assessment shared by many of Isma'il's friends.[6] Some of his colleagues would later portray him as indolent, preferring the discussion of ideas to action, and looking to others to implement his wishes. But there was within him a rigid determination that the NF should become a Marxist vanguard party that would be at the centre of the state, from where it would decide policies for the president and prime minister to implement. Isma'il was one of the many leaders from north Yemen who needed to build up a strong party to compensate for their lack of a regional or tribal base in the south, such as that enjoyed by Salmin and Ali Nasir Muhammad in different parts of Abyan. They also strove with allies over the border to build up a Marxist party that might one day replace the regime in Sana'a.

The third member of the Presidency Council was the prime minister, Ali Nasir Muhammad, whose base lay in the northern part of Abyan, and included groups in Dathina and the Awdhali tribe. It was Isma'il who started calling him 'Ali Marhaba' because of the way he would respond to all requests with the word 'Marhaba' (a word in this context signalling 'at your service') and avoided confrontation. Ali Nasir was and remains a forceful man with restless energy. He was a natural leader with an organized approach to politics and government that was lacking in many of his colleagues. Observers, including a prominent Russian, noted his constantly moving eyes and the two levels within his personality: one a political charmer, the other an intriguer, adventurer and risk taker.[7] He was no intellectual, but had a quick and penetrating intelligence and could spot and exploit the weaknesses in his rivals. There was a Machiavellian streak to his character, and he would appear to be all things to all men – a necessary quality in the lethal politics of the 1970s. He was often misjudged, and sometimes underestimated, because of his emollient personality, as the nickname 'Ali Marhaba' implied.

Restructuring the state

With the defeat of the right, the new leadership could restructure the state's institutions, beginning with the drafting of a new Constitution, assisted by East German and Egyptian experts. It came into force on the third anniversary of independence, on 30 November 1970.[8] It affirmed the commitment to Yemeni unity, and the PRSY became the PDRY. The change of name upset the YAR leaders, who thought Aden was asserting the right to represent all Yemeni people. When Muhsin Alaini, the YAR prime minister, upbraided Haytham and others, they told him that it had been chosen carefully and would not be changed.[9]

The Constitution vested all political power in the working people, defined as an alliance of workers, peasants, the intelligentsia and even the petty bourgeoisie, as well as soldiers, women and students. The Constitution had a key statement: 'The National Front Organization leads, on the basis of scientific socialism, the political activity among the masses and within the mass organizations to develop society in a manner that achieves national democratic revolution following a non-capitalist approach.' Nevertheless, Islam was recognized as the official religion.

Full legislative powers were to be vested in the Supreme People's Council (SPC), whose 101 members were to be elected by local councils and by the trade unions. There were quotas for women, and universal suffrage for all over the age of 18. Pending the election of local councils, the NF General Command selected the SPC members, the trade unions holding elections for their members later. Members of the NF General Command took most of the places. One member each from the People's Democratic Union (PDU) and al-Tali'a and eight non-NF independents were appointed.[10] Twelve were peasants, 20 were from the armed and security services, five were women, and three represented the professions. The SPC would elect the Presidential Council. The SPC had as much power as similar organizations in the Communist world. It was there to approve what the leadership wanted and provide a facade of democracy. It met for the first time in August 1971 to elect Abd al-Fattah Isma'il as speaker, and sanctioned the changes that saw Haytham replaced as prime minister by Ali Nasir Muhammad.

The Constitution was a comprehensive document guaranteeing citizens a wide range of rights and entitlements, though it took some years before the regime was in a position to implement many of them.

The formation of the National Front Political Organization

The fifth NF Congress took place in March 1972 in Medina al-Sha'ab. The language used in communiqués is reminiscent of the Soviet style, with much stress on the principle of democratic centralism. The few really valuable nuggets were embedded in often impenetrable rhetoric that had little meaning to anyone outside the most committed. Abd al-Fattah Isma'il noted that the NF was 'changing its status from being a mass organization destroying everything set up by the feudalist and colonialist regimes and leading the broad mass through the national liberation stage into being a leading force in society directly responsible for authority, drawing up programmes for the broadest masses'.[11] As part of a process of evolution towards a communist-style political party, the NF brought the PDU and the Ba'ath into a closer embrace, and renamed itself the National Front Political Organization. The General Command was replaced by a Central Committee, and the Executive Committee by the Politburo. The final communiqué described the Central Committee as the highest political authority in the PDRY. The party created a secretariat, which included bureaus covering the key areas of internal and external policy normally led by senior members of the NF, and supported by staffs (increasingly recruited from graduates of the Higher School of Scientific Socialism and party schools in the Soviet Union) that could draw up policies in these areas. The Presidency Council was increased in size but the only members with effective power were Salmin, Isma'il and Ali Nasir.

Abd al-Fattah Isma'il envisaged from the outset that there would be in the PDRY a 'vanguard party' that would be made up of the NF, the PDU and the Ba'ath. The leader of the PDU, Abdullah Abd al-Razzaq Ba Dhib, 'the foremost communist in all Arabia'[12] and the man who influenced the thinking of the Adeni fighters and intellectuals of the NF, was appointed minister of education after the Corrective Move. Ba Dhib was a journalist, poet, teacher and administrator.[13] His brother Ali succeeded him on his death as leader in 1976, and both he and another brother Abu Bakr played leading roles in PDRY politics until 1986. The PDU was important in supplying staff for the party school in Aden, and in using its contacts to bring in teachers from other communist parties, notably Iraq's. One leading figure in the NF said that the Ba Dhib's were instrumental in spreading Marxism in the NF in the 1970s.[14] Al-Tali'a had a less comfortable relationship with the NF, but its leader, Anis Hassan Yahya, was appointed minister of economy after June 1969. He served in many PDRY governments, but was less influential than Ba Dhib and was seen as someone who, while competent, was too fond of his own voice.

The Politburo and Central Committee, 1972–75

The Politburo became the main centre of power during the 1970s gradually overtaking in importance the Presidency Council. Salim Rubayya Ali ('Salmin'), Abd al-Fattah Isma'il, Ali Nasir Muhammad, Ali Salih Ubad ('Muqbil'), Salih Muslih, Ali Salim al-Bidh and Muhammad Salih Muti'a were elected to the Politburo. There were two candidate members: Ja'am Salah, and Abd al-Aziz Abd al-Wali, who was also minister of state for the Council of Ministers. Abdullah al-Khamiri and Mahmud Ushaysh were dropped. The Central Committee had 31 full members and 14 candidate members elected by the Congress.[15] The consensus at the time was that supporters of Salmin had done quite well and friends of Isma'il less well in the Central Committee elections.

Muqbil, unlike other historical leaders, was from a landowning family in Abyan, but spent most of his political life in Aden. He was a firebrand associated with some extreme left-wing policies, and was a supporter of Salmin. Many of his colleagues speak of their admiration for his intellect and honesty, which they say had a profound influence on them.

Ali Salim al-Bidh had helped set up the NF in Hadhramaut, and led NF forces in the fight against FLOSY in Lahij in 1967. Al-Bidh himself was briefly minister of defence under Qahtan, then after the Corrective Move a very unlikely minister of foreign affairs. In 1972 he became governor of Hadhramaut before returning to the cabinet as minister of planning in 1973. He had a powerful personality and great determination, and yet was also a difficult character given to unpredictable mood swings. He trusted few people and could bear a grudge for years. His mercurial personality, short temper and a single-minded obsession with his personal interests impeded his personal relationships. In the words of one close colleague, he too often allowed some trivial issue, usually linked to an imagined personal slight, to interfere with his judgement.[16] Another who knew him well described him as 'a man of doubt and suspicion'.[17]

Salih Muslih Qasim (Qasim was only used on formal occasions) was from a Shu'aybi family in Lahij, and was elected to the Executive Committee at the Fourth Congress. After the Corrective Move he was made commander of rural provinces security, and then the first commander of 22 (Abbud) Brigade, a unit formed from NF supporters whose main function was to defend the revolution and the regime. He recruited its personnel mainly from Lahij, which was to prove important in later struggles for power. Salih Muslih had an engaging personality that masked a ruthless streak, making him a dangerous enemy. Ali Nasir said he was the cleverest of his rivals and others have described him as a man of restless intrigue.

Salih Muslih was a close friend and associate of Ali Antar (Ali Ahmad Nasser Antar al-Bishi) from Dhala in Lahij. Ali Antar had left the Presidency Council in 1970 to command the armed forces, and remained one of the most powerful of the historically important leaders. Salih Muslih's election to the Politburo was a reflection of Antar's influence. Muhammad Salih Yafi'i (known usually by his party name, Muti'a) became minister of interior in December 1970, and from 1973 minister of foreign affairs. He was noted for his intelligence, charm and ambition, and had a wide network of friends in the NF and government. He acquired a reputation for ambition and ruthlessness during his period as minister of interior, when he controlled both the police and the Popular Militia, before the militia was transferred to the Ministry of Defence in 1973. He had a good relationship with Ali Antar, but other senior military and security figures were less enamoured of him. In the period of the Salmin presidency, he was seen as a man in the Ali Nasir Muhammad mould, who wanted to back the winning side. He was the leading Yafi'i in the regime, but the Yafi'i never developed an influence in the PDRY to match their apparent numerical strength, their presence in the armed forces, or their links to Yafi'i groups and sources of money abroad.

Ja'am Salih was from the Fadhli area of Abyan, and was a protégé and close friend of Salmin. He kept firm control of the NF in Fadhli, ensuring that it supported Salmin in the power struggles of the 1970s. Abd al-Aziz Abd al-Wali was a northerner close to Isma'il and Muhammad Sa'id Abdullah (known as 'Muhsin'), his brother-in-law and another important northerner throughout the life of the PDRY.

After a reshuffle of the government in 1973, the British embassy noted that, with one exception 'all members of the Politburo now hold key positions, and of the total of 18 ministers the six who are neither members of the Politburo or Central Committee are all in the most insignificant posts'.[18] The one exception that the embassy mentioned was Ali Salih Ubad ('Muqbil').

Government

Ali Nasir Muhammad found that the PDRY was surprisingly easy to govern – the systems, regulations and laws inherited from the British merely had to be adapted to cover the whole country. There was a functioning army, police and civil service, and though many key officials had departed there were enough left to manage; there was also a policy of recruiting people with administrative skills from the Yemeni community abroad. As prime minister, Ali Nasir insisted that the civil service disciplines be maintained; meetings were expected to start on time, minutes kept, and decisions recorded and followed up.[19] The regime encouraged south Yemenis in exile to return to join government and state organizations. From 1975 the regime benefited from a growing number of Yemeni graduates from Soviet and foreign universities and technical colleges. Despite the nationalizations and NF-led uprisings of workers, some brave businessmen accepted invitations to invest, though the few who succeeded often did so because of the patronage of one of the senior figures in the regime.[20]

Government by the early 1970s reached into nearly all parts of the country. There was a gradually improving capacity to draft new laws and devise mechanisms for implementing them. The NF in 1967 ordered the continuation of the previous legal systems until specifically amended. Shortly after the Corrective Move, People's Courts were set up to encourage popular participation in the judicial system, but they were abolished in 1979 once an effective judicial system had been set up, based on the 1970 Constitution and administered by a minister of justice. Great stress was laid on the need to respect the law even if the leaders themselves failed to do so.[21] Compared with the YAR in the early 1970s, the PDRY had an effective government and legal system, whatever their flaws. This remains a matter of pride to many former PDRY ministers and officials.

There was a considerable difference between the attitude of Adenis and those from other parts of the country. The Adenis, who had borne the brunt of cuts in jobs, wages and living standards, were unenthusiastic about the revolution, the NF and its slogans. Despite attempts to prevent migration, there was a constant stream of people leaving, mainly the best-educated and most talented. The NF leaders turned to the provinces to try to counter this and foster the revolutionary spirit that they thought was essential to get through the period of state-building and the hardships that were necessary. Under Ali Nasir, provincial governors were delegated considerable powers, though they had to cope with the limited money available by seeking to mobilize and placate local interests in the name of the NF.[22]

Mass organizations

Mass organizations – a concept borrowed from communist regimes – were established for workers, peasants, students, women and the professions. Their leaders normally had positions on the Central Committee or the Presidential Council. They mobilized support for the regime and helped spread the NF's ideas throughout society under the direction of the general secretary for Mass Organizations, who sat on the Central Committee.

The most successful was the General Union for Women. The PDRY set out to transform the place of women in society. There were women in the NLF before 1967 – some reports speak of 300, and one NLF leader has since named some of those who took part.[23] After independence women were represented at all levels in the party organizations, with at least one woman on all committees though there was only one female member of the NF for every 25 men. However, the General Union was not seen as an organization to represent women, but was designed to recruit and mobilize women for the party. The party itself did much to advance the cause of women, though there were gaps between rhetoric and practice.[24]

Defending the regime from external and internal enemies

Throughout the 1970s the regime believed itself under threat from its neighbours and the south Yemeni opposition groups they supported.[25] The resulting siege mentality was made worse by memories of the struggle against FLOSY in 1967, and awareness that some of the regime's policies created more enemies than friends. This was complicated by the stresses and strains in PDRY–YAR relations that saw the two governments supporting armed opposition groups inside each other's territory, and led to a war between the two in 1972 (see Chapter 5). The response was to devote considerable resources to building up the regime's capacity to defend itself from external and internal threats.

The Popular Defence Forces

The NF had since the Corrective Move consolidated its control of the armed forces (known as the Popular Defence Forces) through purges of officers, a widening of recruitment and the appointment of political commissars to all major units. The military was well represented in the Central Committee (though not normally in the Politburo), and all officers over the rank of major had to be members of the NF. The Haytham government stated in December 1969 that its aim was to rebuild the armed forces 'in accordance with a revolutionary concept to make them a shield in protecting the country internally and externally and to take part in the development plan'.[26] The leadership wanted to create a revolutionary spirit within the armed forces, and make them a servant of the people. The NF was determined to make the army subordinate to the politicians, and it was used to try to stamp out tribalism. There were concerns expressed at party meetings about 'corrupt elements' in the armed forces, but by 1977 the regime was confident that the army had been 'cleansed', and there was no longer any fear of a coup.

The armed forces were reorganized, re-equipped, retrained and indoctrinated after the purges following the Corrective Move (their total numbers by 1978 were 24,000, compared with 14,000 in 1972); two years of military service was compulsory for all. The army was divided into a mechanized brigade, ten infantry brigades and an air defence regiment, equipped with Russian tanks and artillery. There were Soviet and other advisers throughout, and the army gradually took on a more Soviet character. It was supplemented by a small navy with Soviet-supplied ships and an air force with 111 combat aircraft – Mig-17s and Mig-21s, and Su-20s and Su-22s. Soviet and Cuban pilots may have flown some of these aircraft. The armed forces demonstrated their effectiveness in two border wars with Yemen (1972 and 1979). The expansion of the armed forces was clearly dependent on support from the Soviet Union.

Ali Antar was the commander of the People's Defence Forces throughout the 1970s, and Ali Nasir was minister of defence as well as prime minister until 1977. Antar had led the Liberation Army in the independence struggle, and had a forceful, aggressive and sometimes mercurial personality. He was able to inspire loyalty in his followers. Most of his former colleagues in the YSP say that his main problem was a lack of education, and perhaps intelligence; but, as one noted, he had a 'white heart'[27] – though others have spoken of a rough and crude, and even cruel side to his personality. He expressed himself clearly in colloquial language, and could move and motivate people. His speeches were in a completely different style to those of other leaders. He had little guile: he meant what he said. He was given to fits of anger, and could be violent if he was provoked or under pressure.

Antar – working with Salih Muslih and another associate, Ali Shaya Hadi – sought to place officers from Lahij in senior positions within the armed forces. One key post in the People's Defence Forces was that of head of its political department. For much of the early 1970s, the post was held by Ali Shaya Hadi or Fadhl Muhsin Abdullah, one of the few prominent Yafi'I in the NF leadership. He was a brother-in-law of Abd al-Fattah Isma'il, and remained loyal to him in the power struggles that plagued the NF leadership.

To strengthen the country's defences, the People's Militia was rapidly expanded, with recruits from committed supporters of the NF within the provinces. Its job was to defend the party and the regime. It received assistance and training mostly from the Cubans, and became a significant part of PDRY's defence forces from the mid 1970s. The militias in Abyan and Lahij quickly became linked to local leaders, who later deployed them in power struggles. From 1973, the Popular Defence Committees were also created, under the control of the NF Secretariat, and modelled on a Cuban example that set out to solve the problems of people within neighbourhoods, but also seen as part of a wider security apparatus. There was also a 15,000-strong Public Security Force – a cross between a police force and a gendarmerie.

State security

The opposition groups were better at propaganda than at fighting, and helped contribute to wishful thinking in the wider region that the regime might fall. This created paranoia within parts of the government, despite the more detached observations of those such as the British ambassador in Aden who commented in March 1971 that it seemed

> very unlikely that avenging tribes with exiled politicians in their train will rout the armed forces of the Peoples' Republic and sweep into this town or any provincial centre, causing the disintegration or collapse of the regime. They are not strong enough. There are familiar signs of disputation and frustration among the exiles and dissipation of their effort. The wholehearted cooperation of the Yemen Arab Republic is withheld.[28]

He did not detect – nor did other observers – 'any focus of opposition to the NF which seems likely to be blown into flame'. But the NF leaders did not share this view.

The attacks had the opposite effect of the intentions of the PDRY's enemies: they persuaded the PDRY's leaders that they should set aside any personal difficulties and join together to deal with the threat. They set up a National Defence Council that included Salmin and Isma'il, as well as the defence and interior ministers and the chief of staff. They were able to use the menace to work for greater solidarity within the NF, and to justify some of the harsh security measures that were taking place.

Security was entrusted to the Revolutionary Security Organization, led by Muhammad Sa'id Abdullah ('Muhsin'), which in 1972 reported to the newly created Ministry of State Security, with Muhsin as minister. The security service received extensive support and training from the East German Stasi. Its functions were to counter internal and external threats, mount intelligence operations abroad (directed against opposition movements and individuals), and to assist revolutionary movements such as PFLOAG. It rapidly recruited large numbers of informers, and in the early

1970s built up a reputation for its arbitrary and cruel methods. Muhsin was widely feared as the man responsible for detecting, arresting and punishing enemies of the NF and the regime, often brutally and without due process. His friends say that he saved more people than he arrested, and that it was units connected to the army that carried out the worst atrocities.[29] His enemies have no doubt that Muhsin was responsible.

Former PDRY leaders now talk euphemistically of the 'mistakes' or 'excesses' of this period. Others, extolling the rule of law in the PDRY, will give examples of the sons of senior ministers being punished for transgressions in the same way as ordinary people. There is today some nostalgia for a PDRY with strong institutions and a robust legal system, but it mostly harks back to the early 1980s. Things were different in the 1970s. There is ample evidence from Amnesty International reports and personal testimonies of the problems: some disappeared, while others were arrested and died in custody without explanation. Faysal al-Sha'bi, and later Muhammad Salih Muti'a, were 'shot trying to escape' – also the fate of 60 prisoners in February 1983.[30] In the mid 1970s, estimates of the number of political prisoners stood at anything from 2,000 to 10,000. Many others fled the country. The PDRY leaders saw themselves as embattled and dedicated, fighting internal and external foes to create a new society. They justified their actions in terms of the benefits their policies would bring.

Freedom of expression was almost nonexistent; the media were tightly controlled, and there was a widespread fear of the reach of the security services, and later of the Popular Defence Committees. In 1975 a law was passed banning contact with foreigners, mostly directed at Western diplomats in Aden. These were indeed difficult days, and they persisted throughout the 1970s.

5

THE PDRY'S INTERNAL AND EXTERNAL POLICIES IN THE SALMIN YEARS

This chapter will examine the main internal and external policies of the regime in the 1969–78 period, and will concentrate on those issues that were important in the power struggles and personality disputes that will be the subjects of the following chapter.

Internal policies

The government had little money, and the country few resources. GDP had fallen by about 20 per cent since 1966, and foreign exchange earnings by 40 per cent. GDP per capita in 1977 was still only $320. There were high defence and security costs in protecting the regime against external and internal opponents. The recovery of the severely damaged service economy of Aden (which had accounted for over 50 per cent of GDP at independence) would have to wait for the reopening of the Suez Canal in 1975. There were important assets in the agricultural areas in Lahij, Abyan and Hadhramaut, generating around 20 per cent of GDP and 12 per cent of exports. While there was some potential for expansion, the prevalence of desert and mountains, and a lack of water resources, meant that not much more than 1 per cent of the PDRY was cultivable. There were frequent droughts and floods, with an often disastrous impact on local economies. Land ownership at independence was concentrated in the hands of the elite, to which peasants under sharecropping systems gave two-thirds of the harvest. The PDRY's fisheries were promising, but elsewhere there were only limited opportunities for industries based on food processing, textiles or service provision. Aden had the BP oil refinery, one of the most important sources of government income, but it was working at only 70–80 per cent of its capacity in the early 1970s, and much less than that by 1978. Oil prospecting did not take place until the 1980s and the country had to import most of its energy, with the result that electrification developed very slowly. In 1967 the total length of metalled roads in the country was less than 500 km. Many south Yemenis could keep going only because of the inflow of remittances, which averaged about $60 million a year during the 1970s and evaded the grasping hands of the regime.

Creating a socialist economy

In the first few years much of the focus was on slashing costs, mostly by cutting the wages of public sector workers, and on imposing taxes to keep the budget deficit within manageable limits. The NF organized demonstrations by hapless civil servants and workers in the state sector demanding that the government cut their wages. The third such cut was made in 1972. It was thus hardly surprising that relations between the NF and trade union leaders started to become quite tense. The unions objected not only to the cuts in wages, but also to the way that NF-organized committees were sacking workers and civil servants on political grounds.

The political turmoil up to and immediately after the Corrective Move did not inspire either communist or Arab governments to offer significant economic assistance. Planning was dogged by the lack of resources, reliable statistics and expertise in managing an economy. The regime rushed into the nationalization of 36 foreign-owned banks and insurance companies – which included most significant companies, except for BP, the mostly British-owned bunkering companies and Cable and Wireless. The move was pushed through against the advice of some ministers, including the communist Abdullah Ba Dhib.[1] It was literally an empty measure since, for example, the two British banks concerned had long since removed any useful assets out of the country.[2] This measure was accompanied by an investment law to encourage local capital to participate in development – an opportunity that the businessmen who had not fled the country did not take up, to the surprise of ministers! The few who did soon regretted their decision, though there were exceptional cases of investors doing well if, as noted above, they had the protection of one of the NF leaders. An immigration ordinance appeared to encourage those foreigners still working in Aden to leave. The Parsee enterprises that had dominated Aden's trade and retail sectors for decades were taken over either by the state or by their workers in a series of uprisings inspired by the political leadership.

These takeovers were followed by the creation of five 'national companies' dealing with internal trade, external trade, shipping, petroleum and the docks, and a National Bank was set up. Some skilled personnel were retained[3] from the nationalized entities, and others were recruited from the south Yemeni communities abroad, notably from East Africa.[4] Competent junior staff were promoted and given training abroad to improve their skills. At the end of 1970 Aden ceased to be a free-trade port (except for re-exports), as import duties were imposed. In 1972, privately owned buildings belonging to absentee landlords were taken into state hands without compensation, leading to a severe drop in the inflow of remittances, much of which had gone into construction.

The rush of measures led to confusion, and sometimes chaos, with the result that more people left; but this did not deter those in the regime determined to create a truly socialist economy. As ministers gained experience, they adjusted some of their measures in the hope of encouraging an inflow of investment and a higher rate of remittances.

Despite these problems the government set out to look after the poorest people in society. The prices of basic foodstuffs were subsidized through state control of internal trade, and a Price Stabilization Fund, set up in 1974, fixed the prices of wheat, flour, rice, sugar, milk powder, ghee, cooking oil, and later tea; a de facto rationing system governed sales of these goods. Once fixed, prices did not change in the Salmin period.

Agrarian reform and fisheries

Qahtan's agrarian reform law had pleased no one, and the left wanted to implement much more radical measures as soon as possible. A new law was duly issued in 1970. The combined effects of the two laws were to confiscate all land owned by the sultans, their followers and larger landowners. Landholdings were limited to 8.5 hectares of irrigated land and 17 hectares of un-irrigated land per person. Family ownership was limited to 17 hectares for irrigated and 34 hectares for dry land. Most of the confiscated land was allocated to peasants who were brought into various types of cooperatives (some later becoming collective farms). Around half of the country's cultivated area was affected, and was allocated to 26,000 people. One of the better aspects of the law was to give the government control over the drilling of wells – unlike the situation in modern Yemen, where uncontrolled boring of wells is 'mining' the country's rapidly depleting stocks of water. These measures were not allowed to interfere in the export of cotton from Lahij and Abyan as this was a major source of foreign exchange and experienced people managed the new cotton board.

Following a visit to China, Salmin started promoting the Maoist idea of uprisings by peasants to take the land. Land, he said, did not give itself away; it had to be taken through revolutionary violence. Peasants working the land threw out landlords, often led by local NF militants. This concept of a popular revolutionary uprising started in the rural areas, but it entered the cities with uprisings by workers.[5] Such actions were thought to have the additional merit of engendering a revolutionary spirit among the people.

Fishing was the country's major resource, and surveys conducted in the mid 1970s estimated the potential annual catch at around 2.5 times that of current production. The industry employed 13,000 people working for a few boat owners. They were subject to the same uprisings seen in agriculture, which were accompanied by rather more effective moves to organize cooperatives. A Public Corporation for Fish Wealth and a national fleet were set up, the latter soon acquiring modern vessels.

Spending and planning

Planning guidelines were drawn up by the NF, approved by the Politburo, and then put into a national plan by the Ministry of Planning which had then to be endorsed by the cabinet and SPC. An interim first plan was issued to cover the years 1971/2 to 1973/4, with 38 per cent of spending devoted to transport and communications, 31 per cent to agriculture, 17 per cent to industry, and 10 per cent to health, education and other social needs. The plan was designed to create jobs through labour-intensive projects and build up infrastructure and agriculture. It was estimated that over 78 per cent of the funding would come from external sources, but a substantial part failed to arrive. A second five-year plan, covering 1974–78, was more successful, and there was a shift towards more capital-intensive projects, developing agricultural and industrial production and improving government services. Grants and loans from the Soviet Union, the World Bank and Kuwait were the main sources of external assistance.

The economy ten years after independence

The situation in 1978, at the end of the Salmin period and the second five-year plan, was summed up in a study by the World Bank.[6] It described the PDRY as 'one of the least developed countries'. It saw as its main assets a talented workforce (though by now mostly working abroad, and providing a major source of income through remittances), fisheries and its harbour. The report noted that the second five-year plan had done better than expected thanks to the inflow of foreign funds, with a good social balance between targets of investment. It was critical of the plan's focus on what it called horizontal projects – that is, developing a new fishing fleet, for example, rather than spending on the fishing sector as a whole. It noted some positive factors: the effective management of public finance and 'austere' private consumption, balanced by an increase in social services. Investment was 31 per cent of GDP in 1977, compared with 2 per cent in 1970, and there had been 7 per cent annual growth in real terms between 1973 and 1977. Foreign exchange income covered 70 per cent of spending.

Fishing was by 1977 providing 10 per cent of GDP, but agriculture, at 7 per cent, was suffering productivity problems. Transport and commerce were expanding rapidly as a result of the re-opening of the Suez Canal in 1975. Above all, the PDRY's social development was impressive, with adequate food supplies and the rapid expansion of health and education to all parts of the country. Around 49 per cent of the PDRY's economy was in the public sector by 1980 (representing 16 per cent of agriculture, 72 per cent of fisheries, 73 per cent of industry and 30 per cent of trade).[7]

The World Bank was concerned about low productivity especially in agriculture, where investment and the major reforms of the 1970s had not delivered the expected results. Income from agricultural employment was significantly below that in other sectors of the economy and agricultural output per capita fell in the 1970s. The Aden refinery was operating at only a quarter of its capacity, and was not breaking even and significant investment was needed to reverse the situation. The bank wanted the government to find means of directing the flow of remittances into productive investment at a time when the country remained dependent on foreign assistance, and criticized the absence of centralized planning (planning was dispersed over several agencies and ministries) and the poor management levels in the public-sector corporations; but it praised the regime for virtually eliminating corruption and labour absenteeism.

If current policies were not changed, the World Bank judged that the inflow of remittances would grow too slowly, and that foreign aid would stagnate. If the PDRY were to increase productivity (especially in agriculture), as well as stimulating greater foreign assistance and diversifying its sources, that would help lead to increased exports and investment to produce GDP growth of around 9 per cent annually.

The impact on politics

Haydar al-Attas, who was a minister in all PDRY governments from 1969 to 1990, and head of state from 1986 to 1990, believes that there was broad agreement among the leaders over the direction of economic policies after the burst of revolutionary enthusiasm in the early 1970s. Policies were debated vigorously, but once agreed they were laid down in policy statements at party congresses. He argues that the divisions that arose among the leading figures were based on personality and competition for power, not on policy. Ali Nasir Muhammad, on the other hand, who was in all governments from 1969 to 1986, believes that there were significant differences, relating mostly to economic policy. One crucial argument was over the role of the private sector and private investment. Salmin and Ali Nasir – with direct responsibility for the economy, and holding positions in which they had to deal with public opinion – came to favour a more pragmatic approach than did Abd al-Fattah Isma'il and other ideologues. Remittances from migrants remained vital to the economy at a local level. Pragmatists wanted to encourage migrants to invest in the PDRY or put their money into PDRY bank accounts, while the policies pursued by the government led to migrants retaining their money abroad, or trying to remit directly to their families in the PDRY.

There were also differences over the support provided by the Soviet Union and its allies, which was of critical importance to defence and security, and arguably to the development of the party. The USSR was a major provider of economic assistance, but mostly in the form of project assistance and the supply of experts, not in cash. It was enough to keep the regime's head above water, but much more was needed to lift the PDRY out of poverty. The same was true of the substantial aid provided by international organizations designed to develop specific water, agricultural and industrial projects. Aid on the scale required could only come from rich regional states or from the West. This dilemma was reflected in party decisions which spoke openly of the need for balance – but there were arguments behind the scenes between pragmatists, who wanted to do more to attract non-Soviet help, and those committed to the Socialist camp.[8]

Social policies

Though there were obvious flaws in the regime's economic policies, its social goals were both progressive and well-intentioned. There was much less argument over measures to provide jobs, education, health and other social services to people throughout the country. The PDRY may not have had much money, but the aim was to distribute it through services to all on the basis of equality. There was also broad agreement within the NF on how to deal with tribalism, Islam and qat.

Abolishing tribalism

There was a political need to foster nationalist sentiment and abolish tribalism, which was much more fragmented than in the YAR. Whereas there were loose confederations of tribes, such as in Yafi'i and Awlaqi, most tribal units were small. The use of tribal names was abolished: thus Ali Nasir Muhammad al-Hassani became simply Ali Nasir Muhammad. The bearing of arms, including the traditional dagger – *jambiya* – was banned in November 1969. Clubs and organizations based on tribal origins were closed. There were exhortations against using tribal connections for jobs and favours, and it became compulsory to deal with tribal disputes through special tribunals.

In the early 1970s, many NF leaders would exhort the people to abandon tribalism while drawing their own support from family and tribal connections. The old tribal chiefs had gone, but were in effect replaced by NF officials from the tribe: the party secretary was the new shaikh; he was the source of influence and jobs. In return, he expected the loyalty of his beneficiaries. The use of occasional intimidation from the air when disorder threatened might not have seemed too different from what had happened a few years earlier under the British, except that the British normally issued a warning first. In the 1970s the regime had the most difficulty with some of the nomadic tribes close to the Saudi border, and there were cases of whole tribes or sections of tribes working with opposition groups across the border.[9]

Islam

The 1970 Constitution made Islam the official religion, and sanctioned the teaching of Islam as part of the school curriculum. It also charged the government with undertaking to protect the country's Islamic heritage. The NF leaders were secular, and saw Islam as a private matter. They understood the importance of Islam to a great majority of the people – evident from the large number of mosques (18,000 in the mid 1980s) and the sanctuaries in Hadhramaut. Gradually, the regime realized that it could live with this as long as potential opponents could not use Islam to challenge the authority of the regime. There was an initial crackdown on some religious scholars and imams; the tombs of saints were desecrated, and preachers and scholars murdered in Hadhramaut.[10] The tiny Muslim Brotherhood was made illegal. As the regime matured in the 1970s and 1980s it allowed more space for Islam, even though the NF/YSP leaders were determined that Islam should not influence the politics and policies of the state. There was not a single mention of Islam in the 600-page report on the first YSP Congress in 1978, except in an annex containing the constitution.

On the other hand, Salmin would have himself televized at Friday prayers. Abd al-Fattah Isma'il made a speech at the 1972 Congress, not published until years later, telling his audience that East German (and by implication Soviet) leaders had advised the NF to harness Islam for its cause. There were many examples in the Holy Qur'an and the Hadith that could be used to justify the regime's policies, and the writings of well-known historical scholars could be quoted for the same purpose. Some could at the time be found in Tashkent and other parts of the Islamic regions of the Soviet Union. Islam could be adapted to the regime's ideology in what was called 'liberation theology';[11] the state could simply appropriate those beliefs that suited its purposes. Some of the measures taken by the regime provoked criticism from clerics. For example one prominent shaikh criticized the decision to include women in the SPC. This led to media attacks against clerics, who were accused of using their Friday sermons to undermine the regime

As the NF and the PDRY Islamic scholars learned to live with each other, greater mutual toleration developed. Some clerics became members of the NF and the SPC. The NF wanted women to adopt modern dress, and to give women greater rights and access to employment. Isma'il and other leaders took occasional action at a local level to ensure conformity, but the reversion to traditional practices following unification, even in Aden, suggests that the innate conservatism of the population was too deep for the regime to change in its 22 years of rule.

The Islamic revival had begun in other places in the Arab world by the late 1970s, but there was, as yet, little evidence of it in the PDRY's public affairs. It was different in the north, particularly when Muslim Brothers expelled from Syria and Egypt started to arrive, and Yemenis influenced by Wahhabi and Salafi teachings in Saudi Arabia helped to accelerate moves towards more extreme interpretations of Islam than the previously moderate liberal Shafi'i traditions of the PDRY and adjacent areas of the north. These developments then seeped into the south.

Qat

The PDRY government accepted that it could not ban qat, but sought instead to restrict its consumption. Under a law in 1977, qat could only be consumed at weekends and on public holidays in Aden. In the qat-growing areas, Lahij and Abyan, it could be chewed at any time. It was banned in Hadhramaut and Mahra, where at the time it was not widely consumed. Typically, there could be quite draconian measures against transgressors.[12] The PDRY was successful in controlling qat consumption, and thus freeing land and water for exportable cash crops such as coffee. Qat-chewing quickly returned with unification, and is now almost universal.

The status of women

From the outset the regime sought to enhance the status of women, though again the impact of its efforts only became visible much later.[13] The 1970 Constitution guaranteed a broad set of rights to women, making it among the most progressive in the Arab world at the time. Women were given equal access to education and employment, and a Family Law passed in 1974 gave women new rights over divorce and restricted polygamy. Women were a central part of campaigns in the early 1970s to eradicate illiteracy. The General Union of Yemeni Women (led by A'yda Ali al-Yaf'i, who was on the Presidency Council – later the Presidium – for many years) gave women an influence on policy, though its main functions were to mobilize support from the Central Committee and implement its decisions. There is little doubt that women's status and rights greatly improved under the PDRY, though there was always a difference between the situation of a woman working in a government office and her life at home, where traditional practices persisted and became prominent after unity in 1990.[14] There were no female ministers or members of the Politburo in the PDRY.

Education

The PDRY inherited fewer than 400 primary schools of all types, 61 intermediary schools, 19 secondary and technical schools, three teacher training colleges, and no universities. There were no schools of any sort in Mahra. The schools in the old WAP followed a different system from that in Hadhramaut, which was modelled on Sudan's. There was a shortage of teachers. The 1970 Constitution guaranteed education for all, and a 1972 law sought to put education on a modern footing. The state budget gave a high priority to education, so that by 1977 there were nearly 1,000 primary schools, 326 intermediary schools and 23 secondary schools and there were 260,000 pupils in the system, compared with 63,000 at independence. By 1978, participation at primary level was over 80 per cent in Aden and 70 per cent in Abyan, Lahij and Hadhramaut in the 7–14 age group for boys, and 30 per cent or over for girls. There was a sharp fall-off in the 15–18 age groups, especially among women. Aden University was set up in 1975. Like so much in the PDRY, the education system was used to inculcate the party's values, but the party put education at the centre of its social goals and was successful in delivering it. This was accompanied by a campaign in the early 1970s to eradicate illiteracy.

Health and other services

The Constitution guaranteed free medical care for all, but in 1970 there were only 71 doctors in the country as a result of the large-scale emigration of mostly Aden-based health professionals who disliked the regime's restrictions on private medicine and its expectation that they should serve in remote areas. By 1977 there were 222 doctors, of whom 125 were Yemenis, and there were plans for a very rapid increase in numbers as the new medical school at Aden University produced graduates. In the 1970s the number of hospital beds doubled, and health units, health centres and hospitals were set up throughout the country. Social Insurance did not come into effect until the early 1980s.

The constitution also guaranteed housing for all, but little progress was made in the 1970s. After an initial drop in private house-building in the early 1970s, it picked up quickly in later years thanks to a higher inflow of remittances. Many houses, including those built by the British, were nationalized under the 1972 Housing Law. These were made available to people at very low rents, though they suffered from a lack of maintenance.

Foreign policies

The broad direction of policy was laid down at the NF congresses, which clearly put relations with the Soviet Union and the communist world at the heart of the PDRY's foreign relations but spoke of the need to improve relations with neighbouring and regional states in order to obtain economic assistance. At the same time it was also seeking to export its revolution to these states.

There was some confusion about who took the lead in foreign affairs. The NF view was that the Politburo, as advised by the party secretary for foreign affairs, would draw up policy guidelines which the minister of foreign affairs would then implement. A powerful minister, such as Muhammad Salih Muti'a, would demand a major voice in policy, but for most of the 1970s the party post was held by his friend and protégé Salim Salih Muhammad, a fellow Yafi'i, and there were few difficulties. In practice the party often took the lead in dealing with the socialist states through its relations with the Communist Party of the Soviet Union (CPSU), while the Ministry would be responsible for dealing with Arab countries, international organizations and the West.

Salmin, as head of state, believed he was responsible for foreign affairs, and in his later years he took the lead in seeking better relations with the Arabs. Presidents and kings were accustomed to a personal style of diplomacy, ignoring foreign ministers and dealing directly with each other through meetings, phone calls and special envoys. This style of diplomacy suited Salmin, but he encountered trouble because he often refused to give his NF colleagues a full account of his contacts and did not keep records. There is little in NF public statements to show that Isma'il opposed moves to build better relations with Arab donor states. He clearly gave a much higher priority to the alliance with Moscow, but his outright support for revolutionary movements in the Arab world and beyond undermined Salmin's diplomacy with Arab rulers.

War and unity with the Yemen Arab Republic

In the late 1960s the YAR and the PRSY appointed ministers of unity affairs, and frequently spoke of the high priority they placed on achieving unity. Ali Nasir Muhammad is among several former leaders who say that they always wanted a proper negotiated union, but believed that northern leaders wanted to swallow the south.[15] Writings and comments by northern leaders show that they considered the government in Aden as being in temporary control of a part of the Yemeni homeland, to be incorporated when the time came. Some will admit that unity in the 1970s would have been a distraction at a time when the NF was trying to establish its rule, and the regime in Sana'a to recover from the civil war. On the other hand, Mohsen Alaini recalls that, when he met Muhammad Ali Haytham and Muhammad Salih Awlaqi in May 1970, he told them:

> You should not think that, through unity, we aim to control you although the population of the north is larger. We are ready to accept unification with Aden as the capital, your government as the Yemeni government and your flag as the Yemeni flag. If partition continues, it will become impossible to unify. The differences between us today are few and easily resolved, but as time passes they will grow and become more difficult to eliminate.[16]

He added that he had to reject the counter-offer from the PRSY that the currencies of the two countries be united, noting that the PRSY leaders must have known this was impossible. The constitution setting up the PDRY in 1970 caused dismay in Sana'a, since it seemed to assert that it was a regime with aspirations to rule the whole of Yemen, not just the south. Aden objected to an article in the YAR Constitution that set up a Consultative Council with 20 seats allocated to southern members. Both parts of Yemen aspired to rule the other.

In the north, the coup of November 1967 brought into government the so-called 'third force' of republicans and royalists. But these had divided by mid 1968 into groupings that essentially represented the major Zaydi tribes of the northern part of the country and some of the Shafi'i interests in the south, and drove into opposition more militant left-wing groups that formed the Revolutionary Democratic Party (RDP), the MAN-inspired forerunner of the National Democratic Front. In the ensuing conflict, the RDP and its allies were defeated and the Yemen government drew closer to Saudi Arabia, whose subsidies were important to the major tribal confederations. The NF thus quickly found itself supporting the opposition to the new regime in Sana'a.

Shortly afterwards, the RDP and another left-wing group (the Yemeni Revolutionary Resistance Organization) launched a guerrilla campaign in the Damt region, with covert support from the PDRY. In response, the YAR government allowed PDRY exile groups access to facilities, arms and propaganda in the north. Meanwhile, the leaders of both Yemens continued to pay lip-service to Yemeni unity, but failed to meet each other except at Arab summits.

Relations deteriorated even further during 1972, following the killing in February by PDRY soldiers of the leading shaikh from the Bakil Tribal confederation (Ali bin Naji al-Kadr), and up to 70 others, in circumstances disputed by the two governments.[17] Tensions eased in subsequent months, but when RDP opposition groups moved from bases in the PDRY to the border areas and occupied some north Yemeni territory, YAR troops were mobilized and sent to the border. The PDRY responded by reinforcing its positions. Hostilities broke out in September 1972, and in the course of a two-week war mostly in the border region, PDRY forces got the better of their opponents. Sana'a was able to occupy the island of Kamaran in the Red Sea and refused to give it up, arguing that its inhabitants had requested its transfer to Sana'a, and that it was of little importance to the PDRY.[18]

The short war was ended through mediation by Arab states, leading to peace talks in Cairo where, to general astonishment, the two prime ministers, Ali Nasir Muhammad (Abd al-Fattah Isma'il was also present for part of the time) and Mohsin Alaini, agreed to unite their two states.[19] This was followed up by a summit meeting held in Libya, where the two presidents – Salmin and Abd al-Rahman al-Iryani – agreed to achieve unity within a year, and to set up a process to do so. The half-hearted attempts to follow this up were stymied by the growing instability in the YAR, caused partly by opposition to the agreement from northern tribal leaders and senior military officers.

Salmin and al-Iryani had formed a good relationship, and agreed to stop supporting each other's dissidents. In 1973, Salmin became the first PDRY head of state to visit Sana'a. Salmin was able to establish even better relations with President Ibrahim al-Hamdi, after he had overthrown al-Iryani in a coup in 1974. They used their relationship to prevent further quarrels between the governments, allowing both to concentrate on pressing internal issues. Neither was seriously interested in union. Al-Iryani and al-Hamdi realized that, despite the YAR's much greater population and economy, its military and administrative capacities at the time were weaker than those of the PDRY.

Salmin and Ali Nasir Muhammad were willing to work with the government of the YAR in a pragmatic fashion, taking into account the pressures on the YAR leaders from Saudi-backed tribal leaders and other interests. Unity could wait. Isma'il and his allies – many of whom were from the north or, like Salih Muslih, from tribal areas of the PDRY bordering the YAR – envisaged unity following the installation of a left-wing government in Sana'a. Salih Muslih was responsible within the NF for organizing political and military support for the RDP and other left-wing groups in the north. Salmin may have objected, but could see the value of using PDRY support for the RDP as a useful tool to put pressure on al-Hamdi to be more helpful to the south. Despite Mohsen Alaini's words to Haytham, there was not much enthusiasm for unity in the north throughout the 1970s.[20]

By 1975, al-Hamdi had proved himself to be an astute and popular leader capable of building a strong central government and reducing the influence of the northern tribes and their Saudi backers. With his encouragement, leftist groups in February 1976 merged to form the National Democratic Front (NDF) to offset the influence of the Saudis. It included the YAR versions of the PDU and al-Tali'a, which in 1975 merged with the NF in Aden (see Chapter 6).[21] The NDF exploited al-Hamdi's policy, but its aim was to take power in Sana'a and then unite with the south. Al-Hamdi must have known that the NDF was virtually a northern extension of the NF, but also that Salmin was opposed to both the formation of the YSP and the inclusion of the NDF or its constituent parties within it.

The assassination of al-Hamdi on 11 October 1977 affected Salmin deeply on a personal level. He returned from his funeral suppressing a deep anger, and eager to take revenge on the perpetrators. Who did it and why has not been established, but the cause was probably linked to internal rivalries, and many concluded that it was his successor Ahmad al-Ghashmi who was the culprit, allied with other army officers and interests thought to oppose closer relations with the south and favour better relations with Saudi Arabia. The fact that he was killed a day before he was due to visit Aden for important discussions was seen as circumstantial evidence of such a plot.

Ahmad al-Ghashmi pursued a more pro-Saudi policy, and he alienated a key ally, Colonel Abdullah Abd al-Alim, who led a revolt against him. Al-Ghashmi routed his forces, but they retreated to the PDRY, and the probability of armed confrontation between the two sides loomed. The head of the forces defeating Abd al-Alim was Ali Abdullah Salih, the president of the YAR from 1978.

For Salmin, this was all a disaster. He had built up a great rapport with al-Hamdi, and with his death Salmin's strategy for Yemen disintegrated. He was realistic enough to know that he would have to deal with al-Ghashmi even if – as some allege – secretly he might have been planning to avenge the death of his friend al-Hamdi.

Thus, at the end of the Salmin presidency, the two Yemens had fought a short war and signed a unity agreement. The south had a much greater influence over the situation in the north than vice versa; its regime was stronger and better organized. It was never in a position to impose itself on the north, but was well able to resist any northern attempt to absorb it.

Regional relations

In the early years the PDRY had ambitions to export its revolution and seek allies among movements and governments close to its ideological aims. Later, these policies were partially abandoned, as the PDRY came to terms with its neighbours and learned to adapt itself to a world it could do little to influence.

Oman

There had been links through MAN since 1965 between the NF and the Popular Front for the Liberation of Dhufar, which later became the Popular Front for the Liberation of Oman and the Arabian Gulf (PFLOAG). Soon after the PRSY became independent it provided logistical and political support to PFLOAG, and helped facilitate the flow of arms to the front from China and the Soviet Union. There were bases in Mahra province and an office in Aden. In the first few years of the PDRY, PFLOAG achieved undeniable success, exerting some form of influence over most of Dhufar outside Salalah. In that period there were clashes between soldiers from either side, and attacks on PFLOAG facilities in the PDRY by British-piloted aircraft. In 1970 Sultan Qaboos overthrew his father and, using the new oil revenues, started modernizing the Omani administration and enhancing its armed forces, with British, Jordanian and Iranian support. An Iranian brigade was moved to Dhufar. Gradually, PFLOAG was pushed back towards the PDRY border, until in 1975 the war came to a virtual end. The PDRY continued to support PFLOAG (which divided itself into the Popular front for the Liberation of Oman and the Bahrain Liberation Front). Saudi Arabia insisted that the PDRY end its support for PFLOAG as part of its agreement to establish diplomatic relations with Aden in 1976. However, the PDRY continued its backing until 1981, long after such assistance had any great significance or served the national interests of the PDRY. It was reluctant to abandon the principle of assisting a like-minded organization to overthrow a reactionary regime in which British influence was only too visible.

Saudi Arabia

King Faysal had lobbied against British withdrawal from Aden as late as May 1967. Saudi Arabia did not recognise the PRSY/PDRY, and set about frustrating its aims in the YAR and Oman, and undermining the regime itself. It was resolutely against the Yemeni unification, and lobbied to get the Yemeni prime minister, Mohsen Alaini, sacked after he had signed the unity agreements in Cairo.[22]

Saudi Arabia provided the many Yemeni exiles in Saudi Arabia with arms, bases, training and logistical support, and helped set up Radio Free South Yemen. There were clashes along the borders between exile groups and PDRY armed forces. Saudi armed forces were rarely involved, except for a major incident in Hadhramaut in 1969, in an area that Saudi Arabia had claimed as part of its territory long before 1967. In 1973 Salmin asserted that the Saudis wanted to annex Hadhramaut, a fear long nourished in the PDRY and heard even today. Control of policy towards Yemen at that time was in the hands of the defence minister, Prince Sultan, who wanted to keep the PDRY weak and unable to threaten Saudi or YAR security.

The first contacts between PDRY and Saudi leaders appear to have taken place at an Arab summit in 1974, but it was the assassination of King Faysal in April 1975 that offered the prospect of change in Saudi policy to the PDRY and the YAR. King Khalid and his advisers were prepared to try to woo the PDRY with what was called 'riyalpolitik'.[23] The opportunity was provided by the defeat of the PFLOAG rebels in Oman in 1975. Riyadh began to mediate between Aden and Muscat, leading to a visit to Riyadh by the PDRY foreign minister, Muhammad Salih Muti'a, in December, following a chance encounter with a Saudi diplomat on an aircraft. In early 1976, the leadership authorized Salmin to enter a dialogue with Saudi Arabia. Diplomatic relations were established in March 1976, and there were reported to be promises of Saudi project aid for the PDRY. There may also have been an understanding that part of any rapprochement would involve a weakening of Soviet–PDRY relations, and the withdrawal of Iranian forces from Oman. During 1977 more concrete steps were taken to provide assistance, and for a time Saudi support for the south Yemen opposition was suspended. Though neither side fulfilled these promises, enough was done for Salmin to make a state visit to Riyadh on 31 July 1977, after which Saudi Arabia undertook to provide oil to Aden's refinery. The Saudis found Salmin to be pragmatic, with a much greater understanding of regional politics than any of his colleagues. They did not see any trace of the Maoist Salmin of the early 1970s.

By this time Salmin's position was weakening. The Saudis, by some accounts, felt that the changed conditions in the YAR would enable them to extract more concessions from Aden in return for economic support. The unintended consequence of this was to undermine Salmin, who was criticized by his colleagues for not extracting enough from the Saudis, and cutting back too far in PDRY support for organizations like the PFLOAG. His critics accused him of pursuing a personal foreign policy, and even of taking Saudi bribes. He did not help himself by refusing to give details to the Politburo of his dealings with the Saudis.

Other Gulf states
At the time of independence, Kuwait was the only formally independent Gulf state. It quickly recognized the PDRY and, consistent with its policies at the time, it provided economic assistance without strings. In PDRY eyes, the rest of the Gulf states were de facto British colonies. It did not recognize the independence of these states or the formation of the UAE in 1971, and vainly campaigned to persuade the Arab League not to recognize them. These states, close to Saudi Arabia and the UK, and supporters of Oman, were deeply suspicious of the regime in Aden. During the early 1970s there was a gradual shift in policy as the PDRY saw these states benefiting from the oil boom. The PDRY foreign minister visited the UAE, Qatar and Bahrain in early 1975, and the UAE president visited Aden in March 1977. There was some UAE aid, but there were unsubstantiated accusations by the internal rivals of Salmin and foreign minister Mutī'a that they had received bribes from the UAE.

The wider Arab world and the Horn of Africa
The PDRY joined the Arab League and became active in Arab politics soon after independence, but its role in the region was limited by its small size, its distance from the centre of events and its impoverishment. It was associated with the more radical forces in the region and was closer to Libya,

Syria and Iraq than to Egypt. From the mid 1970s, Libya took an interest in PDRY affairs that lasted, in the mercurial fashion of Libyan policies, until unity in 1990. Aden seemed close to Baghdad for a time, but Iraq was more interested in the north, and did not like the presence of pro-Syrian Ba'athist ministers in PDRY governments or of Iraqi communist lecturers at the Higher School of Scientific Socialism. There was a public row when the PDRY protested at Iraq's brief reconciliation with the Shah of Iran (whose troops were in Oman) in 1975. The PDRY welcomed the Iranian Revolution, despite its Islamic character, and was the only Arab state that spoke out against Iraq in its war with Iran in the 1980s. President Sadat had little time for either the PDRY or its Marxist pronouncements. During the Ramadan (Yom Kippur) War of 1973, when Egypt, Syria and Jordan fought Israel, the PDRY helped Egypt blockade the Bab al-Mandab. There were discussions in March 1974 about the possibility of Egypt leasing Perim, a PDRY island off the YAR coast, occupying a strategic position close to the Bab al-Mandab. Aden, like most Arab capitals, cut links to Cairo after President Sadat's visit to Israel in 1977.

In the early 1970s, the PDRY gave strong support to the PFLP and PDFLP, led respectively by the MAN patrons of the NLF, George Habbash and Nayif Hawatmah, who at the time had strained relations with the PLO led by Yasir Arafat. In 1971 PDRY helped the PFLP launch an attack on Israeli-bound tankers in the Bab al-Mandab. From 1973, however, Aden recognized the PLO, which opened an office shortly afterwards. In 1976 a detachment of PDRY forces was sent to Lebanon as part of an Arab Deterrent Force to provide protection to the PLO. When the PLO armed forces were expelled from Lebanon in 1982, PDRY provided a camp for some of these forces near Aden.

Relations with Somalia were close in the early 1970s, as its president, Siad Barre, like the PDRY regime, was drawn into the Soviet camp. The success of the Dergue in Ethiopia in overthrowing Emperor Haile Selassie in 1974 offered an opportunity to form a socialist bloc embracing Ethiopia, Somalia and Yemen. The PDRY drew closer to Addis Ababa and cut its support to the Eritrean rebels fighting the Ethiopian regime, causing complications in its relations with most other Arab states, which continued backing the Eritreans. When war between Somalia and Ethiopia broke out in the Ogaden in 1978, the PDRY backed the Ethiopians, and at Soviet request sent troops to assist the Addis Ababa regime. The Saudis and most Arab states backed the Somalis, helping to isolate the PDRY and undermine Salmin's efforts to build relations in the Arab world.

The PDRY and the Soviet Union

By 1978 Moscow was the PDRY's most important ally and source of military and economic support. Between 1967 and 1978, Moscow's policy towards the PDRY evolved from an early period of puzzlement, through a sceptical welcome and cautious opening, to a gradual warming and deepening of relations. Its policies were much influenced by its strategic and regional interests and its confrontation with the United States, and both were profoundly affected by developments in the Middle East and the Horn of Africa. Moscow regarded the YAR as a potential regional ally, and provided it with military and economic support; up to the early 1970s it had close relations with Egypt, and up to the mid 1970s with Somalia. The Russians wanted to keep some balance in their relationships between the two Yemens; they also wanted a degree of stability in the peninsula. Ali Nasir has described how the Soviet leader Leonid Brezhnev told him in 1973 that the PDRY should stop exporting revolution to its neighbours if it wanted Soviet help in exploring for oil.[24] A year later, however, in response to Oman's deepening relationship with the USA and the Shah's Iran, it was providing support to PFLOAG through the PDRY.

Moscow saw the Corrective Move as helpful to its aims, even if it had reservations about the extreme ideas of Salmin and other leaders.[25] As it later admitted, it had some worries about the way the PDRY took 'radical measures without regard to the socio-economic foundations, seeking to do away with backwardness at one stroke'.[26] Soviet commentators in the early 1970s warned that the non-capitalist approach was complex, and that parts of it could not be skipped. It was aware of the internal divisions, and worried about the stability of the country. It thus favoured an approach of gradually increasing its economic support for the PDRY. In October 1969 relations between the PDRY and the USA were finally broken. There was a three-week visit by Isma'il to Moscow in April 1970. One outcome was the agreement by the CPSU to help build the NF's cadres through special educational courses, and to provide support for the Higher School of Scientific Socialism. From then on, there were close relations between the NF and the CPSU, as well as between the two governments. There was a string of visits by PDRY leaders to Moscow in the early 1970s, each generating more military and economic assistance, and with the PDRY leaders being received at an increasingly higher level in the Soviet leadership.[27]

Soviet commentators writing in the media suggested that the 1972 Fourth Congress was an important milestone, in that the PDRY was adopting an approach favoured by the Russians and moving away from some of the Maoist and extremist ideas of its recent past. This may have been prompted by a change in Chinese policy, which saw it developing relations with other countries in the region, cutting its aid to PFLOAG and giving a lower priority to its relations with the PDRY. When Egypt expelled Soviet advisers in July 1972 and the YAR resumed relations with the USA, Soviet interest in the PDRY increased. Agreements were signed in 1972 for a loan of $20 million to build relations at party and government levels. Soviet arms were then finding their way to PFLOAG through the PDRY. By the end of 1972 there were 200 Soviet military advisers in the PDRY, and East Germany was assisting the PDRY's police and security services. In the following year there was an agreement to provide MiG-21 aircraft, and a PDRY leader (Ali Nasir Muhammad) finally met Brezhnev. The Moscow press spoke of the PDRY's commitment to scientific socialism.

Moscow's interest in the region increased further after the 1973 Ramadan War. Its main focus was Somalia, with which it signed a Friendship and Cooperation Agreement in July 1974. Abd al-Fattah Isma'il rushed to Moscow immediately after that, and received assurances that there would be no diminution of Soviet interest in the PDRY. Moscow reportedly cancelled a $50 million PDRY debt, and offered enhanced defence and technical support. Soviet commentators showed increasing concern from 1973 at the power struggle developing between Isma'il and Salmin, and at a government level were aware that Salmin, while talking of his belief in the critical importance of the PDRY–USSR relationship, was trying to strengthen relations with the richer Arab countries.

Despite the importance of Soviet assistance, there was disappointment in the PDRY that it was not more substantial. Soviet aid, in the words of the British ambassador, was 'life saving' but 'would not, I believe, be enough to reverse the downward trend in the economy and the regime's popularity'.[28] Salmin was clearly conscious of this criticism of Soviet and communist economic support, and used it to justify pursuing a more diversified foreign policy. The PDRY's economic survival owed as much to the World Bank and other international agencies as it did to the Soviet Union.

The Soviet government gave a cautious welcome to the PDRY's attempts to build better relations with its neighbours, although wary of Saudi attempts to use its contacts with Salmin and Muti'a to draw Aden away from its orientation towards Moscow. In March 1976, a month after Egypt had terminated its friendship treaty with the Soviet Union, it cancelled access to Egyptian ports for the Soviet navy. Moscow responded by increasing its use of Aden. Ali Nasir says that the Soviets wanted additional facilities in the PDRY, and that Aden refused because of concerns about the likely impact on its relations with its neighbours. The Soviets were allowed to use Aden for naval support and supply, and to base Antonov aircraft for patrolling the Indian Ocean. Soviet aircraft might use Aden, but were told to keep well away from PDRY's land borders with its Arab neighbours.[29]

The CIA estimated that in 1977 there were 1,000 Soviet, East European and Cuban economic advisers in the country, together with about 350 Soviet and 350 Cuban military advisers. A further 875 south Yemenis were on training courses in Communist countries.[30] It was developments in the Horn of Africa that persuaded Moscow to invest more in the relationship after 1976. Military aid was increased in 1977. In the same year, the PDRY started backing Ethiopia in its struggle with Somalia, following the Soviet line. PDRY troops were sent to Ethiopia, and Moscow provided more arms to the PDRY. Moscow's support for Ethiopia lost it access to facilities in Somalia, thus giving the PDRY greater strategic importance. The PDRY's backing for Ethiopia and the Russians put an end to any chance of rapprochement with Saudi Arabia. At the end of 1977 Siad Barre finally ended Somalia's Treaty of Friendship with the USSR and threw out remaining Soviet advisers. In January 1978, PDRY troops sent as part of a peace-keeping force to Lebanon were withdrawn and transferred to Ethiopia. In February Ali Nasir Muhammad went to Moscow and left with a major new aid package, said to be worth $90 million.[31] More tanks and aircraft were promised, and there were reports that Ali Antar, then the defence minister, had negotiated a broader agreement for military cooperation.

Thus, by the time of Salmin's downfall, Soviet–PDRY relations were closer than they had been since independence, and the PDRY's attempts to improve relations with selected Arab countries had largely failed. The PDRY was virtually in the Soviet camp. There was no Soviet defence guarantee to Aden, and economic aid, though substantial, fell a long way short of the PDRY's needs, and probably represented no more than a quarter of aid received in the 1970s. There was as yet no Soviet–PDRY Friendship Treaty. The relationship was of growing importance to both countries, but there were reservations on both sides. Moscow was worried about the personality clashes within the PDRY leadership, and some in Aden felt that the PDRY should be wary of becoming a pawn in the wider Soviet confrontation with the West.

Other socialist states
East Germany and Cuba, in particular, became close supporters of the PDRY in the 1970s, providing aid, training and education. The East Germans were the main advisers to the security services, while the Cubans provided training for the militias and the armed forces. The PDRY was

active in pursing relations with Vietnam, North Korea and others, and in the Non-Aligned Movement. From these flowed important personal relationships, such as the affection that Fidel Castro had for PDRY leaders and the influence of such people as George Hawi, leader of the Lebanese Communist Party. By 1978 the PDRY was part of the communist world, led, as the PDRY constantly said, by the 'Great Soviet Union'.

China

It seemed, up to the Corrective Move, that China's position in the PDRY was at least as strong as that of the Soviet Union.[32] China had supported the NLF before 1967, but relations took a new turn after a visit to Beijing by Salmin in August 1970. He was deeply impressed by the Cultural Revolution and China's 'self-reliance policies'. China provided the PDRY with weapons for 5,000 soldiers, and with substantial loans – Salmin obtained one of $43 million on his visit. The Chinese were subsequently engaged in building the road from Aden to Mukalla, a textile mill, a hospital and salt works. By the end of the 1970s, China had provided roughly $84 million in assistance; it helped train the People's Militia and worked with the PDRY to support PFLOAG and Eritrean rebels.

Like Moscow, Beijing advised the PDRY to be self-reliant and avoid 'infantile leftism'; it should instead concentrate on practical development projects, and avoid provoking social unrest and stirring up problems with its neighbours. At a time when groups of Chinese diplomats and experts were jogging around Aden each evening chanting slogans from Mao's Little Red Book,[33] Chinese officials were advising the PDRY not to pursue a Cultural Revolution in their country.

While China continued its economic support during the 1970s, it appeared to downgrade the importance of the PDRY as it pursued better relations with other Arab states and reacted against Aden's close links with Moscow. For the rest of the PDRY's existence, the Chinese played a relatively minor role when measured against their apparent ambitions in the early 1970s.

The PDRY and the West

The PDRY's relations with the West were affected by its alignment with the Soviet Union, its support for revolutionary movements throughout the world, its habit of giving refuge to what Western countries regarded as terrorists, and the higher priority given by the West to relations with Saudi Arabia, Egypt and other regional powers. The British and French retained small embassies in Aden. Aden's support for international terrorism started to cause problems in the mid 1970s. In 1974 the PDRY allowed into Aden wanted terrorists associated with Palestinian movements, the Japanese Red Army Factions, and in 1975 five members of the Baader-Meinhoff group. Carlos, 'the Jackal', carried a PDRY passport. Towards the end of the 1980s the regime saw that this was counterproductive. It did not expel the terrorists, but the word went out that new arrivals would be unwelcome. An attempt by Palestinians in 1978 to bring a hijacked aircraft to Aden was rejected.

Despite the PDRY's alignment with the Soviet Union and its allies, its main trading partners were the major industrialized countries of the West, with the UK, Japan and China among the main sources of imports. In 1974, US congressman Paul Findlay – who had been to Aden to get the government to release one of his constituents arrested for photographing Aden harbour – met Muti'a and brought letters from the US secretary of state. When the Carter administration took over in 1977, Findlay arranged a meeting between Salmin and the secretary of state, Cyrus Vance, at the UN that September. Findlay followed this up with a visit to Aden in January 1978, and a second mission set off in June 1978, led by a senior State Department official, though it never arrived because of the removal of Salmin.

6

WHO LEADS – THE PRESIDENT OR THE PARTY? THE DOWNFALL OF SALMIN

Much of the politics of the 1970s was dominated by the competing visions and ambitions of Abd al-Fattah Isma'il and Salim Rubayya Ali (Salmin). At the Sixth NF Party Congress in 1975, Isma'il declared that it was for the NF to formulate long-term policy, for the Presidential Council to set the tasks, and for the cabinet to implement these through the collective leadership. Salmin, however, while paying lip-service to the role of the party, saw himself as the leader who decided policy and set the tasks, which he often sought to implement through his own patronage networks. As a British government document put it,

> Salmin, with his roots in the hinterland, derives much of his support from local loyalties, respect for his achievements and personal ties. An additional factor is that he had always been a practising Muslim ... He has favoured a Maoist philosophy, one in which political initiatives originate at the lowest levels, with the leadership responding to rather than directing the masses.[1]

The rivalry started almost immediately after the Corrective Move.[2] The PDRY leaders tried to suppress all discussion of it, but could not prevent it becoming part of the daily diet of the media and opposition abroad, and in Aden behind closed doors. The British ambassador noted in his annual review of 1973 that 'I can only report – once again – that the rivals are still hanging together'.[3] A year later he reported that the conflict had intensified. Their NF colleagues believed that neither Salmin nor Isma'il would allow the conflict to get out of hand. They united in the face of external enemies, who helpfully remained divided and ineffectual, but active.

In the early 1970s, Salmin was much influenced by his personal interpretation of Maoism. His approach was epitomized in the 'Seven Glorious Days' of July 1972. These saw demonstrations in Aden and elsewhere, often in front of government offices, of 'workers and peasants' once again demanding 'lower' wages and an end to 'bureaucracy'. These were clearly inspired by Salmin in a bid to assert his authority over the party. By appealing directly to the masses, he appeared to be drawing on what he had witnessed during a recent visit to China; he may also have wished to show that the regime would best survive and thrive by mobilizing popular opinion, rather than passing resolutions at stage-managed Congresses. Isma'il later accused Salmin of using the Seven Glorious Days to seek personal prominence and 'one-man leadership', with the aim of destroying the cadres of the political organization.[4] Although Salmin had acquired great charisma from his role as head of state when major transformations of society were taking place after the Corrective Move, his opponents later contended that 'from the outset [he] lacked the background of the ideology of scientific socialism – his revolutionary zeal being spontaneous and anarchist'. He was accused of being corrupted by the pomp of high office, and of surrounding himself with tribal and self-seeking elements.[5]

Former party officials speak of Salmin's lifelong concern for the poor, and his conviction that the PDRY's policies should be focused on relieving their plight.[6] Salmin was a man who had 'faith in the revolutionary spirit of the masses which could be used to counter the new privileged elite'. His strength lay in his 'popularity in the country and his revolutionary vision'.[7] He did not work to a clear ideological system, within a defined system of government, or in an organized way. He preferred a more inspirational approach, appealing directly to the people. Western ambassadors judged that he was less intelligent than his rivals.

The power struggle between Salmin and Isma'il and his associates reflected their different personalities, political attitudes and styles of leadership. In interviews 30 years after these events, former PDRY leaders say that the most sensitive issue between the two men was Salmin's opposition to the creation of the Yemeni Socialist Party (YSP) as the new vanguard party, so long espoused by Isma'il. After 1978, Isma'il accused Salmin of working to block its progress, despite speaking up for it in public. Salmin, of course, was well aware that Isma'il would use it to undermine Salmin's position and reduce the powers of the presidency.

The Sixth Congress and the Unification Congress

The main objective of the Sixth Congress, held in March 1975, was to get the NF to agree formally to incorporate the PDU and al-Tali'a into the NF, which would then become known as the United Political Organization of the National Front (UPONF). The Unification Congress, held in October, completed the process, and the leaders of the PDU and al-Tali'a were given positions in the UPONF, as well as retaining their cabinet posts. They were firm supporters of Isma'il and stuck with him over the next few years, though there was a purging of 'self-seeking elements' from the ranks of both parties during internal party elections in 1976 and 1977. Isma'il saw unification as a major step towards his ambition of turning the NF into a vanguard party.

The Sixth Congress was preceded by a series of open meetings to allow people to show their solidarity with the NF. People were 'encouraged' by the NF to work longer hours than they were paid for. This campaign was deemed so successful that the government announced that the working week would be increased to 48 hours. Wages were raised by 5 per cent, but the small print required that in future 5 per cent of wages would be clawed back by a new social security law.[8] Unlike the Seven Glorious Days, these developments were initiated by the NF, and served to highlight the PDRY's continuing economic problems and the need for austerity.

Diplomatic observers at the Sixth Congress commented on the popularity of Salmin, whose pronouncements were greeted with much greater (and apparently genuine) warmth than those of Isma'il.[9] However, in voting for members of the Central Committee and Politburo, Isma'il and his associates won around one-third of the members of the Central Committee, with about 20 per cent of the rest thought to be favourably disposed to him. Salmin received the applause, but Isma'il was thought to have a greater share of the seats. Changes to the government tipped its balance slightly in favour of Salmin, though this was at a time when the institutions of the party were gaining the capacity to play a greater role in policy-making. Observers at the conference thought that Isma'il's supporters were generally better educated than those of Salmin, and included a number of people who had attended courses at the Higher School of Scientific Socialism. One observer believes that the formalization of political life, with the training of cadres, helped estrange members of the NF from ordinary people.[10] This was something that Salmin had noticed and started to exploit.

The existing members of the Politburo were re-elected, and the candidate members of the Politburo and Central Committee were promoted to full members, thus making both bodies slightly larger – at 9 and 41 members respectively.[11] Isma'il remained secretary general of the party, and Salmin merely assistant secretary general.

The resolutions of the Congress followed those of 1972, though there were subtle changes. The NF was evolving from being a socialist revolutionary movement into a Leninist vanguard party built on a basis of 'scientific socialist ideology', desired by Isma'il but anathema to Salmin. The Congress stressed the importance of 'democratic centralism', which rejected 'anarchic democracy and laxity' and took 'a firm stand against bureaucratic centralism'. Democratic Centralism, in the NF view,[12] was the

> commitment of the minority to the majority, the implementation of directives from the Central Committee and Politburo by the local cells, and the right of these bases to elect the leadership and to initiate and discuss views, raise reports and practise criticism and self-criticism.

It also attacked individualism. Isma'il probably had one person in mind when he wrote:

> No individual, whatever his qualities of leadership, his genius or feeling for the masses, can ever be a substitute for the collective ... however long his revolutionary experience of the stage of the struggle which follows national liberation may be, no individual can match the peoples' experience of revolutionary transformation. Everything done by the individual ends with the individual.[13]

Isma'il expanded on his vision in a report he delivered to the Sixth (Unification) Congress, held under the ponderous slogan 'Struggle to defend the Yemeni revolution, implement the Five Year Plan and build a vanguard party'. A great deal, he declared, had been achieved since 1967 and the Corrective Move, but much more remained to be done, which would require effective leadership by the party and greater revolutionary commitment by the people.[14] The UPONF was a transitional stage towards the establishment of a vanguard party:

> [I]t is a tool of the national democratic revolution within the general framework of a broad class alliance between all social

democratic forces who have a real interest in the national democratic revolution – that is the workers, peasants, soldiers revolutionary intellectuals and the petty bourgeois'.[15]

The leadership of the party was to be armed with scientific socialist ideology and it was essential that the NF build its organizational and policy-making capacity 'in setting the government along the right path of serving the interests of the people'.[16] The party should be dominant, and must not be allowed to become a mere adjunct of the executive – as had happened before the Corrective Move. There were, he noted, in an obvious allusion to Salmin's actions, dangers of this happening again:

> our state executive, even after the Fifth General Congress, still suffered from some incorrect manifestations. Some elements acted without due regard for, and responsibility towards, the progressive measures decreed by the government and went so far as to act on their own subjective convictions.[17]

Isma'il believed that the leadership must fire the party with the spirit of revolution, inject this into the government system, and mobilize the people in support of the NF's aims. One way forward was to organize elections for the SPC and local councils. But, at the same time, he wanted to see greater 'democratic centralism' to foster more effective relations between the legislative and the executive organs, and to inculcate greater discipline and devotion to their tasks and responsibilities.

Isma'il confirmed that the military and security forces 'have been purged militarily and reformed politically and have become a force able to defeat the class enemies of the revolution'.[18] He recognized the need to improve the ideological and political consciousness of the People's Militia. The Popular Defence Committees, which had only recently been set up, were hailed as signs of democratic progress. They could solve local problems and deal with issues such as literacy, but no mention was made of their security function. As elsewhere in reviewing the system, Isma'il sensed a lack of revolutionary zeal among those involved, and the need to 'overcome the negativity and apathy of the past'.[19]

Isma'il acknowledged that there had been problems with the leadership of the trade unions, who had objected to the cuts in wages and jobs imposed in the early 1970s. He extolled the role of workers' committees in factories, which were more responsive to NF wishes. He referred briefly to organizations among peasants, but saw the need to develop a mass organization to defend their interests, starting with those working on collective farms and within cooperatives. He placed great emphasis on education, and talked of the fine work of the Higher School of Scientific Socialism, which now needed to be extended to involve the Bedouin tribes.[20] As always, he stressed the importance of raising the political consciousness and status of women through the General Union of Yemeni Women. He discussed the role of culture not simply in terms of improving government and society, but as a vehicle for indoctrination and communicating the NF message.

Salmin's attitude to the PDU and al-Tali'a

Salmin went along with all this in public, but his colleagues in the NF leadership were in no doubt that he was, at best, lukewarm about the idea of unification with the PDU and al-Tali'a and the expansion of the NF organization, which would strengthen the hand of Isma'il and others who lacked a tribal or regional power centre. He accused members of the PDU and al-Tali'a of seducing the young in the NF with their Marxism. The Central Committee said of Salmin, after his downfall in 1978:

> Sometimes he would wear the veil of an extreme leftist in front of the democratic vanguards; on other occasions he would wear in an exaggerated manner the veil of bogus realism. He opposed the unity of the groups of national democratic action, which we regard as a first basic step towards the establishment of a brand new party.[21]

Salmin was well aware of his personal popularity, and he had sufficient political clout to make sure, for example, that 'virtually all of the party secretaries in the Governorates, the people who wielded effective power outside Aden, were associates of his'.[22] He had his own budget that he could use for development programmes of special concern to him. Salmin is even reported to have suggested at the Unification Congress the restoration of some of the nationalized properties to previous owners, the return to the country of selected political exiles, and a broadening of the government base by including some non-party members.[23]

Writing in 1979,[24] Isma'il criticized Salmin for lacking a coherent ideology based on scientific socialism. His ideas were rooted in petty-bourgeois thinking, whereas Isma'il believed in 'true revolution' and the importance of a firmly based ideology that could change people's attitudes and mobilize them for the good of the party. Salmin wanted to create a state around the office of the presidency. The earlier right-wing opposition led by Qahtan had been easy to detect, but Salmin 'had worn the clothes of revolution'. He had worked against the party, the mass organizations, the workers and trade unions. He had links with those trying to create chaos in the Arab and international revolutionary movements. He rejected the strategic alliance with the 'Socialist movement led by the Soviet Union'.

The economy

It was clear to all the NF leaders in 1975 that eight years of independence had not brought any prosperity to the country. Arguably, the little income it had was now distributed much more equitably, with Politburo members and ministers earning very little more than civil servants or military officers, and there were clear improvements in education, health and other government services, at least outside Aden. The 1975 Congresses wanted the regime to focus on the economy, improve living standards and eliminate the differences in these standards between Aden and the rest of the PDRY. The five-year plan had been launched in April 1974, but progress was not satisfactory. There was a role for the private sector, and a realization that the success of the plan would require its implementation in stages, improved bureaucratic practices, the ending of corruption, and much more commitment – with the NF leading the way. The trade unions, now firmly under NF control, should be given more attention and a greater role. The role of the mass organizations in the economy must be enhanced.

All Salmin's critics agree that, whatever his faults, he genuinely believed that the regime should place the relief of poverty at the centre of its economic agenda. His problem was that he lacked the patient and bureaucratic approach of the NF as portrayed in Isma'il's 1975 Political Report, and wanted to use his presidential authority and his contacts to speed up the process and give people the means and motivation to do more themselves. Like other regional leaders, he would often help people directly when they appealed to him personally or through his supporters for assistance.

Foreign policy

After 1975 the central issue was often seen – not always correctly – as a competition between Isma'il's policy of building relations with the Soviet bloc and Salmin's policy as head of state of cultivating personal relations with other regional leaders as and when the opportunity arose.

The potential role of foreign governments in relieving the economic problems of the PDRY was on the agenda of the 1975 Congresses and subsequent meetings of the Central Committee. The general orientation towards the socialist camp and commitment to revolution remained, but there were changes in outlook towards the Gulf states, whose riches provided a potential source of investment. The 1975 Congresses praised Arab states for using the oil weapon in 1973, even if the PDRY shared a view heard at the time that the oil should be seen as a common resource of the Arabs, not merely of the states in which it happened to be found. The Congresses reaffirmed their support for PFLO (the 'AG' had been dropped in 1974), but called on the government to explore the possibility of establishing diplomatic relations with the UAE, Qatar and Bahrain (its support for the Bahrain Liberation Front was clandestine). Isma'il said in 1975, 'For our part we will make every effort to develop relations with these sister states on the basis of mutual benefit, respect for national sovereignty and non-intervention in the internal affairs of other states'.[25]

Isma'il criticized Saudi Arabia for its aggressive actions against the PDRY, but added that

> natural relations with the Kingdom of Saudi Arabia, as we see the situation, are conditional on Saudi respect for our independence and national sovereignty, non-interference in our internal affairs, a solution to border disputes, and an end to persistent aggressions against us, an end to mercenary camps on the borders and an end to the propaganda campaign directed at us.[26]

It was a long list of conditions, but it was a first weak signal of greater pragmatism in Aden – which Salmin wished to promote. This was in line with the lecture he had received from President Anwar Sadat on the need to create an alternative source of support to the Soviet Union in the Arab world. The Russians might well have encouraged this (the Chinese certainly did) as a means of relieving pressure on their financial resources, providing it did not go too far. Riyadh, for its part, was aware of the good relationship between Salmin and President al-Hamdi which the two Yemeni leaders used to prevent problems between their regimes from turning into crises.

Relations with Yemen

Isma'il reminded the audience of the stance of the NF at the Fifth Congress, before the fighting of 1972, using rather typical NF language: 'The strategy of the Yemeni revolution is organically related to the unity of the 26 September and the 14 October revolutions. This is based on the shared interests and unity of the Yemeni people and territory.'[27] This was hardly a ringing endorsement of the unity agreement signed only three years earlier, and acknowledged the divergent political systems in the two Yemens.

What Isma'il failed to mention was that he and his asociates were examining ways of extending support for the Revolutionary Democratic Party and the National Democratic Front and integrating their activities more closely with those of the NF. These efforts did not come to fruition until 1978, but many in Aden and the Yemen Arab Republic were aware of what was being planned. It showed that the NF was committed to supporting the NDF, thus justifying the north's fears that the PDRY had ambitions to govern the whole of Yemen. Salih Muslih was responsible for handling relations with the NDF, including the supply of arms and training.

Salmin and others in the NF leadership, including Ali Nasir Muhammad, were not associated with support for the NDF; they much preferred to deal with the Yemeni president directly, and cultivated good relations at first with President al-Iryani, then and more closely with al-Hamdi, and apparently with President al-Ghashmi. It is not clear what Salmin really felt about Yemeni unity, but his actions and his dealings with the Yemeni presidents suggest that he saw Yemen as two states that should cooperate closely while working in the longer term for unity.

1975–78: Salmin's power wanes

These issues continually surfaced in the power struggle inside the regime after 1975. The story of the conflict between Salmin and Isma'il, and increasingly others in the leadership, has been told mainly in documents written after 1978 by Isma'il and the winners, who clearly wanted to heap all blame on Salmin for what had gone wrong. Salmin's former colleagues in the party and government now acknowledge that there were faults on both sides, and regret that the NF leaders allowed their personal rivalries and policy differences to lead to violence. There was more talk of a collective leadership after 1975, but it came to mean a gathering of those opposed to Salmin.

Salmin increasingly acted in the same way as other Arab leaders, preferring to operate through networks of patronage. Salmin at heart remained a revolutionary leader who never quite adapted to the disciplines of government. He antagonized not only leading NF figures, but also ministers and government officials. The powers of the presidency after 1975 were offset by the growing efficiency of the NF political machine. The impact of the improvements in party organization, the powers given to its specialized secretariats and the investment in training led to the emergence of a cadre of better-educated and better-indoctrinated individuals who would have greater affinity with Isma'il. Isma'il noted in his report to the Unification Congress that nearly 5,000 people had attended courses at the Higher

School for Scientific Socialism, and 163 others had been sent abroad for longer-term party studies. The civil service was rapidly expanding and improving. Ali Nasir Muhammad, who had remained neutral in the power struggle before the mid 1970s, grew increasingly impatient with Salmin's working methods, and started with other ministers to turn against him, or at least neutralise his actions.

In 1976 and 1977 there was criticism of Salmin's negative role on the economy, and Isma'il and Ali Nasir managed to divert to Salmin blame for the PDRY's failure to use its better relations with the Arab world to extract support for the government budget and development spending. He became a scapegoat for the PDRY's economic failures, which were heightened by serious flooding in 1977. Gradually, during the 1970s, the PDRY became more dependent on support from the Soviets and their allies. Salmin played a much less significant role in this than either Isma'il or Ali Nasir Muhammad, and his interference in military and security matters alienated some key senior figures in their ranks, notably Ali Antar and Salih Muslih.[28]

Many of his former colleagues have said in interviews that they admired Salmin's leadership and his unwavering commitment to helping the poor, but add that he was quick to anger and could deal with opposition ruthlessly. They agree that he was responsible for some of the human rights abuses in the mid 1970s by the security forces. Isma'il later accused Salmin of responsibility for arbitrary arrests and killings, and for fomenting trouble in the YAR and Oman, for committing unspecified terrible crimes, for disobeying the Constitution and the law, and causing major losses to the country and its people. He had tried to concentrate power into his own hands and divide the army. More neutral colleagues say that Salmin gradually became more arrogant and more difficult to deal with and could treat party officials and senior civil servants callously.

Though he remained popular in the country – and toured the provinces regularly – his powers outside his home base in the Fadhli area of Abyan began to wane. His arbitrary actions gave rise to a loose alliance of people who opposed him for different reasons. One official who had known him for many years says that he often insulted his colleagues, stopped listening to others, and saw himself as the only leader.[29] His colleagues would later cite examples of the way that he used the power of the presidency to try to force ministers and officials to pursue his pet projects, mostly in the cause of helping the poor.[30] Salmin was angered when a deputy minister of education rejected a demand that a boy should be allowed to pass an examination because he was from a poor family. Shortly afterwards, Isma'il phoned the deputy minister to say he had arranged for his transfer to a diplomatic because he was from a poor family. Shortly afterwards, Isma'il phoned the deputy minister to say he had arranged for his transfer to a diplomatic appointment abroad – which he advised should be taken up immediately if he valued his freedom.[31] A senior minister has described how he was given a diplomatic posting at short notice after Salmin took a dislike to him. Others describe how Salmin protected them from threats made by other leading NF figures.

A Russian expert quotes a statement of Isma'il's at the time which condemned 'left-wing extremists [who] play on revolutionary sentiments of the masses and call for a more or less immediate establishment of socialism, jumping across the stages of development necessary in this country'.[32] He meant Salmin.

Isma'il, with core support only from Adeni northerners like Muhsin (see Appendix B) and his acolytes in the NF, would not have been a match for Salmin in a straightforward power struggle. The powerful figures in Lahij, such as Ali Antar and Salih Muslih, with their strong base in the army and security forces, turned against Salmin even though they had strong reservations about Isma'il and his policies. Even Ali Salim al-Bidh, in many respects similar to Salmin, stopped supporting him. Ali Nasir, who now had a powerful network of his own in Abyan, the government and the army, sat on the fence as long as he could, but in the end moved to Isma'il's side. In cabinet changes after 1975 there were fewer places for people closely identified with Salmin.

Isma'il, in 1977 and early 1978, intensified his preparations for the formation of the Vanguard Party. He toured the provinces building support among party workers, and organized successful local elections in several provinces, which were seen as a test for elections to the Supreme People's Council envisaged in the 1970 Constitution. Salmin was criticized for trying to delay or block the creation of the YSP at a Central Committee meeting held in September 1977.

By the beginning of 1977 there were instances of decisions made by Salmin being reversed by NF committees. He was outmanoeuvred when his rivals called for the return from Moscow of Abdullah al-Khamiri – a noted intellectual and an Adeni northerner known for his support for Isma'il – after he had been removed from his position as minister of information by Salmin. In September 1977, Salmin was stripped of some of his functions on grounds of administrative failings. This was a sure sign that Ali Nasir had finally lost patience and was siding with Salmin's enemies. In October, Ali Nasir gave up the defence portfolio he had held since 1969 to Ali Antar, who had had been antagonized by what he regarded as interference in military matters by Salmin. Antar used his new post to remove Salmin's supporters in the armed forces. Salmin, it seemed, had lost the support and even the friendship of many of the historical leaders of the NF. Salmin opposed the decision to send troops to Ethiopia in 1977, but was ignored, as Isma'il insisted that the PDRY respond positively to this Soviet-sponsored request. Salmin's authority was reduced at a Central Committee meeting in January 1978, when he was reminded of the need to work through proper organizational channels. In the spring of 1978 the NF appointed a close associate of Isma'il, the Yafi'i Husain Qumatah, the head of the People's Militia, to run the Armed Forces Organization Committee, replacing Salmin, who had refused to hand over a report on the Committee's activities to the Politburo. In that position, Qumatah could assist Antar in purging the military of Salmin's military supporters. In May 1978 up to 150 military officers – all loyal to Salmin – were arrested. A reshuffle of the cabinet and the NF secretariat in March 1978 further undermined Salmin's authority. In June 1978 the Central Committee issued instructions that restricted the powers of the president to act in the prime minister's absence. Significant supporters of Salmin were removed from their positions in the NF and government.

By June 1978 Salmin's position had become almost untenable. This was made explicit on 21 June, when it was announced that the new vanguard party would be established at a party Congress in October. While it might seem that it would be only a matter of time before Salmin was removed (one version is that he was under de facto house arrest from mid June), he was probably still the most popular of the PDRY leaders. He had significant support in Abyan and allies elsewhere. A minority on the Central Committee backed him, and his support in the army had been reduced but not eliminated. He was no longer dominant, but he could not easily be removed.

The downfall of Salmin

On 24 June 1978 the YAR president, Ahmad al-Ghashmi, received an envoy from the PDRY carrying a briefcase. When that case was opened in the president's office it exploded, killing both al-Ghashmi and the envoy. The YAR investigation into al-Ghashmi's death reports that Salmin telephoned al-Ghashmi on 23 June to say that an envoy would arrive on 24 June carrying a message.[33]

The Politburo had to act quickly to avoid a war with Yemen, and called an emergency meeting of the Central Committee for the next day, spending the intervening period demanding that Salmin resign and leave the country. It sent a three-man delegation consisting of Muhammad Ali Ahmad, soon to be governor of Abyan, Ali Shaya Hadi, soon to be governor of Shabwa, and Husain Qumatah, head of the Popular Militia, to demand that Salmin resign.[34] He refused to do so, and there were prolonged negotiations up to and during the Central Committee meeting. When Salmin finally understood that the Central Committee would expel him if he did not step down, he wrote a letter of resignation, which was submitted on his behalf by Salih Muslih, the minister of the interior.[35] Other reports at the time said that the Central Committee passed two resolutions: one suspending Salmin, and the second appointing a committee to investigate his actions.

Salim Salih Muhammad, who was present at both the Politburo and Central Committee meetings, says that Salmin's resignation was accepted, and he was removed from all official and party posts. The Central Committee agreed he would be given funds and allowed to leave for Addis Ababa in an aircraft to be provided by the Ethiopian leader.[36] Isma'il confirmed in 1979 that it was agreed that he would go into exile.[37] All members of the Central Committee were then told to go home and stay there while preparations were made for Salmin's departure.

Later that night, rockets hit the Central Committee meeting room and the residences of Abd al-Fattah Isma'il and Ali Nasir Muhammad. These were the first moves in an attempted coup in Aden and an uprising in the Fadhli tribal district of Abyan. One witness said that members of the Central Committee were asked at 3 a.m. on 26 June to go to the headquarters of the People's Militia because Salmin had broken his agreement with the NF. Army units loyal to Salmin had launched the attacks.[38] There were reports of other units loyal to him moving towards Aden. Isma'il said that officers helping to organize the 1969 coup attempt against the NF leaders had been involved.[39]

The Central Committee ordered the armed forces and local militias to suppress the attempted coup. Both sides used heavy weapons, but within a few hours units loyal to Isma'il had taken control of most of Aden. Salmin and around 700 of his supporters were forced to retreat to a stronghold around the presidential palace, where, after 12 hours of fighting, including aerial and naval bombardment, they surrendered. Around 1,000 people died in this violence, which continued sporadically for a further two days in Aden. Ali Antar said some years later that the army had lost only 68 of its men.[40] The People's Militia in Abyan prevented an armed group of Salmin's Fadhli tribal supporters from marching on Aden. There were reports that a Yafi'i militia joined the forces opposed to Salmin in Abyan.[41]

The Politburo tried Salmin and two of his close associates – Ja'am Salih a member of the Politburo and a former leader of the Peasants' Organization, and Ali Salim Law'ar, secretary of the presidential office. The Politburo agreed unanimously that they were guilty, and sentenced them to death. The Presidential Council confirmed the verdict, and they were executed by firing squad shortly afterwards.

This whole episode is thus presented as an attempted coup by Salmin, who realized that his position had become untenable. The suggested motive is that he had taken an oath to avenge the death of President al-Hamdi – and, like many others, believed that al-Ghashmi had organized that killing.[42] Salmin, it was said, wanted to create mayhem in the north and use this to regain his position in the south. At the time, many in the YAR believed this version of events. Halliday, writing just after the events, noted that some accounts suggested that the bomb carrier was Mahdi Ahmad Salih, who thought that he could step back after delivering the bomb. Most saw the venture as a desperate attempt by Salmin to provoke a crisis in the north that he could exploit to save his position in the south. If this version of events is correct, then he would have instigated the coup, as claimed.[43]

Supporters of Salmin, on the other hand, believe that the briefcase, or in some versions the envoy (one official in an interview said that Salmin had ordered Ali Salem Law'ar to act as the envoy) was substituted at Aden airport, and that the whole affair was a plot by Isma'il's supporters organized by Salih Muslih to get rid of both al-Ghashmi and Salmin. One leading north Yemeni figure at the time, Yahya al-Mutawakkil, believes that al-Ghashmi and Salmin had developed a good working relationship which Salmin's colleagues in the leadership saw as a threat.[44] Salim Salih Muhammad says that Salih Muslih told the Politburo that Salmin had asked him to prepare the explosive briefcase, but had not explained why he needed it. Another prominent member of the Central Committee said that Salih Muslih had gone further in admitting responsibility for the assassination, claiming he was acting under Salmin's orders.[45] Muslih was also responsible for NF support for the NDF, which had been suffering at the hands of al-Ghashmi. One leading figure said that Ali Antar believed Salih Muslih had been responsible, and would in private conversation refer to Muslih as the 'errand boy' of Salmin's opponents.[46]

Salmin's supporters claim that he got wind of a plot in Aden against al-Ghashmi, and was trying to warn him of the details. Others think that the two may have been plotting a joint move against Isma'il and his supporters as a prelude to calling for unity. Other more elaborate conspiracy theories exist, involving an intrigue by the Russians and East Germans.

From many interviews with surviving PDRY leaders, it is clear that they believe that Salmin was responsible for al-Ghashmi's assassination, and that his motive was to avenge the death of al-Hamdi. They see it as a symptom of his mental state at the time. It was the last straw, and gave Salmin's many opponents in the leadership the pretext to remove him.[47]

The aftermath

This was not the end of the affair. Supporters of Salmin, especially in Abyan, opposed government forces for several weeks, and there were defections of military, security and political figures to the YAR, Oman and the opposition abroad. The two Yemens came close to war, and the PDRY was for a time put into a state of diplomatic isolation by Arab states for its role – no matter who carried it out in particular – in killing an Arab president.

The Central Committee began a campaign to blame Salmin for all that was going wrong in Yemen, north and south. He was vilified for allowing personal ambitions to damage the state and party. His economic policies had caused chaos and confusion, and he was responsible for the failed attempts to improve relations with the PDRY's Arab neighbours, and for trying to provoke a war between the two Yemens. Isma'il would refer to him as a 'the deviationist leader of a left opportunist plot', or a 'left opportunist' or an 'infantile leftist', and 'given to acting spontaneously', which in Isma'il's eyes was perhaps the greatest sin.[48] His deviations caused divisions, tensions and problems, and led to the 'sacrifice' of party members and others.

Many of the policies closely associated with Salmin had failed by mid 1978. The economy remained in dire straits; the move towards the Arab world had not provided much in the way of economic benefits, and events in the region had put the process into reverse. Yemeni unity remained a distant aspiration, and Salmin's cultivation of Iryani and al-Hamdi, and finally al-Ghashmi, had come to nothing, thanks to the vicissitudes of YAR politics at the time. Events flowed in the direction of Isma'il. The relationship with the Soviet Union and its allies was producing economic, military and security support. The PDRY, thanks to events in the Horn of Africa, had become much more important to the Soviet Union, offering hopes of more economic assistance.

Several leaders believed that the tensions at the top had brought proper government to a standstill. They felt that something had to give even if they regretted that it had to end in the death of Salmin and so many others. On the other hand, Anis Hassan Yahya, the al-Tali'a leader and a member of the Politburo after 1978, believed right up to 24 June 1978 that the differences between the leaders could be solved by negotiation.[49]

Salmin was accused of exploiting tribal and regional loyalties. There is no doubt, in Salmin's case, that his power base was in the Fadhli area of Abyan. A different personality might have tried to build alliances with other powerful leaders in Lahij, or even parts of Abyan. Up to 1975, his relations with Ali Nasir, Ali Antar and Salih Muslih had been good. The problem was that a growing arrogance and assertion of presidential power antagonized his potential allies and pushed them into an alliance against him.

In June 1978, Ali Nasir Muhammad had the backing of Dathina, parts of the army and most of the civil service, as well as the increasingly powerful Muhammad Ali Ahmad, the leading Awdhali in the regime. Ali Antar and Salih Muslih – respectively ministers of defence and of interior – had turned against Salmin. Prominent Yafi'i such as Husain Qumatah, head of the People's Militia, the rising Salim Salih Muhammad and Fadhl Muhsin, Isma'il's brother-in-law, backed Isma'il. The position of another Yafi'i, Muhammad Salih Muti'a, was more ambivalent. As foreign minister he had been a key figure in the contacts with the Saudis and other Arabs, and was associated with Salmin in the mid 1970s. It seems that, like Ali Nasir Muhammad, he was something of an opportunist, and perhaps entertained his own ambition of winning a top job.

PART C

THE STRUGGLE FOR POWER

7

THE PRESIDENCY OF ABD AL-FATTAH ISMAʿIL AND THE FORMATION OF THE YEMENI SOCIALIST PARTY

On the death of Salmin, an interim Presidential Council was formed under the chairmanship of Ali Nasir Muhammad (as prime minister he became chairman for a period of 90 days) with Abd al-Fattah Isma'il, Ali Antar, Muhammad Salih Muti'a and Ali Abd al-Razzaq Ba Dhib as members. Its tasks were to stabilize the regime and to prepare for the next Congress, due in October, which would see the formation of the new vanguard party. The vilification of Salmin and the purging of his supporters within the NF, armed forces, militias and central and local government continued for several weeks. Sporadic resistance to the new leaders was confined to the Fadhli area of Abyan, and there was an upsurge of cross-border activity in Shabwa and Hadhramaut, partly inspired by the reorganized United National Front, now based in Cairo and led by Abd al-Qawi Makkawi (the former head of FLOSY) and Muhammad Ali Haytham. The Front's secretary general was Najib, a son of Qahtan al-Sha'bi, who stood against Ali Abdullah Salih in the Yemeni presidential elections of 1999.

Nine members of the Central Committee were expelled, together with some leaders of the mass organizations. There were defections of officers, men and even units of the armed forces to the north. Up to 250 officers loyal to Salmin were executed without trial by State Security (see p. 118). Four provincial party secretaries loyal to Salmin were removed, including Hassan Ba'um from Shabwa (who in 2012 was a leader of the southern movement in Yemen) and Abdullah al-Bar, one of the firebrand Hadhrami extremists of the late 1960s. Isma'il and Ali Nasir were made brigadiers – the most senior rank in the PDRY military structure – and the defence and interior ministers, Ali Antar and Salih Muslih, were made colonels, an interesting comment on their relative standing at the time. Officers loyal to the historical leaders were promoted to fill the posts vacated by Salmin's followers.

There were no trials, and very few remained in detention for long. Salmin may have been popular in parts of the country, but the regime's measures were successful in preventing his residual supporters from becoming a threat. After 1978 there were only occasional references to this 'infantile leftist', and by 1980 some of his supporters were rehabilitated as new rivalries developed within the leadership.

Formation of the Yemeni Socialist Party[1]

With Salmin out of the way, the leadership could move ahead with the formation of the YSP and hold the first congress of the party in Aden, on 11–13 October. By October 1978, the NF had 25,683 members, of whom 1,068 were women. In addition, some of the mass organizations had significant memberships: 84,000 in the General Yemeni Workers' Union; 21,000 in the Youth Organization and 15,000 in the General Union of Yemeni Women.[2]

At the opening ceremony, Isma'il spoke of the centrality of scientific socialism and Yemen's attachment to the international socialist movement headed by the Soviet Union. He emphasized the need to continue fighting imperialism, colonialism and reactionary elements in the Arab world and beyond.[3] He claimed to draw inspiration from the great enthusiasm with which people greeted the new party – though neutral observers failed to notice. He urged delegates to incite greater dynamism and commitment to the party among the wider public as a means of achieving its economic and social aims. Though Isma'il had made speeches like this before, he had rarely given such strong emphasis to scientific socialism, the paramount role of the party and the leadership of the Soviet Union. This and subsequent writings were even more densely packed than previous speeches with socialist rhetoric and terminology. He had a clear view of the world, but had difficulty in conveying this to all but graduates of the Higher School of Scientific Socialism. He left it to others in the party to translate these musings into practical programmes. He wanted a party made in his image.[4]

Despite the triumphalism of some of the speeches and documents, the congress did not make any major new policy announcements. It was very much business as usual. Summing up in 2001, Abd al-Wakeel al-Sururi, a member of the Central Committee from al-Tali'a, and thus perhaps not as keen a Marxist as some of his colleagues, described the main results as:

1) bringing together the leadership of the state and the party;
2) establishing the centrality of scientific socialism;
3) making the party the highest authority in the state;
4) committing the PDRY to a strategic alliance with the Soviet Union and the Soviet bloc;
5) bringing the PDU and al-Tali'a fully into the YSP and its leaders into the top leadership of the party;
6) joining the revolutionary elements from the south and the north into a single party.[5]

This final point was a reference to the merger of the political groups in the NDF with the YSP to become the Northern Branch of the YSP.[6] In the words of Jarallah Umar,

> We unified into one party – the Yemeni Socialist Party – in 1978 and constituted a single leadership, but we did so, of course, in secret. These were exceptional circumstances, in many ways similar to the situation in Vietnam (despite the differences to which Giap pointed): the Party governed in the South and participated in armed struggle in the North. Our goal was to unify Yemen. We had one Politburo. I was chosen as the First Secretary of the Northern Branch of the party in 1979. I was also the person responsible for the NDF in the North.[7]

None of these arrangements were publicized. The Northern Branch members of the Politburo and Central Committee were required to leave the room when photographs were taken of the leadership, but their presence was hardly a secret and the regime in Sana'a knew about it.[8]

Organization of the state

The congress agreed amendments to the Constitution (ratified by the Supreme People's Council in December), which put the party at the heart of the state:

> The YSP, armed with the theory of Scientific Socialism, is the leader and guide of society and the state. It will define the general horizon for the development of society in line with the state's internal and external policy ... [It] shall lead the struggle of the people and their mass organizations towards the absolute victory of the Yemeni revolution's strategy and

the achievement of the tasks of the national democratic revolutionary stage for the purpose of accomplishing the construction of socialism.

The main policy-making body was the Central Committee of the YSP whose members were to be elected at party conferences. It elected the Politburo, which retained all its previous powers. The congress approved changes to the party structure, which had the effect of increasing the powers of the secretariat and the bureaus that worked out policies to be implemented by ministries once they had been sanctioned by the Politburo.

The SPC became the highest legal authority, and defined the political principles of the state. It had to approve changes to the Constitution, economic and social development plans, budgets, and international agreements. It would elect the Presidium and approve appointments to the Council of Ministers. The SPC was to meet four times a year, with direct elections and universal adult suffrage. Of 111 elected members, 40 would not be YSP members. Elections were scheduled for December 1978.

The Presidium, which replaced the Presidential Council, could have between 11 and 17 members. Its chairman would be the head of state. It would elect a deputy chairman and a secretary. Though it appeared to have similarly wide powers to the Presidential Council, in reality its chairman was less powerful than in the Salmin period. The prime minister's powers, on the other hand, were increased, and he or she would also be 'appointed' by the SPC.

These changes were designed partly to prevent the emergence of another Salmin, who might use his position as head of state to bypass party and government processes. The SPC remained little more than a rubber stamp controlled by the YSP, though it could witness some heated debates and frank appraisal of government policies. In reality, the Politburo proved to be the main decision-making body, and the Central Committee was less influential than previously.

The party congress was followed in December 1978 by the first elections to the SPC. The successful local elections in 1977 had inspired some confidence in the electoral system and the possibility – for the first time in South Arabia – of conducting elections involving not just Aden, but the whole country. The elections were fixed, to the extent that people voted for candidates from approved lists. There was a deliberate effort to get voters to support the party, rather than local leaders, so that on most regional lists there were some people from elsewhere in the PDRY. The first meeting of the elected SPC took place on 27 December 1978.

New fractures emerge

The Presidium elected by the SPC in December 1978 was led by Abd al-Fattah Isma'il (chairman) and Ali Nasir Muhammad (prime minister and deputy chairman) and Fadhl Muhsin Abdullah (Isma'il's brother in law).[9] The other members were from the Central Committee or heads of the mass organizations. All subsequent Presidiums were similar in structure. Apart from Isma'il and Ali Nasir (and Fadhl Muhsin), there were no major historical leaders of the NF or people with real power.

They were on the Politburo: Abd al-Fattah Isma'il, Ali Nasir Muhammad, Ali Abd al-Razzaq Ba Dhib, Anis Hassan Yahya, Muhammad Salih Muti'a, Salih Muslih Qassim, Abd al-Aziz Abd al-Wali, Ali Salim al-Bidh, Muhammad Sa'id Abdullah (Muhsin) and two candidate members Ali Antar and Salim Salih Muhammad. Isma'il was secretary general of the YSP, with Ali Abd al-Razzaq Ba Dhib, Ali Salim al-Bidh, Anis Hassan Yahya and Salim Salih Muhammad as secretaries. There were also members of the NDF on the Politburo and Central Committee; there were at least three (and perhaps up to five at times) on the Politburo.

The SPC approved a new Council of Ministers in December, chaired by Ali Nasir Muhammad, who was also minister of finance. The key members were Muhammad Salih Muti'a (minister of foreign affairs), Salih Muslih (minister of interior), Ali Antar (minister of defence), Muhammad Sa'id Abdullah ('Muhsin', minister of state security), Mahmud Ushaysh (minister of communications), Haydar al-Attas (minister for construction), Rashid Muhammad Thabit (minister of information), Ali As'ad Muthana (minister for cabinet affairs), and Abd al-Ghani Abd al-Qadir (al-Tali'a, minister of industry).

By the beginning of 1979, the regime had recovered from the events surrounding the overthrow of Salmin. The state and party had been reorganized, with the powers of the key posts more clearly defined and broad agreement on the main directions of internal and external policy. It could now look forward to a period of stable development.

However, new cracks were opening up beneath the surface. Ali Nasir was reluctant to give up his position as interim president to Abd al-Fattah Isma'il and almost from the outset worked to manoeuvre himself back into the position of head of state. Ali Nasir's personal and political standing had been strengthened by the removal of Salmin and the greater powers given to the post of prime minister. Though he gave every appearance of being as committed as Isma'il to the development of the party, to the alliance with the Soviet Union, and to Yemeni unity, his years of trying to turn ideas into practical policies had given a pragmatic edge to whatever ideology actually drove him. For long the apparent quiet man of PDRY politics, he had used his time to build up support in the country and form alliances with other leading figures in the regime, notably Ali Antar and Salih Muslih. He showed considerable political skills both in surviving for so long and in emerging in a strong position from the mayhem of June 1978. Ali Nasir was now the leader of Abyan, and made moves in 1979 and 1980 to win over Salmin's remaining supporters. Ali Nasir had also built up a strong constituency in Aden among civil servants, state factory managers and the small private sector, and was a much more popular politician than Isma'il.

Isma'il was a man who believed in ideology, commitment to the party and effective organization. He was known in the late 1970s as 'al-Faqih' (one learned in Islamic jurisprudence), perhaps a compliment today but not in the late 1970s, when it implied he was more interested in Marxist doctrine than the realities of government. He may have placed too much stress on ideas and the organization of the NF and YSP and not enough on the cultivation of personalities, especially outside Aden. The changes since 1967 had given greater weight to the hinterland, where many of his rivals in the Politburo had their regional and tribal support. Leading figures respected Isma'il, but they did not like him. They felt that his rhetoric and lack of charisma undermined the popularity of the YSP among ordinary citizens. Whereas people worried about making ends meet, Isma'il seemed interested only in ideology and doctrines. His colleagues gradually came to see him as a person best fitted for a background ideological role, and not as the leader of the party and the state. His friends now say that they advised him not to become head of state, but that he had insisted on taking up a role for which he was not suited. Among the memoirs and accounts of Arab leaders who had to deal with Isma'il over the years, there is little to suggest they warmed to him, and few appear to have trusted him. Younger people, however, found him inspiring.[10]

Ali Nasir, in arguing that he should be made president, pointed out that he was a southerner. This reflected a growing resentment among PDRY leaders from Abyan and Lahij at the influence of politicians, such as Isma'il, who were Adenis of northern origin. From at least 1978 the term 'northerner' was being used by southern politicians to disparage their Adeni rivals and the growing influence of the politicians from the NDF in the Politburo. One Central Committee member noted that the northern ministers – Muhsin, Abd al-Aziz Abd al-Wali and Mahmud Ushaysh – were trying to weaken the position of Ali Nasir Muhamad and bolster that of Isma'il.[11]

The YSP organization was strong in the armed forces and security forces, but both were clearly influenced by the personalities of the ministers responsible, namely Ali Antar and Salih Muslih, and by Ali Nasir's long stint as minister of defence. Antar and Muslih were developing their own political ambitions. Their influence would need to be won by the two contenders for power, or they would need to be neutralized.

The inevitable conflict re-emerged quite quickly over the economy, relations with the YAR, and foreign policy.

Poor economic performance

There was much debate at the October congress on the economy. The problems outlined in the World Bank report of 1978[12] were sapping the morale of the YSP and affecting its popularity. There was severe pressure on the budget caused by the need to increase defence spending as relations with the YAR deteriorated: it rose from 19 per cent of the budget in 1977 to 28 per cent in 1979. The financial difficulties were heightened by disastrous droughts in 1976 and 1977. If Salmin had failed to persuade the Arab states to provide assistance and investment, there was no prospect of these countries helping Isma'il, whom many regarded as a communist and a Soviet stooge. Moscow and its allies provided project aid and assistance in kind, but not the cash that the PDRY needed. In a rather typical move by Isma'il, there was an amnesty in 1979 for those who had migrated despite a ban on such movement having been imposed in 1974: rather than providing incentives for people to return and invest remittances, he promised stiff penalties for those who emigrated in future. Despite this, remittances remained the most important source of foreign exchange. The government was forced to postpone the implementation of a new five-year plan until 1981, to focus instead on trying to complete unfinished business from the previous plan. Development spending was reduced, and urgent reforms delayed or not implemented. Meanwhile, social consumption rose.

The political significance of these developments was that, in the perception of most people, the poverty of the PDRY became more acute in the period between 1978 and 1980. It was obvious to ordinary south Yemenis that the PDRY was impoverished, while the states in the rest of the peninsula were enjoying a major boom. In 1977 the PDRY's per capita income was one-fortieth of Saudi Arabia's, and only a tenth of that of Oman. Ali Nasir, who understood how to communicate, could deflect the blame on to the unpopular Isma'il. It became politically opportune to do so in 1979, when declines in both imports and local production led to shortages of goods.

The YAR

Sanaʻa was greatly angered by the assassination of al-Ghashmi, and had little doubt that the PDRY had been responsible, either directly through the hand of Salmin or indirectly as a result of machinations linked to the power struggle in the PDRY. The YAR media highlighted the continuing fighting in the south, and the defections of southerners loyal to Salmin to the north. Tension was very high in the months after June 1978. Though there was talk of war, the first priority of the new YAR leader, Colonel Ali Abdullah Salih, was to consolidate his own position before considering what to do about the south. Sanaʻa helped ensure the isolation of the PDRY by the Arab League until March 1979, when it was accepted that the assassination of al-Ghashmi had not been a state act, but that of an individual acting unconstitutionally. There were some in the YAR who felt that fighting should be avoided, as the experience of 1972 had shown that the YAR army was not fit for purpose. Some thought that the Saudis, who accused the PDRY of assassinating al-Ghashmi and Moscow and Havana of organizing the assassination of Salmin, may have egged on the YAR to fight.[13]

At its October congress, the YSP made many references to unity, but it was clear that by that it meant a Yemen united under a YSP-led regime:

> The YSP is convinced that nothing but a broad-based popular movement backed by all popular forces can achieve unity for the Yemeni homeland, can set up a single centralized state with its various organs to be formed and run by the popular masses as they build an independent national economy free of world capitalism and developing a scientific base according to plan.[14]

The open participation of the NDF in the YSP Congress, the formation of the northern branch of the YSP and the presence of 'secret' members of the NDF in the YSP Politburo were highly provocative. A group of armed northern tribesmen, said to be 2,000-strong, came to Aden to show their support for the YSP at the time of the Congress – even though the bearing of arms was illegal in the PDRY.

In October 1978 there was an attempted coup against Ali Abdullah Salih, mounted by a group of leftists among whom was by Mujahid al-Kuhhali, a once close associate of al-Hamdi. It was defeated with some difficulty, and its surviving instigators moved to Aden, where they formed the 13 June Front. Fighting between government forces and the NDF and its allies broke out in the YAR in late 1978, with the NDF clearly having facilities and a radio station inside the PDRY. Following a meeting between Ali Abdullah Salih and Abd al-Qawi Makkawi, of the United National Front, the YAR gave assistance to groups opposed to the PDRY regime, and allowed an anti-PDRY radio station to broadcast from its territory. The media in the PDRY openly supported the NDF, asserting that the NDF was implementing a comprehensive social revolution in the lands it controlled.[15] The 13 June Front joined the NDF in January 1979.

Ali Nasir has said that PDRY leaders believed the position of Ali Abdullah Salih and his regime was weak. The YAR armed forces were in some disarray as a result of the divisions in their ranks that had been exposed since the death of al-Hamdi.[16] President Salih was untested, and appeared to be yet another middle-ranking army officer from a small tribe who would not be able to impose his authority on the country. Few at the time gave him much chance of survival. The PDRY was united behind a new leadership with a clear vision, support in the north, and above all armed forces that had been professionalized and strengthened by the Soviet Union, and had proved their loyalty in the events surrounding Salmin's fall. The PDRY could bid for the leadership of Yemen from a position of relative strength, despite the disparities in the populations of the two Yemeni states.

The inevitable war broke out on 24 February 1979, and the NDF, with PDRY support, made major gains quickly, occupying Qataba and other towns and soon threatening to cut off Ta'izz from Sana'a and Hodaida. The YAR was facing defeat, though tribal militias were soon moving to stiffen its army.

The PDRY failed to take into account the speed of international reaction at a time when its left-wing policies and closer relations with the Soviet Union were antagonizing regional and international powers (Libya was one of the very few to offer it support). A group of Arab countries put great pressure on Aden to halt its offensive and agree to a ceasefire. Washington ordered an airlift of supplies to Sana'a and moved a naval force into the Red Sea. It supplied two AWACS aircraft to Saudi Arabia, and it later transpired that President Carter had approved a covert operation against the PDRY.[17] Moscow gave some verbal support to the PDRY, but called for a negotiated settlement;[18] it was trying to improve its relations with Saudi Arabia in the wake of the Camp David Accords. The PDRY thus had to agree a ceasefire and open negotiations with Sana'a.

These took place in Kuwait on 28–30 March 1979, with Isma'il, Salih Muslih (who remained responsible for the NDF within the YSP) and Ali Abdullah Salih attending. Both delegations were thus led by north Yemenis, albeit with very different backgrounds, personalities and ambitions. In

Kuwait Isma'il pushed hard for immediate union but Salih, despite being under-prepared, was able to resist this. They accepted the terms of the 1972 unity agreements (Cairo and Tripoli) and set up a Constitutional Committee which was tasked with drawing up a constitution for a united state within four months. The two presidents were to lead the process and not, as in the 1972 agreement, leave matters to numerous committees of officials. Before going to Kuwait, Salih, in a gesture of good will, had removed two FLOSY members from his government – Abdullah al-Asnaj and Muhammad Salim Ba Sindwah.

The follow-up took a similar course to that of 1972: much activity and little action. There was no agreement within four months, merely the start of another long and intermittent series of meetings spread over several years. The YSP continued to support the NDF, which in its turn tried to undermine the regime. A Saudi delegation turned up in Sana'a soon after the unity agreement seeking an explanation.[19]

In practice, it was Ali Abdullah Salih who got most out of this development. He bought himself the time he needed to build up his regime and consolidate the support of the northern tribes. Not only did he receive US and Saudi support, but Moscow started to supply arms. There was no way that the powerful Zaydi tribes in the Hashid and Bakil confederations, which were an essential part of the YAR regime, would ever work with the NDF, and Ali Abdullah Salih was eventually able to use militias from these tribes to harass the NDF.

The pendulum swung clearly in favour of the regime in late 1979, and, after a period of fighting between the NDF and the government, the NDF agreed in January 1980 to abandon its armed struggle and engage much more fully in the political process. The radio station in Aden was closed, and the PDRY seemed to be trying to improve relations with Sana'a. Ali Abdullah Salih was growing more confident in late 1979 and early 1980, and was clearly waiting for an opportunity to hit the NDF, egged on by Zaydi tribal leaders. Salih was no doubt aware that Isma'il's position in the PDRY had weakened during 1979, and that Ali Nasir and other southern leaders were growing disenchanted with the influence of the northerners in Aden. Ali Nasir, like Salmin, seemed ready to work at a government-to-government level towards an eventual union; the northerners were more interested in stimulating revolution in the north.

In March 1979, during the fighting, the NDF created its own vanguard party, called the Yemeni People's Unity Party (YPUP), which, like its PDRY equivalent, was now an integrated political group within which the five original members of the NDF had merged; it was in fact the northern branch of the YSP. It posed the question, debated within the YSP well into the late 1980s, of how the YSP could operate as a governing party in the south and an opposition party in the north. Many in the north saw the YPUP as a threat to the regime. It appears that, for a time, the NDF continued to operate in the north as a guerrilla force, leaving political action to the YPUP – though both were intimately connected with the YSP.

Soviet relations and the Treaty of Friendship

At the YSP Congress, Isma'il's speeches underlined the need to be guided by the experiences of Moscow. He spoke of relations with Moscow as strategic, a term that was not used at any time by the Soviet Union in reference to the PDRY. Though Moscow, as always, remained cautious in what it said in public, the PDRY was seen by Soviet writers as a country of 'socialist orientation', that is, a country on its way to socialism.[20] After the congress, Soviet and other communist parties increased their support for the YSP.

The concrete results were promises of more Soviet weaponry (MiG-23s and Su-22s) in January 1979. Later in the year new tanks, helicopters and patrol boats were also promised. Soviet military aid in 1979 reached $250 million – double the 1978 figure – and there were more Soviet and foreign pilots training and flying PDRY aircraft.[21] A British government briefing document published in September 1980 said:

> The PDRY's armed forces, which today number some 22,000 men (there are a further 20,000 in the People's Militia), have over the years received more than 300 Soviet tanks, over 100 Soviet combat aircraft and a variety of other sophisticated equipment. A substantial number of Soviet advisers (estimated at 400 to 500 at any one time) have been provided; the PDRY air force is particularly dependent on Soviet training, supervision and technical support.[22]

Calls by Russian ships and exchanges of visits between delegations and leaders continued. Ali Nasir Muhammad attended a meeting of the Soviet-led Council for Mutual Economic Assistance (COMECON) as an observer, the first time that this honour had been conferred on any Arab country. Isma'il received the Order of Friendship among Peoples (another Arab first). Alexei Kosygin visited the PDRY in September 1979, though the Russians by then were trying to improve their relations with both the YAR and Saudi Arabia. Moscow supplied, for example, $500 million worth of arms to the YAR in late 1979. This has to be seen against the background of events at the time: the Camp David Accords, the Soviet invasion of Afghanistan, and the explosive impact on regional politics of the Iranian Revolution.

In October 1979 there was an agreement to strengthen links between the Soviet Communist Party and the YSP, and a separate department was set up in the Soviet Communist Party secretariat to deal with the PDRY. The culmination of the process came in a visit by Isma'il to Moscow in October 1979, when he and Kosygin signed the 20-year Treaty of Friendship and Co-operation, celebrated by a dinner at which Leonid Brezhnev spoke of the Soviet Union being a true and reliable friend.[23] This represented a significant step upwards in the relationship, and ushered in a period of PDRY diplomatic and political support for Moscow, in exchange for economic and political benefits. It was highly symbolic – and the symbolism was not lost on the PDRY's neighbours or the West. Their attitude to the PDRY hardened notably, and despite overtures by the PDRY it remained isolated in the Arab world. There was again an increase in Soviet military assistance, but no new economic aid despite the fact that the need for it was becoming more apparent in late 1979. Soviet companies started exploring for oil in the PDRY. Relations with other communist states improved, and the PDRY signed friendship treaties on the Soviet model with East Germany in November 1979 and with Ethiopia in December of the same year. By 1980 the PDRY was clearly in the Russian Camp, and relations with China, which maintained a small aid programme, had become correct rather than warm. By 1980, total Soviet aid to the PDRY had reached $152 million – about one third of the total received, and nearly double China's $84 million.[24]

The relationship was not without its tensions. One former official described a meeting he attended with Isma'il and Kosygin in this period. Isma'il complained about Soviet assistance to a specific project: much of the equipment supplied did not work and was not suited to the PDRY's climate. Kosygin responded roughly, saying that the PDRY had nothing and should not make demands. He asked what the NF/YSP had achieved: only 'a party school'. Later in the meeting, Kosygin advised Isma'il not to make trouble for its neighbours. They were living in an era of détente, and the world was too small for wars. He added that Moscow was keeping a close eye on Aden. Isma'il was not at all put out by the Soviet leader's disobliging tone, and over a drink afterwards said the conversation had been 'routine'.[25]

Poor relations with the Arab world and the West

Relations with the Arab world and the West deteriorated. This was mostly expressed in coolness or absence of contact, but in the case of Iraq there was a major dispute. The PDRY had given refuge to members of the Iraqi Communist Parties throughout the 1970s, and some were teaching at the Higher School for Scientific Socialism. In November 1978 an Iraqi Kurd teaching at Aden University was assassinated in Aden, almost openly, by people attached to the Iraqi embassy. The PDRY responded in a singularly undiplomatic way, storming the embassy and seizing three suspects.[26] Meanwhile, the PDRY continued to support revolution in Oman, but this seemed increasingly counterproductive since PFLOAG had been defeated and the sultan was wooing some of its leaders into his government.

Any slim US hopes of a possible opening to the PDRY were dashed with the disappearance of Salmin and the emergence of Isma'il. Concerns about the PDRY were growing in Washington partly because of Saudi hostility, but mostly because of worries about its increasingly close defence relationship with Moscow. The US had intervened indirectly in the fighting between the two Yemens in February and March 1979. Washington had earlier placed the PDRY on a list of states supporting or sponsoring terrorism.

Internal political developments: the isolation of Isma'il

In 1979 and early 1980, the policies associated with Isma'il drew the PDRY closer to the communist world, but without producing the investment and assistance needed to lift the PDRY out of poverty. Isma'il's policies had isolated the PDRY from Saudi Arabia and other countries with the resources to help it, with the exception of Kuwait and the UAE. The PDRY's action in the north had neither achieved unity nor enhanced the YSP's influence.

Inevitably, Isma'il and his northerner associates were blamed for these problems, even though many others in the regime had supported the policies towards the north (notably Salih Muslih and Ali Antar). Ali Nasir and others backed the strengthening relations with Moscow, but while arguing – as had Salmin – for a more balanced approach that might encourage a greater degree of economic assistance from the PDRY's rich neighbours.

Policy failures turned the cracks in the regime into major fault-lines during 1979. There was increasing talk in Aden of differences between northerners and southerners. It was recalled that Ali Nasir had argued against Isma'il being made head of state partly on the grounds that the northerners were gaining too much power. In 1979 this resulted in accusations that the Adeni northerners had too much influence in the Politburo, the Cabinet and State Security.[27]

In a later commentary, the YSP summed this situation up in its own arcane language:

> Relations between the principled elements began to witness some sensitivities arising out of weak adherence to party principles, democratic traditions and respect for the opposing view. Isolationist tendencies, minimizing the opponent's strength and hasty resolutions of issues without care for collective agreement began to prevail. The opportunist right (i.e. Ali Nasir) and the counter-revolution took notice of these trends and employed them to turn the principled elements against each other and open up the way for the domination of the right seeking to abort the party's revolutionary class content.[28]

Against this background – or 'sick atmosphere'[29] – there were continuing tensions at the top, and one Arab communist leader claimed that Isma'il resigned 'four times' before his eventual demise in April 1980.[30] The first sign that serious problems might be developing came in August 1979 over a dispute about control over military intelligence. Al-Bidh, speaking after 1985, referred to it as a problem over the respective roles of the military and security. Members of the Central Committee who participated in these events said that a 'dangerous confrontation'[31] developed between Muhsin and Ali Antar over the role of State Security in the armed forces. The origins of the dispute went back to allegations that State Security, led by Muhsin, had been responsible for executing around 250 military officers, in the aftermath of the overthrow of Salmin, without trial or reference to the Central Committee. The dispute became highly personal, and an armed confrontation seemed possible. Ali Nasir perhaps saw a chance of removing one of Isma'il's key supporters. Some felt that he encouraged Ali Antar to think that Isma'il was backing Muhsin as a means of extending his influence into the armed forces.[32] A party committee was set up, with Ali Nasir in the chair, to solve the dispute. It recommended that Muhsin be suspended from his post (he was made ambassador to Hungary). State Security was put under the authority of a new committee headed by Ali Nasir, with the Hadhrami Salih Munassir al-Siyayli as head of State Security, from 6 January 1980. Like nearly all Hadhramis apart from Ali Salim al-Bidh, he was essentially a technocrat, and at this stage was not regarded as a major figure in the regime, despite his position.

Figure 1: Mentors and rivals. From left to right: George Habbash, Nayif Hawatmah, Ali Nasir Muhammad, Muhsin Ibrahim, Ahmad Haydarah Sa'id, Ali Antar and Muhammad Ali Ahmad.

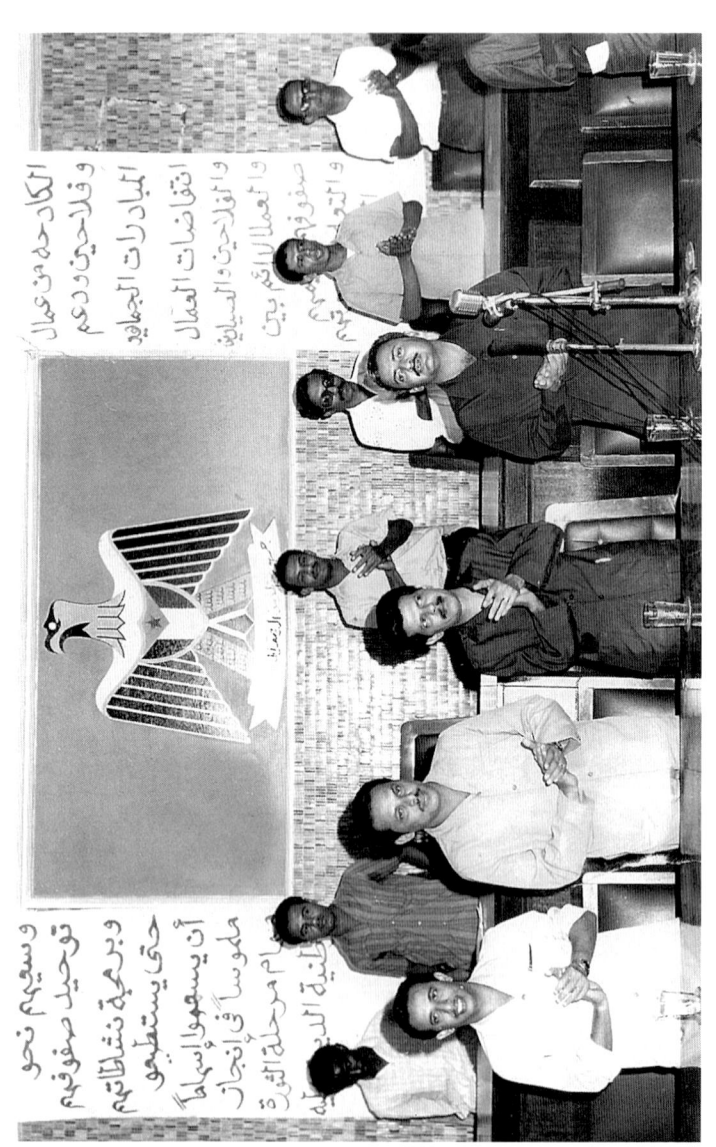

Figure 2: Front, from left to right: Muhammad Salih Muti'a, Ali Nasir Muhammad, Abd al-Fattah Isma'il and Salim Rubayya Ali (Salmin) celebrating a peasants' uprising to seize land in 1970.

Figure 3: From left to right: Salim Rubayya Ali (Salmin), Abd al-Fattah Isma'il, Ali Nasir Muhammad and Ali Antar.

Figure 4: Salim Rubayya Ali (Salmin) in Abyan. Muhammad Salih Ubad (Muqbil) is on his left (in a jacket). Muhammad Ali Ahmad is immediately behind Muqbil.

Figure 5: Ali Abdullah Salih and Ali Salim al-Bidh sign the Aden unity agreement.

Ali Nasir used the incident not only to get a grip on the security apparatus, but to strengthen his position as prime minister through the cabinet reshuffle that was necessitated by Muhsin's dismissal. Muti'a, the foreign minister, exchanged places with his protégé Salim Salih Muhammad as party secretary for foreign affairs. This could be interpreted as a promotion, since under the YSP the party secretary had become more powerful than the minister. Muti'a was at the time thought to be an ally of Ali Nasir, but events after 1980 indicated that Ali Nasir did not trust him.

Salih Muslih was dismissed as minister of interior, possibly as part of a wider reform of the security apparatus, which was thought to have become too repressive and to have perhaps begun to operate too independently. It might also have reflected the need to remove from such an important position the person responsible for supporting the NDF. Others think that Ali Nasir had doubts about Salih Muslih's 'abilities' (a euphemism for loyalty since even Ali Nasir subsequently said that Muslih was one of the cleverest people in the leadership). Muslih joined the Secretariat of the Central Committee and retained his command of the important Abbud Brigade. Like Muti'a, he was replaced by a close associate, Ali Shaya Hadi, a former head of the political department of the armed forces who was governor and party secretary in Shabwa province.

Abd al-Aziz Abd al-Wali, a northerner and close friend of Muhsin, lost his position as minister of planning and industry, was moved into a post in the YSP, and went to eastern Europe to pursue his studies. He was replaced by his highly competent deputy, the Hadhrami technocrat Faraj bin Ghanim (later a prime minister in a united Yemen), who had a PhD in planning from Poland. The Mahra leader Muhammad Salim Akkush was sacked as fisheries minister, and replaced by the voluble Anis Hassan Yahya. Fadhl Muhsin was removed from the Presidium, but appointed minister of agriculture – in effect a demotion for the brother-in-law of Isma'il, and a sign that his influence might be waning. It was around this time that the al-Tali'a and PDU members of the YSP became more closely identified with Ali Nasir than with Isma'il. Ali Antar was said to have been unhappy about the appointment of a Hadhrami as director of the army's political department behind his back by Ali Nasir.[33]

These changes strengthened the hand of Ali Nasir, but only exacerbated the tensions within the regime. There were rumours that Isma'il might even have tried to arrange for the assassination of Ali Antar.[34] Moscow became seriously concerned, and may have tried to intervene to prevent the dispute getting out of hand. Even so, the difficulties increased towards the end of 1979, and there were warnings from within the party that the divisions would only help the PDRY's enemies. Government business became paralysed. It was clear that something had to change, and there were reports of negotiations over Isma'il's future. A coalition had developed that wanted to see him 'retire', but without the potential violence of 1969 or the real violence of 1978. It appears that Muti'a was the most outspoken critic of Isma'il, with Ali Nasir, as usual, playing the Machiavellian diplomat.

The removal of Abd al-Fattah Isma'il

Matters came to a head in April 1980. Isma'il left for an Arab summit conference in Libya on 13 April (Muti'a, who should have accompanied him, withdrew at the last moment). In his absence, Ali Nasir arranged a series of Politburo meetings to investigate what were described as irregularities. When Isma'il returned to Aden, he was told by friends that he should resign. The most influential of these was said to be Abu Bakr Ba Dhib, leader of the PDU and a long-time friend of Isma'il. If such a person had turned against him, Isma'il must have realized the degree of his isolation.

On 20 April, at an emergency meeting of the Central Committee, Isma'il tendered his resignation 'for health reasons'. It was accepted by a narrow majority. He had never enjoyed robust good health (he was reported to have had tuberculosis and chronic stomach ulcers), but his departure was interpreted as meaning that if he did not go to Moscow for 'treatment', his health might become very poor indeed. In the post 1986 analysis, the YSP said that the April Central Committee meeting was 'convened under an atmosphere of terror and [acted as] an indication that force would be used in the event of the committee rejecting the resolution' that Isma'il should leave. Isma'il, it said, was prevented from attending the meeting;[35] but he was also said to have resigned to avoid an armed clash.

Isma'il was sent into exile in Moscow rather than locked up or killed. Moscow, which tried to intervene at one stage, concluded that his departure was necessary because of the shifting balance of support among the PDRY leaders. It judged that his removal would not materially affect its interests if he were replaced by Ali Nasir, a politician Moscow knew well and one whose long stint as defence minister had made him fully aware of the importance of Moscow for the PDRY's armed forces. Isma'il was given a medal and the title of honorary chairman of the YSP as he left for Moscow. The recently elected SPC confirmed the decision a few days later.

The YSP later described Ali Nasir as the principal architect and driver of the April Central Committee resolution. He had been 'striving after exclusive control of the first position in the party and the state'. He used conspiracy to win over 'principled elements' motivated by self-interest. The lesson for party stalwarts was that, when internal regulations were violated, party militants fell into 'a maze of self-contradictions'. This paper, however, acknowledged the fact that, whatever Ali Nasir's faults, he had proved himself adept at building a coalition to oust Isma'il and exploiting the weaknesses of Isma'il's leadership.[36] The SPC elected Ali Nasir as both chairman of the Presidium and party secretary, while he remained prime minister.

Former colleagues of Isma'il look back on his period of leadership in mostly sympathetic terms. He was the visionary who helped turn the NF in 1967 from a successful guerrilla movement into an effective political party 12 years later. He was the main ideologue, and understood the need for a properly organized and disciplined party. The YSP owed him a debt of gratitude. They also judged that his personality and talents were not suited to government. He could not handle the powerful personalities around him. A more adept leader might have exploited divisions among them to stay in power, whereas his actions and policies played into Ali Nasir's hands and isolated him from the historical figures who might have backed him. Isma'il, like Salmin before him, became a scapegoat for the PDRY's many problems. Though his colleagues did not question the need for a strong relationship with Moscow, they wanted to see more balance in the PDRY's foreign relations. He was seen as giving too great a priority to Yemeni unity through the YSP, rather than first developing the PDRY state and lifting its people out of poverty.

Though some former members of the Central Committee say that Ali Antar wanted him executed, the bulk of the leadership had sufficient respect for Isma'il (and perhaps no great fear of him) to allow him to go into exile. He was able to leave with honour. He remained an important figure in the YSP, particularly for those who had graduated from party schools and now populated many of the offices of the party. As Ali Nasir and his rivals engaged in a renewed power struggle within weeks of his departure, each came to understand that Isma'il still had a significant following and symbolic importance.

In the longer-term context of PDRY politics, Isma'il failed to divide the leaders of Abyan and Lahij, or to win over the main YSP leaders from Hadhramaut. His core support came from Adeni northerners and loyalists within the party. He appears to have made several attempts to extend his influence into the armed forces, but this served only to antagonize Ali Antar. He was perhaps too focused on the party and on the tribe-less Yemen he aspired to create, rather than on the realities of trying to lead a Politburo composed of powerful personalities with deep support in the provinces and the military.

One of Isma'il's last acts, on 5 March 1980, was to give the PDRY provinces back their traditional names: Aden, Lahij, Abyan, Shabwa, Hadhramaut and Mahra.[37]

8

ALI NASIR MUHAMMAD AS SUPREME LEADER

In April 1980 Ali Nasir Muhammad was, at least on a temporary basis, president, secretary general of the YSP and prime minister. He immediately set about consolidating his grip on power, and winning formal endorsement for holding the three most important posts in the PDRY. His enemies after 1986 acknowledged his political skills, but saw him as devious and ruthless. Ali Nasir proved more adroit than his rivals in exploiting and manipulating the divisions within the leadership and had sufficient support in the ministries, state organizations and armed forces to outweigh other contenders for his posts.

Ali Nasir knew how to appeal to the wider public. His speeches contrast sharply with those of Isma'il and Salmin. They are expressed in simple and direct language, and discuss how policies should be applied, rather than ideas and ideology. They did not list the many 'achievements' since 1967, but described what needed to be done to improve living standards. A political manager and a pragmatic leader more interested in tactics than strategy, he knew how the PDRY worked, and how to make it work for his objectives. Ministers in the YAR felt that his references to unity were not serious.[1]

He retained the structures he had inherited from Isma'il, but operated them differently. He sat at the top of government and the party, and the key people in both reported to him. Power came from his position: chairmanship of the Presidium, and the command of army, security and militia units, central government departments and the secretariats in the YSP. There was collective leadership, but Ali Nasir especially between 1980 and 1982 made the big decisions.

The Exceptional YSP Party Congress of October 1980

This Congress was exceptional in that it was supposed to discuss the deteriorating economic situation, whereas it became the vehicle for redistributing seats in the Central Committee and the Politburo in the light of the expulsion of Isma'il. It was a highly orchestrated event. In the weeks before the Congress, there were signs of a growing confrontation between Ali Nasir, on the one hand, and Ali Antar, al-Bidh and Muti'a on the other, as they jostled for power. Al-Bidh and Muti'a both wanted to be prime minister; Ali Antar may have had ambitions to be president. Both Antar and Ali Nasir appointed people loyal to them and removed potential opponents in the armed forces. At the congress, delegates were presented by al-Bidh with a list for voting for the 47 full and 11 candidate members. They were told to accept the list on offer or try to produce an alternative. It was clear that Ali Nasir, Ali Antar and al-Bidh, and possibly others, had negotiated how many supporters each would have on the Central Committee, reflecting the balance of power at the time. In those elections, Ali Nasir came first, al-Bidh second, and Ali Antar seventh. The YSP later claimed that Ali Nasir had used irregular means to make sure that he had a majority of delegates at the Congress, and thus on the Central Committee and Politburo. Despite this, even his opponents acknowledged that the policy decisions made were in line with those of the first YSP Congress, which they saw as a victory for 'principled ranks'. Policy differences did emerge later, and are considered in the next chapter, but were usually secondary to the ambitions of PDRY leaders in determining the politics of the period.

The Politburo was reduced from nine to five members: in order of precedence, Ali Nasir Muhammad, Ali Antar, Abu Bakr Abd al-Razzaq Ba Dhib (PDU), (who replaced his brother Ali), Salih Munassir al-Siyayli, and Abd al-Ghani Abd al-Qadir (al-Tali'a), with Ali Shaya Hadi and Abdullah Ahmad al-Khamiri as candidate members.

These appointments need to be seen alongside the cabinet as reflecting the position, influence and power of individuals.[2]

Al-Bidh, who had been at the centre of the negotiations, was not himself re-elected to the Politburo, and had to be content with the post of deputy prime minister and membership of the Presidium, instead of being prime minister. Ali Antar was rewarded for his role in removing Isma'il by being placed second in the Politburo list. Salih Munassir al-Siyayli, a non-Sayyid Hadhrami of Yafi'i origin, retained the key post of minister of state security, and was promoted to full membership of the Politburo by Ali Nasir to ensure that his support might neutralize any resentment on the part of al-Bidh. Salih Muslih remained out of the Politburo, but returned to the interior ministry he had left in August 1979. He replaced his close ally Ali Shaya Hadi, who became a candidate member of the Politburo. Abu Bakr Ba Dhib and Abd al-Qadir were the PDU and al-Tali'a members of the Politburo, though the actual leading figures in their groups – Ali Ba Dhib and Abd al-Qadir – were removed from the Politburo and given ministerial appointments. The northerners lost out, with only al-Khamiri (who was widely respected for his intellect and moderation) and Abd al-Aziz Abd al-Wali in senior positions (with Ahmad Abdullah Abdillahi in the party secretariat). Haydar al-Attas, who was a friend and supporter of Ali Nasir at the time, said much later that Ali Nasir had made an error in not appointing people with deeper roots in the party to the Politburo.[3]

The northern branch of the YSP retained up to one-third of the seats in the Politburo. One southern member of the Politburo at the time said that the northern branch, which he referred to as the NDF or YPUP, was a considerable nuisance: it took part in discussions and contributed to decisions. It was not always united, and Ali Nasir could exploit its divisions, but it always put the interests of the north before those of the south.[4] The branch's leader Jarallah Umar, a true intellectual, was effective in articulating opposition to some of Ali Nasir's policies.[5]

Death of Muti'a

Where was Muti'a in the new Politburo, Central Committee or government? He had suddenly become a non-person, after playing a big part in ousting Isma'il and making little secret of his ambition to be prime minister. There was no news of him until February 1981, when it was revealed that he had been put under house arrest in the late summer of 1980. He was accused of illegal dealings with Saudi Arabia during the visit of a delegation led by Ali Nasir Muhammad in June 1980. It was said that he had had a number of unauthorized meetings with Saudi intelligence. Muti'a had been in touch with Saudi Intelligence since 1975, but his friends say that Ali Nasir and Salmin had authorized these contacts, which were used as channels of communication and not for espionage.[6] He was also accused of other corrupt and illegal activity designed to finance subversive political objectives.[7] There were claims of documentary evidence to back up the accusations. He was sentenced to death at a secret trial conducted by the Central Committee in February 1981. Shortly afterwards, YSP members were told that he had been 'shot while trying to escape'. Ali Nasir was later accused of having had Muti'a murdered to remove him as a potential threat to his retention of the premiership.[8] There is no evidence for this, but Ali Antar, for one, appears to have been convinced that his friend Muti'a had been eliminated. Muti'a was the leading Yafi'i in the leadership, but the other senior Yafi'i such as Salim Salih Muhammad, kept their positions. In the later power struggles, leading Yafi'i backed Ali Nasir's opponents.

Al-Bidh resigns

The next senior figure to be discarded was al-Bidh, another man who wanted to be prime minister. In January 1981, he resigned from the government and Presidium and was suspended from the Central Committee for a 'moral offence' after he had taken a second wife (who was herself removed from the Presidium with him) in the secular PDRY. Others think that this was a convenient pretext (at least two other senior YSP members had second wives, but kept it secret) to get rid of a rival who was starting to make common cause with Ali Antar. Outside Hadhramaut al-Bidh was not very popular, and there were not many tears shed over his demise, which proved to be temporary. Al-Bidh had not been able to mould the Hadhramis into a power bloc to match those of Abyan and Lahij, and the many Hadhramis in the upper reaches of the party and government, such as al-Attas or al-Siyayli, or those in the army and civil services, functioned as individuals valued for their technocratic skills rather than their political weight.

Ali Antar departs

The relationship between Ali Nasir and Ali Antar rapidly deteriorated after April 1980 and even more so after the Exceptional Congress. Ali Antar removed from the army people known to be loyal to Ali Nasir, in part of a struggle for control of the army and the militia. Ali Nasir appears to have surprised Ali Antar by appointing a deputy minister of defence and chief of staff without first clearing it with Antar. There were reports in January 1981 of a major security alert linked to rumours that Antar had tried to rally support within the armed forces for a possible coup or threat of a coup, but had found that he could not.[9] Ali Antar decided to leave the country in early 1981, stayed in India for several weeks; he was clearly worried what might happen on his return.[10] Ali Nasir used Antar's absence to strengthen his position in the armed forces by dismissing at least 50 officers loyal to Ali Antar. When Antar returned from India on 28 February, he may have tried to mobilize his remaining support in the armed forces to try to reduce Ali Nasir's powers, but Ali Nasir was strong enough to nip this in the bud. Antar attacked Ali Nasir in an interview he gave at the airport upon his return, but he issued a 'correction' later.[11]

Ali Nasir used his power to persuade a Central Committee meeting in April 1981 to replace Ali Antar as defence minister and suspend his membership of the Politburo, accusing him of showing disloyalty to the party and its decisions. Antar, it appears, had no option but to accept this humiliation. In May, Salih Muslih was moved to the defence portfolio (thus maintaining regional balance), and Antar took over al-Bidh's former position as deputy prime minister and minister of local government. He insisted, however, that he stay in uniform and remain a member of the armed forces. A close associate of Ali Nasir, Abdullah al-Battani from Abyan, succeeded Muslih as minister of interior.[12] A few days later, Ali Nasir praised Ali Antar's role in the PDRY and his willingness to give up the defence portfolio.

Antar, however, was clearly furious. His colleagues always spoke of the need to handle him with the greatest care. He was given to fits of anger, sometimes violent if provoked or under pressure, and he was a dangerous enemy. Ali Nasir must have assumed he had the power to neutralize any threat Antar might pose. Ali Antar told his associates that Ali Nasir had to go. It was clear that Antar meant what he said.

Thus, one year after taking over Isma'il's posts, Ali Nasir was in the ascendant and, being confident in his own political abilities, felt he could manage the rivalries within the regime. He was now the only member of the historical leadership left in the Politburo. In achieving this, he had alienated Antar and al-Bidh. Isma'il was alive and well in Moscow. If these rivals could make common cause, they and their allies within the system, such as Salih Muslih and Ali Shaya Hadi, could challenge Ali Nasir's power.

The reality of politics in the PDRY was that no one leader could dominate for very long. Ali Nasir might hold the top positions, but he still had to take into account the influence of politicians from Lahij with their presence in the armed forces, the interests of other historical leaders, and the need to placate a variety of other regional interests

Ali Nasir's power

In the shifting alliances of PDRY politics, Ali Nasir's core support came from his strong position in Abyan and in the early 1980s from technocratic ministers, the civil service and the managers of state enterprises, members of the old PDU, and the Ba'athists, who usually had no option but to support the dominant YSP figure. The state establishment grew in the 1980s under his premiership, and many of the top bureaucrats looked to him for patronage and protection from the followers of his political rivals. His economic policies and his control of some state enterprises provided funds that could be used to reward allies outside the government structure. Interviews with members of the leadership and memoirs like that of Abdul Wakeel al-Sururi show how even members of the Central Committee and cabinet ministers had to use their links with the major figures for promotion and protection. Ali Nasir has since said that he was also trying to advance the careers of able people from the second generation, many of whom resented the way the historic leaders retained a hold on the key positions in the regime. Some might argue that rather too many of the second generation seemed to come from Abyan.

There was a big increase in membership of the YSP during Ali Nasir's period: it had reached over 34,000 by 1985, and it appears that many had joined for careerist rather than ideological reasons. In 1985, for example, the class composition of the YSP was 13 per cent workers (compared with 17.4 per cent in 1980); 10 per cent farmers (11 per cent in 1980); 17.2 per cent intellectuals (10.2 per cent in 1980) 38.6 per cent military (28.2 per cent in 1980); 13.2 per cent functionaries (27.2 per cent in 1980) and 8 per cent petty bourgeoisie (6 per cent in 1980).[13] Ali Nasir's rivals later used these figures to claim that he had been prepared to sacrifice quality for quantity within the YSP, admitting richer farmers and businessmen. What is interesting is that over a third of the YSP were in the military. Many may have been obliged to join the party, but the army, during the period when Salih Muslih was minister of defence, recruited a high proportion of middle and junior officers from Lahij. The core of party members educated abroad and at the renamed Abdullah Ba Dhib School for Scientific Socialism was increasing, and Ali Nasir was trying to reach out to them. Despite this, the regime organized local elections in 1983 when about half of those elected were members of the YSP.[14]

The PDU and al-Tali'a had smoothly transferred their allegiance to Ali Nasir, and were rewarded with party and government posts that seemed to go beyond their numbers in the YSP. There were eight PDU members and seven from al-Tali'a on the Central Committee. Ali Nasir could normally muster a majority of the Central Committee elected in 1980. He had a core support base of up to 25 members mostly from Abyan and Aden and 15 members from the PDU and al-Tali'a (there were 13 northerners and around 20 from Lahij and Hadhramaut). If he could not get his way in the Politburo (which he normally managed to do in the early 1980s), he could muster his majority on the Central Committee, which had endorsed the removal of Muti'a, Antar and al-Bidh.

One of the key supporters of Ali Nasir was Muhammad Ali Ahmad, the governor of Abyan. He had been a successful police and army officer, and had been governor of Mahra before moving to Abyan. He used this position and his Awdhali tribal origins to build what was later seen as a coalition of local interests – mostly though not exclusively tribal – in Abyan. He had a network of supporters in the armed forces, many from the Awdhali and Awlaqi tribes, who were promoted by Ali Nasir into top positions, including for example Ahmad Abdullah al-Hassani, commander of the navy; Ahmad Musaʻid Husain, an Awlaqi who later became minister of state security; and Muhammad Abdullah al-Battani, the minister of interior. Muhammad Ali Ahmad was something of an anti-intellectual (he never went to school as a boy in the Sultanate of Lawdar), but was seen as a coming man and future minister of the interior. He was highly ambitious, and had a forceful, dynamic and charismatic personality whose influence in the armed forces made him an enemy of Ali Antar and Salih Muslih. Though it is difficult to find direct evidence (other than as to who did what in January 1986), it seems that Muhammad Ali Ahmad built up support in the People's Militia in Abyan on behalf of Ali Nasir.

Ali Antar, Salih Muslih and Ali Shaya Hadi also had a network of supporters in the armed forces – mostly junior and middle-ranking officers, with a concentration in certain brigades. A Yafiʻi, Husain Qumatah, now party secretary in Abyan, was close to Ali Antar, and no doubt was there partly to keep an eye on Muhammad Ali Ahmad. There were others in the Central Committee, especially from Hadhramaut, who were neutral in the power struggle in the early 1980s but turned against him later. These included substantial figures such as the Hadhrami Salih Abu Bakr bin Husainun, the chief of staff and later a cabinet minister. There were also people like Ali Asʻad Muthana, who was from the same district as Salih Muslih, but as minister of state for cabinet affairs in the 1980s worked alongside Ali Nasir, and appeared to be loyal to him.

The influence of the northerners had been greatly reduced by the removal of Ismaʻil, and by the posting of Muhsin as ambassador to Hungary. There were still important northerners in the Central Committee and government, including highly experienced politicians such as Mahmud Ushaysh, minister of communications and a *bête noire* of the southerners, and Sultan al-Dawsh, a trade union leader who had been too close to Ismaʻil to be trusted. Abdullah Ahmad al-Khamiri, a candidate member of the Politburo and once a friend of Ismaʻil, quickly made himself useful to Ali Nasir, who protected him from his enemies. Ahmad Abdullah Abdillahi was in the YSP secretariat, as was Abd al-Aziz Abd al-Wali, who later left for eastern Europe, where he died. Fadhl Muhsin, linked to them as a brother-in-law of Abd al-Fattah Ismaʻil, was not popular, but perhaps because he was a leading Yafiʻi he proved to be a great survivor.

An alliance of the disgruntled was starting to emerge, embracing Ali Antar's supporters from Lahij, Ali Salim al-Bidh, some other Hadhramis and those northerners remaining in the system. There was a gradual building of this alliance in 1982, which coalesced around a demand that Ali

Nasir should give up one of his three posts. They also opposed in party and government meetings some of his moves to liberalize the economy, mend relations with Oman, and draw closer to Ali Abdullah Salih's regime in the north. They claimed that he was not adhering to the principles of democratic centralism and the collective leadership, the same accusations made against Salmin before his demise.

Ali Nasir was able to maintain his grip through a combination of concession and compromise, and security action. Following party elections for the Central Committee in August 1982, Ali Antar was given the honorary position of deputy chairman of the Presidium, and thus deputy head of state. In a government reshuffle, al-Bidh returned to the cabinet and Abd al-Aziz al-Dali, the moderate and able Adeni of northern origin (a dentist by profession), was recalled from Moscow to become minister of foreign affairs, replacing Salim Salih Muhammad, who saw his demotion as part of the continuing power struggle.[15]

At around this time there were reports of a plot against Ali Nasir. Muhsin was summoned from Budapest and arrested with others, including Mahmud Ushaysh, on suspicion of being involved. Husain Qumatah, the former head of the People's Militia who had been YSP party secretary in Abyan, committed 'suicide' in prison.[16] It is not clear when he was arrested. There were reports that Muhsin and the others had been making discreet calls for the return of Abd al-Fattah Isma'il. Whatever the circumstances, Ali Nasir was still strong enough to handle this real or imagined threat, and used it to isolate, demote and lock up some of his enemies, mostly northerners. Memoirs of PDRY officials refer to the atmosphere of tension, manoeuvre and counter-manoeuvre. The differences started in the Politburo, but went all the way down party and government to the smallest branches.

Ali Nasir's grip loosens

During 1983 Ali Nasir's rivals rallied around a demand that Abd al-Fattah Isma'il be allowed to return to resume party work. The first approaches to Isma'il himself were made in late 1981 or early 1982 through Isma'il's brother-in-law, Fadhl Muhsin. Antar met Isma'il in September 1983 in Moscow despite the fact that he had called for his execution three years earlier.[17] From around this time, and into early 1984, there were signs that the anti-Nasir alliance was consolidating and mobilizing support throughout the country. By mid 1984 the situation had become so difficult that outside observers were speaking of a paralysis of government.[18] This period was later said to have seen greater party vigilance, with meetings of the Central Committee 'characterized by frankness, vitality and the exercizing of criticism and self-criticism exposing the opportunist right deviations and underlining the need for adherence to the party programme and internal regulations'.[19] It was a fight to bring Isma'il back.

The pressure on Ali Nasir began to tell. In July 1984, two of the northerners who had lost position and even their freedom in 1982 were brought back into the cabinet: Muhsin and Mahmud Ushaysh. They were highly experienced politicians, well able to challenge Ali Nasir in cabinet. A senior member of al-Tali'a, Abd al-Wakeel al-Sururi, relates how he was recalled from his post as ambassador in Algeria by Ali Nasir, who wanted to make him minister of housing. When he arrived in Aden, Ali Nasir told him he would be ambassador to East Germany instead, because 'elements of Abd al-Fattah Isma'il are stronger and more prominent than me', and because he needed to keep 'a political balance'.[20] At the same time, Ali Salim al-Bidh returned to the Politburo and there were five additions to the Central Committee, though Ali Nasir still had a majority. Ali Nasir released and rehabilitated some of the previous supporters of Salmin, presumably in the expectation that they would support him and contribute to his strength in his home base in Abyan.

The return of Abd al-Fattah Isma'il

Throughout the rest of 1984 relations at the top continued to be tense. Abd al-Wakeel al-Sururi, for example, spoke from Berlin of the growing danger of an armed confrontation, as did journalists and diplomats reporting from Aden. There were attempts by so-called national and neutral factions (which appear to have included members of the PDU and al-Tali'a) to try to bring about compromise, but neither side was interested. One leading figure from Lahij, who was a relative of Salih Muslih and friend of Ali Nasir, reports how he organized a meeting in his house to bring the rivals together. This helped lead to the agreement described below, but he said that it had been difficult and 'had solved nothing'.[21] There were signs, too, that Moscow was becoming increasingly alarmed at the divisions, and intervened on at least two occasions to prevent the two sides attacking each other.[22] George Habbash and Nayif Hawatmah tried at different times to mediate. By the autumn of 1984, Ali Nasir realized that he would have to allow Isma'il to return. He met him in Moscow in October, though discussions were said to be inconclusive.

The compromise of February 1985

In February 1985 the two factions negotiated a compromise. Abd al-Fattah Isma'il was appointed to the position of secretary of the general directorate of the YSP, joining six others.[23] Isma'il returned a month later from his five-year exile. There were changes to the Politburo, with Salih Muslih and al-Bidh returning and Ali Shaya Hadi and al-Attas joining for the first time as full members. This tipped the balance in favour of Ali Nasir's opponents, but they remained weaker than Ali Nasir in the Central Committee.

Ali Nasir was finally forced to yield the post of prime minister. His opponents wanted to put Mahmud Ushaysh into the position. He had served as minister of finance for a long period in the 1970s, and was one of the better-educated members of the first PDRY government. He was an unusual northerner, in that he was a Zaydi (as was Jarallah Umar). Ushaysh, like many pre-1967 migrants from the north, regarded himself as an Adeni, and resented being labelled a northerner. Appointing Ushaysh was, however, a step too far for Ali Nasir. A compromise figure was selected: the Hadhrami Haydar Abu Bakr al-Attas. Al-Attas was smooth, patient, cautious and good at building networks of support within the party and government. He was widely respected, and had been a minister in most PDRY cabinets since 1969. He had steered a careful path between the two sides in the power struggle, but was closer to al-Bidh than to Ali Nasir.

Ali Nasir's reluctance to cede power was demonstrated when he proposed that al-Attas should be appointed as a candidate member of the Politburo. Al-Attas refused, on the grounds that he would lack full authority, as others in the cabinet were full members of the Politburo.[24] Al-Attas worked well with Ali Nasir for a short period, but then turned against him because Ali Nasir would not relinquish control. A new government was formed with a mixture of technocrats and supporters of the two sides. Ali Nasir's supporters had the two key posts: Mohammad Abdullah al-Battani remained minister of interior, and Ahmad Musa'id Husain became head of state security. Also in the cabinet were Antar, Muslih, al-Bidh, Muhsin and Ushaysh, who were by now working actively and openly against Ali Nasir. Two technocratic appointments were worth noting for their role in later events: the Subayhi Yassin Sa'id Nu'man as deputy prime minister, and the Hadhrami ally of Ali Nasir Abd al-Qadir Ba Jamal as minister of energy and minerals.[25]

Isma'il quickly gave more bite to the campaign against Ali Nasir though it was Ali Antar that led it. Isma'il was able to articulate more clearly the case against Ali Nasir's policies. He did so largely in obscure YSP-speak ('allowing petty bourgeois tendencies to roam'), but Ali Nasir was accused of rejecting democratic centralism and the collective leadership, and of failing to follow party procedure, preferring bureaucratic centralism, one-man rule and pragmatism. The attack extended to Ali Nasir's economic policies, which led to 'corruption, nepotism, favouritism and laxity of control'. Powerful party figures were allowed to abuse the system to build up wealth. The

PDRY, after 16 years of independence, was starting to look like other Arab revolutionary regimes, where those in power used their position to provide patronage to their supporters. Social networks often based on tribal and family links were more important than those of the party.

Policy issues are discussed in more depth in the next chapter, but as so often in the PDRY concerned the relative weight to be given to the Soviet bloc and regional alliances in foreign affairs, the role of the private sector in the economy, and relations between the YSP and its northern branch, the YPUP/NDF. Ali Nasir believed in working with the Yemeni president, Ali Abdullah Salih, while the northerners, Ali Antar and Salih Muslih, encouraged the YPUP/NDF either to overthrow the regime or force it to change its policies. There were also a few who objected to Ali Nasir's reconciliation with Oman and courting of the UAE and other Gulf states. Though disputes over policy played a role, it was chiefly a fight for power: Ali Nasir, Isma'il and Salmin followed broadly similar policies. The disputes were over what positions they and their supporters occupied.[26]

The compromise of February 1985 calmed the situation for a while, but over the next few months there were rumours of an attempted coup by supporters of Ali Antar, and reports that both sides were acquiring weapons and preparing for the contingency of an armed struggle. Details of what Ali Nasir's supporters were up to were brought out in the reasonably open trials that took place in 1986/7, but there has not been a similar description of what his opponents were doing. To many of those working for the PDRY government, this was a time of great difficulty. Decision-making had become almost impossible. Relations between people within the party and ministries were linked to the faction they supported and neutrality was not an option. Government was, in the words of one Arab diplomat, functioning at only 10 per cent of its capacity.[27]

One assessment in mid 1985 gave Ali Nasir's key allies as mostly military officers from Abyan.[28] Those lined up against him included the usual suspects: Antar, Salim Salih Muhammad, Salih Muslih al-Bidh and Ali Shaya Hadi. In addition there was Haytham Qasim Tahir, a Radfani who commanded the Armoured Brigade, and Sa'id Salih Salim, a leading security official from Lahij. They had the backing of most leading Hadhramis and the northerners.

A top military officer from Abyan claims that in 1985 he and others were approached in secret by Salih Muslih, the minister of defence, with the suggestion that they plan an attack on the north using all arms of the PDRY's forces. It would have the effect of uniting the army, which he said was split down the middle, with half backing Ali Antar and the other Ali Nasir. The proposal was rejected mostly because the senior officers did not trust Muslih, 'who was highly intelligent but was a man of intrigue', and always argued for imposing PDRY control on the north. However, the top military officer agreed that Muslih's assessment was correct: officers from Abyan and Shabwa were with Ali Nasir, and those from Lahij with Ali Antar.[29]

In the midst of this tension, preparations were being made for the Third YSP Congress (the Exceptional Congress of 1980 was retrospectively renamed the Second, seen as a victory of sorts for Ali Nasir).[30] Both sides were said to be energetically recruiting support in their home regions, within the armed forces and the People's Militia. Ali Nasir wanted to use this to bolster his position, but the pendulum was swinging against him as the alliance of opponents developed. There was a meeting of the Politburo in June 1985 at which a paper proposing a compromise between the factions was discussed, but no decisions were made.[31] Ali Nasir's opponents proposed that he cede the presidency to Ali Antar, and make other concessions. Ali Nasir refused, and as tensions rose both sides decided to step back from the brink and agreed a process to allow for a series of preparatory conferences to elect 426 delegates to the Congress from the provinces, the armed forces and external branches. Further efforts were made by figures inside and outside the country to help negotiate a compromise. One member of the Politburo said that he had asked the Soviet ambassador to persuade Ali Nasir to give up one of his two remaining posts. The Russian said he could not interfere in a manner that would so blatantly 'clip the wings of Ali Nasir'.[32] Ali Antar, on the other hand, complained to the Soviet ambassador that Isma'il was not being active enough against Ali Nasir.[33]

The congress was eventually held in October 1985, in a very difficult atmosphere. The YSP leaders did not appear together except when absolutely necessary, and their body language reflected the fractiousness of their personal relations.[34] One Central Committee member said it was a piece of theatre: the scenery, the settings and the sounds were all present, and the actors were reading the appropriate scripts, talking of achievements and plans. Ordinary members had no part to play, other than as spectators. They were not allowed to speak or express their views, or even to ask questions. In every corner there was fear about the now inevitable confrontation. But the supporters of Ali Nasir felt that he had managed to outmanoeuvre his opponents, and had emerged from the congress in rather better shape than he had entered it.[35]

A compromise of sorts was again reached, with changes to the YSP and government reflecting the shifting balance of power. In light of what happened subsequently, it is worth looking at the membership of the new Politburo in more detail.[36] It consisted of:

1) Ali Nasir and his supporters, including Abu Bakr Ba Dhib, Anis Hassan Yahya, Ahmad Musa'id Husain and Abd al-Ghani Abd al-Qadir;
2) Ali Nasir's opponents – Ali Antar, Salih Muslih, Salih Munassir al-Siyayli, Haydar al-Attas, Salim Salih Muhammad, Abd al-Fattah Isma'il, Ali Shaya Hadi and Abdullah al-Khamiri (a candidate member);
3) the neutral Abd al-Aziz al-Dali (but leaning against Ali Nasir);
4) the undeclared members from the old northern branch.[37] This had now split but the majority were against Ali Nasir.

Ali Nasir still had a slight advantage in the Central Committee, which now had 77 members,[38] but his lack of a majority in the Politburo made his position precarious, particularly as the majority of the historical leaders were now lined up against him. After January 1986 his opponents claimed that the elections of delegates to the congress were an 'outright rejection' of Ali Nasir's nominees – and he reacted by freezing elections for new YSP committees at district and provincial level until a compromise could be worked out.

A meeting of the Politburo held in November 1985 discussed a paper examining how to introduce a more democratic atmosphere into its deliberations, in what appears to have been a final effort at compromise, but each side apparently thought the proposal was directed against themselves.[39]

The struggle continued, now centring on an allocation of responsibilities within the new Politburo and the internal organization of the YSP. A group of Ali Nasir's supporters on the Central Committee produced a paper that called for a thorough investigation of a series of events dating from 1979, including the process for electing members attending the Third YSP Congress.[40] It proposed the strengthening of the office of Ali Nasir and a purge of the YSP's old guard to clear the way for a new generation. It attacked Ali Antar, demanded an investigation into the activities of several of Ali Nasir's rivals, including Isma'il and al-Attas, and recommended that Ali Shaya Hadi, Salih Munassir al-Siyayli and Ali al-Bidh be expelled.

His opponents were now openly criticizing Ali Nasir for belittling Isma'il and trying to push him onto the 'back benches', while pursuing economic policies leading to consumerism and subservience to capitalist reactionaries. Ali Nasir had 'eliminated' party militants and promoted tribally loyal officers in the armed forces. He was corrupting the state apparatus, neutralizing the influence of the party, and undermining the authority of ministers. In one speech to party members in Aden, on 13 December 1985, Ali Antar accused Ali Nasir of deceiving Antar and others at the 1978 Exceptional Congress, and ignoring the decisions of the Third YSP Congress. Ali Nasir seemed to think he could issue orders to the party and ignore the views of the majority. Antar demanded that Ali Nasir give up either his party post or chairmanship of the Presidium, implying that blood would flow if Ali Nasir refused.[41] A member of the Central Committee, speaking in 2009, confirmed that a majority on the Politburo wanted Ali Nasir to give up one of his two remaining posts, adding that Isma'il had suggested a compromise whereby Ali Nasir could keep both as long as he obeyed the decisions of the party.[42]

There were reports that both Ali Antar and Ali Shaya Hadi were saying openly – even at diplomatic receptions in Aden – that Ali Nasir would have to give up the party post or face the consequences.[43] On a visit to Berlin in December 1985, Ali Nasir told the PDRY ambassador that Isma'il was trying to push the PDU and al-Tali'a members out of the secretariat of the party. He spoke of his concern about the tension and disturbances, but he was still confident that he could control matters. On the other hand, one of the ministers accompanying him – Salih bin Husainun – said that things were going very badly and that an explosion was inevitable and would take place soon. He was right.[44] On 9 January a meeting failed to allocate new responsibilities within the Politburo and Central Committee. The key issues were the possible appointment of Isma'il to be responsible for internal YSP matters, and the move of Salim Salih Muhammad from secretary for ideology to secretary for foreign affairs.[45] Ali Nasir realized he would lose any vote, and called for the postponement of further discussions until after mid January on the grounds that al-Attas and al-Dali were travelling abroad. Though Isma'il and Antar agreed at the time, they later demanded that the meeting be held, as previously scheduled, on 13 January.

By then an explosion was widely expected, and a last-minute attempt was made by a leader of the Lebanese Communist Party to mediate between the two sides. Ali Antar reportedly told him that if Ali Nasir refused to accept the view of the 'majority in the Politburo, he would kill him and shoot himself'.[46] One account says that the visitor relayed the conversation to Ali Nasir, who appears to have spent 10–12 January polishing details of a coup he may have been planning for some time.[47] A warning of a possible attack by the Israelis on Palestinian installations in Yemen either caused or was used to cause a state of alert. Whether as a result of the internal situation or the state of alert, the tank brigade commanded by Haytham Qasim Tahir, an Ali Antar loyalist, moved into positions near Aden, and some militias were put in a state of high readiness. Ali Nasir made a secret visit to Sana'a at the end of December to seek the support of Ali Abdullah Salih and to brief him on the situation. The tension by the morning of 13 January was almost unbearable; it was a matter of who would move first and who would prove stronger.

9

POLICIES IN THE ALI NASIR YEARS

Haydar al-Attas, who was in all PDRY governments between 1969 and 1990, asserts that the turmoil in the Ali Nasir years was essentially a struggle for power. Nevertheless, Ali Nasir's opponents attacked his policy actions over the economy, Yemen and foreign relations, and Ali Nasir himself now says that the differences between him and his opponents over these issues were profound. The record suggests that al-Attas's assessment is correct. This chapter will examine the three main issues and their impact on the power struggle.

Economic policy

The Exceptional Congress had been arranged ostensibly to discuss economic matters, and Ali Nasir's speech as prime minister concentrated on the economy, dwelling on what needed to be done to raise living standards. The PDRY had not been able to attract sufficient investment to lift the country out of poverty, or to sustain a long period of growth. Economic difficulties had been exacerbated by an increase in the military budget in the Isma'il period, and without new sources of external income there would have to be cuts in development spending to preserve the sums allocated to health, education and social development.

Ali Nasir concluded that changes of policy were required, and he cajoled his colleagues into allowing greater participation of private and foreign capital and modest moves towards less rigid state policies in agricultural and industrial development. He had to overcome the lack of domestic resources for investment. There was a persistent budget deficit, and debt servicing at $27 million in 1981 was becoming a burden. The economy was plagued by low productivity, poor educational standards and shortages of capacity. The state sector could not deliver equipment on time, or even provide enough houses for foreign experts.

The second five-year plan (1981–85) had the highly ambitious goal of generating GDP growth of 11 per cent annually. Spending was forecast at nearly 60 per cent more than the previous plan. The allocation of money between the sectors was subject to big changes: 30 per cent on social development (as against 17 per cent in the first five-year plan), 23 per cent on transport and communications (against 29 per cent), 17 per cent on agriculture and fisheries (against 36 per cent) and 30 per cent on industry and minerals (against 17 per cent). Apart from grants and loans, spending was to be financed by encouraging foreign investment from a diversity of sources, and by persuading Yemeni expatriates to invest in productive development. The state would take the lead, but incentives were provided to the small private sector to contribute to development.

Ali Nasir believed that progress in the PDRY was only possible – without the discovery of oil – if the government could attract enough external funding. He needed to maintain relations with the Soviet Union while looking for new sources of money in the Arab world and beyond. He was not able to make much headway with Saudi Arabia (except for emergency aid to deal with floods), but the PDRY did attract significant sums for projects, but not budgetary support, from the Gulf states. The PDRY had received $94 million from the Kuwait Fund for Arab Economic Development and $56 million from the Abu Dhabi Fund for Arab Economic Development out of a total aid figure of $506 million by 1984. In that year, money from Arab sources exceeded that from the Soviet Union for the first time.

One of Ali Nasir's main achievements was to persuade Yemenis abroad to send more money to their homeland through remittances and investment. In 1984 the PDRY, which had a visible trade deficit of goods and services of $877 million, received around $480 million in remittances and $166 million in grants and loans, and had $29 million in foreign exchange reserves. Remittances in the 1970s had averaged around $60 million per year. In 1984 they were the equivalent of one-fifth of the PDRY's GDP. The PDRY government organized in November 1980 what was the second conference of emigrants, and took its advice in drafting a new investment law. The PDRY government asked what other measures would encourage migrants to invest and remit more, and implemented many of their suggestions. Expatriates were offered special rates of interest if they deposited money in PDRY banks. The PDRY joined international organizations protecting investments. Most remittance money continued to bypass the government, but more of it was diverted into productive investment in the Ali Nasir years.

Implementation of the five-year plan was much more successful than that of earlier plans, thanks to the regime's more practical approach and to reforms in administration. All went well in the first two years, but the country was deeply affected by disastrous flooding in 1982. Rising political tensions began to take their toll after 1983, as did falling oil prices in the Arab countries assisting the PDRY and providing jobs for its workers. There were problems over electricity supply and industrial expansion, but by the end of 1985 the PDRY was richer, better financed and better managed than it had been in 1980.

In the agricultural sector Ali Nasir initiated reforms to reverse the centralization measures favoured by Isma'il. Farmers were allowed to distribute up to 40 per cent of their fruit and vegetable production independently of the state, at higher prices than those officially decreed. Bonuses and piece-work wages were brought into the state farms, and some cooperatives were reorganized into smaller producing units. Much more investment was put into training agronomists and skilled professionals to help improve the output of state and collective farms. Efforts were made to boost farm output, reduce food imports and make more food available to the rapidly growing urban population. There were only small increases in the prices of subsidized goods. Fisheries, which had always received special treatment, continued to flourish under Ali Nasir, with output in the period 1980–85 substantially higher than in the previous five years. Fishery cooperatives were permitted to dispose of 40 per cent of their total production on the open market. The remaining 60 per cent was bought by the state at slightly increased prices. A new fishing port at Nishtun was completed in 1984, and important improvements were made to port facilities in Aden and Mukalla. Ali Nasir's reforms and the flow of remittances stimulated the service sector and housing, and led to a rapid increase in smaller private-sector enterprises. By the end of the Ali Nasir period there were 35,000 enterprises, of which 75 per cent were private and about a quarter of the workforce was in the state sector.

Prospecting for oil and gas got underway during Ali Nasir's period, but there were no major discoveries until after his downfall. A Ministry for Minerals and Energy was created in 1983. Ali Nasir became frustrated at the pace of Soviet oil companies working in the PDRY, and found that they had to buy in Western technology. He therefore opened up the field to Western companies, and Total started to explore for oil towards the end of his period of rule. The main contributor to GDP was the oil refinery, which began to receive significant quantities of heavy oil for processing after Ali Nasir improved relations with the Arab states (and Iran). There was also significant new investment in the refinery, so that by 1985 its output was around 3.9 million tons, compared with 1.8 million in 1979 (and 6.2 million in 1967).

Despite visible improvements in parts of the PDRY, particularly in Aden, which had suffered in the 1970s, there were problems. While money was found for public parks, shanty towns appeared around Aden as people moved from the rural areas in search of work. As the political rivalries intensified after 1984, there were complaints from within the YSP about a state within a state, in which people linked to Ali Nasir appeared to acquire buildings, money, goods and cars. The governor of Abyan, Muhammad Ali Ahmad, was singled out for criticism over what was described as a palace he had built for himself.[1] Later there were claims that government spending was focused on Aden and Abyan to the exclusion of other parts of the country – in particular Lahij and Hadhramaut. Ali Nasir, it seemed, was directing spending and investment towards building political support in his home province and the capital, and consequently restricting the funds available to the regional bases of his political opponents. Investment had become part of the political battle.

There were claims that consumerism was growing, and the arrival of Palestinians fleeing from Beirut in 1983 reportedly contributed to this. These criticisms started to bite as deteriorating economic conditions in the region in the mid 1980s reduced the flow of funds into the PDRY. Critics argued that neither Ali Nasir's economic policies nor his attempts to build relations with states in the region had produced much improvement in the lives of ordinary Yemenis. The left claimed that consumerism and the presence of foreign oil corporations would undermine the revolutionary zeal of the young.[2]

The Ali Nasir period was distinguished by a greater adherence to the rule of law, with harsh punishments for those who transgressed, but with more transparency and less arbitrariness in the system. There were commissions to investigate abuses within government, and a policy was pursued of stricter adherence to regulation. Many former PDRY leaders talk with some nostalgia about a vaguely remembered utopian state in which the rule of law prevailed.[3] Time has redacted memory and abuses still occurred, but under Ali Nasir the government was better managed. The gaps between the very poor and the wealthier grew, and those with links to Ali Nasir and his close associates were perceived to receive favourable treatment. After 1986, the new leaders spoke of the nepotism, patronage and favouritism of the Ali Nasir period.

Relations with the YAR

Ali Nasir's accession was welcomed in Sana'a, where he was well known for his pragmatic approach and had a wide circle of contacts. He had negotiated the Cairo unity agreement in 1972, and strongly backed the Kuwait agreement. He went to Sanaʿa in June 1980 to sign agreements on economic cooperation and integration. At the YSP congress in October, Ali Nasir spoke of the determination of the YSP to give the highest priority to implementing the agreements on unity.

The Yemeni People's Unity Party was the 'tactical name'[4] for the northern branch of the YSP. Its leaders were on the Politburo and Central Committee, and played a full role in policy discussions. In the early 1980s many in the YSP still believed it was possible for the PDRY to impose unity by force on the north. Ali Nasir later spoke of the presence of extremists within both the northern and southern regimes who thought that their interests were served either by war or by creating tensions between Aden and Sanaʿa.[5] He judged that Ali Abdullah Salih, like himself, put regime stability and economic development at the centre of his agenda. Both wanted greater assistance from the oil-rich states in developing their economies. The best way forward was for the two regimes to work together to solve problems, implementing unity agreements gradually and preventing 'extremists' from disrupting the process. Ali Nasir also understood that Soviet support for the regime in Sanaʿa, including the provision of arms, was evidence that Moscow was not interested in seeing Ali Abdullah Salih being overthrown. For Ali Nasir, it was better to work with Ali Abdullah Salih than against him. It is not certain if his sense of realism went as far as preventing Salih Muslih and others from assisting the YPUP/NDF. On the one hand, it would be useful to have a means of putting pressure on Ali Abdullah Salih when necessary, and, on the other, he may have wanted to avoid a dispute with Salih Muslih and his friends until he was ready. Ali Abdullah Salih appears to have understood Ali Nasir's position. Others in Sanaʿa clearly saw that the PDRY was pursuing two options simultaneously: continuing to give support to the YPUP/NDF, and talking to Sanaʿa about unity.

Under an agreement with the YAR government in January 1980, the YPUP/NDF was given greater freedom to operate in Yemen politically. But it was handicapped by the loss of its radio station in Aden.[6] The Saudis put pressure on Sanaʿa not to allow the YPUP/NDF a greater political role in the YAR.[7] However, fighting between the NDF and the government forces (supported on occasion by militias from the Hashid tribal confederation) broke out in late 1980 and continued sporadically until April 1982, when the YPUP/NDF was defeated and forced to give up the fight. Under an agreement with Ali Abdullah Salih, it was allowed to withdraw 2,000 men into the PDRY, and given a broader opportunity to operate in the YAR as an organized political faction.

Sometime between meetings with Ali Abdullah Salih in Kuwait in October 1981 (in which there may have been secret talks involving the YPUP/NDF) and in Aden in November 1981 and May 1982, Ali Nasir acted to reduce PDRY support for the YPUP/NDF. He persuaded a reluctant Politburo to integrate the northern branch into the main body of the YSP.[8] His objective was to prevent the YPUP/NDF from causing further problems with Sana'a and bring it under closer control. Jarallah Umar, secretary general of the northern branch, said that there was also pressure from Moscow for the YSP to cut its support for the NDF.[9] In order to do so, Ali Nasir appears to have been forced to give the remnant YPUP/NDF additional places on the YSP Politburo (and presumably the Central Committee). Ali Abdullah's priority at the time was to continue to build up the power of his regime, and to keep the PDRY and YPUP/NDF from threatening this.[10] Ali Nasir used his meetings with Yemeni leaders to ask that individual YPUP/NDF leaders, if not the NDF, be allowed to play a greater role in YAR political life. Later on he must have regretted allowing the leaders of the YPUP/NDF such a significant voice in the YSP, though Yassin Sa'id Nu'man, for one, says that they were careful not to intervene on matters that concerned the internal policies of the regime.[11]

In their November 1981 meeting in Aden, Ali Nasir and Ali Abdullah Salih established the Supreme Council of Yemen, which they would chair and which would supervise the work of the unity committees, meeting twice a year. Reporting to the Supreme Council was a joint ministerial committee led by the two premiers, and including the two chiefs of staff. A draft Constitution was prepared, though it was not published. After 1982 they started to travel together to Arab summits as a demonstration of their commitment to unity. Neither president, however, was seriously pursuing unity at the time.

Throughout the rest of Ali Nasir's presidency, Ali Abdullah Salih consolidated his regime, snuffing out the NDF as a potential threat. Gradually there was a shift in the balance of power between Sana'a and Aden, linked closely to the success of Ali Abdullah Salih in building internal and external support for his regime. From around early 1982, the risk that the PDRY might force its version of unity on the YAR had been reduced, although the reverse was also true: the PDRY was far too strong for Sana'a to force it into unity.

The relative positions of the two regimes continued to change after 1982 in favour of Sana'a. Major floods had a devastating impact on the PDRY economy in 1982. After 1984 the regime was weakened by the disputes within the leadership. The PDRY's economy improved under Ali Nasir, but the transformation of the northern economy was much greater. The YAR came to the help of the PDRY during the floods, and when there were problems over electricity production at a plant near Aden. By 1985, there was a greater sense of regime stability and control in the YAR as Ali Abdullah Salih had proved a much more adept leader than many had estimated. Thanks to the remittances from emigration and the flow of aid, the YAR economy began to overtake that of the south and was likely to continue to do so after oil was discovered in the YAR in 1984. People in the south may have had better social provision, but life started to seem better in the north.

For the rest of the Ali Nasir period, relations between the two Yemens were peaceful and largely cordial, and important steps were taken to implement the unity agreements. In January 1985 they agreed to set up a joint economic zone along their borders, and to share any revenues from oil in that zone. There was greater coordination of foreign policy, and in some respects the policies of the two states became more closely aligned over the Palestinian issue, while Sana'a drew closer to Moscow. The two Yemeni presidents took to travelling together to attend Arab summit meetings.

Towards a greater balance in foreign relations

The Soviet Union

Ali Nasir, like Salmin, wanted to diversify the PDRY's foreign relations without damaging its ties with Moscow. He knew he would have to proceed cautiously, given the importance of Moscow's defence, security and economic support. Between 1967 and 1980, Soviet aid amounted to $152 million – a third of the total received by the PDRY. In 1980 there were 24 main projects, of which the most important were a joint permanent fishing expedition and a fish cannery in Mukalla.[12] Moscow had no objections to efforts to obtain more economic support from Saudi Arabia and the Gulf Co-operation Council (GCC, formed in 1981), or indeed Western Europe, as long as Aden remained tied to the Soviet camp. Ali Nasir later said that Brezhnev and Gorbachev had encouraged him to continue with his external and internal policies.[13]

The Soviet leaders had known Ali Nasir since 1969, and had awarded him the Order of Friendship among Peoples medal in 1979. They might have preferred that Isma'il had stayed in power, but they were able to work with Ali Nasir and knew they could do little to influence the highly personalized rivalries in leadership. They opted for good relations with all the key figures, and tried to mediate in disputes when they judged these might get out of hand. Ali Antar and Ali Salim al-Bidh, like Ali Nasir, visited Moscow and were received at a high level in 1980 and 1981.

Ali Nasir's first visit as president and party leader was in May 1980, a few weeks after the departure of Isma'il. He was accorded the level of reception reserved for special friends, though there was some bargaining about this beforehand.[14] The practical outcome was the formation of a new committee to handle economic and technical cooperation, and a promise to construct the long-delayed power station at Hiswa, which had become a bone of contention between the two governments after the failure of the Soviet Union to make good on promises given as far back as 1972. Ali Nasir was aware that many south Yemenis compared Soviet aid unfavourably with what was received from other socialist and regional states, often citing Hiswa as an example. There were also problems over the costs of gold-mining in Hadhramaut.

Despite the official warmth, some Soviet commentators blamed the PDRY for its own problems, caused by the left-wing extremism of Salmin and perhaps by Isma'il's over-dogmatic approach. Soviet writers could also be quite unflattering in their assessment of PDRY leaders: in their view, they took radical steps without fully understanding the backwardness of their country and realizing that it would takes years of hard work and sound administration to bring about change. Fred Halliday describes how Soviet analysts looked at the PDRY at this time as a state on a 'socialist-orientated path'. Such analysis can seem arcane today, but at the time these theoretical considerations had an important bearing on Soviet policy.[15] Whereas defence and security support might depend on an analysis of Soviet strategic interests, the level of economic aid did depend on where along the path the PDRY was located. If it had become a 'socialist state', for example, it would have qualified for aid on a much larger scale. In the eyes of the Soviets, the PDRY had moved perceptibly along the path in the 18 years of its existence at the end of the Ali Nasir period, but was not quite there. Whether anyone in the PDRY fully understood this thinking is moot, but the complaints about the quality and effectiveness of Soviet aid remained strong, if not always given public expression.

In September 1982, two months before the death of Leonid Brezhnev, Ali Nasir made his most successful visit to Moscow. At this time the Soviets were happy with the close identity of their views with those of the south Yemenis on a range of issues. They were also happy with the PDRY's friendship with other Soviet allies, notably Ethiopia. Ali Nasir departed from

Moscow with a substantial credit for the construction of the Hiswa power station, which some sources said was worth $320 million.[16] By the end of 1982, the number of Soviet aid projects to the PDRY had risen to 50. A little later, the Soviet Union agreed to put more effort into oil exploration.

The Russian leaders expressed mild concern in the September 1982 meetings about aspects of the PDRY's attempts to improve its Arab position. These anxieties became more evident in 1983, after Yuri Andropov had replaced Brezhnev. Relations were cordial on the surface, but Ali Nasir did not meet Andropov on two visits to Moscow, and shortly afterwards Moscow asked the PDRY to start repaying some of its debts. Moscow was said to be unhappy at the PDRY's reconciliation with Oman (see below) and its agreement to give the PLO sanctuary in 1983.

Criticisms of the effectiveness of Soviet aid continued for the rest of the Ali Nasir period. The Soviets were not popular among ordinary people, who could not see the impact of their aid but had noticed, for example, a growing number of Kuwaiti- and UAE-funded projects, and even Saudi and Omani support to deal with the disastrous floods of 1982. There were temporary hiccoughs in Ali Nasir's attempt to persuade the GCC states to give more aid, so that by September 1983 he realized he needed to talk much more about the importance of PDRY–Soviet relations. He was duly rewarded with a brief call on Andropov, followed by a high-level Soviet visit in October 1983. There were generally correct relations after 1985, once Chernenko had succeeded Andropov, and was then succeeded by Gorbachev. Ali Nasir got on well personally with Gorbachev, who, after listening to Ali Nasir's exposition of his internal, regional and international policies, promised that Moscow would continue its support.[17] Ali Nasir interpreted this as Soviet acquiescence in his attempts to diversify relations without undermining the most important one, with Moscow. By then, the increasing tensions within the PDRY leadership were causing concern to Moscow, which itself was feeling the strains of its competition with the West.

Warmer relations with Saudi Arabia and the GCC

Ali Nasir made his first presidential visit to Saudi Arabia in June 1980, with the clear intention of resuming the level of contact established by Salmin. The Saudis were prepared to maintain a dialogue, but showed little interest in providing support for the regime as long as it was seen to be so close to Moscow, and siding with those regimes and left-wing parties in the Arab world that Saudi Arabia most disliked. The PDRY did not endear itself to the Saudi leaders by its support for the Soviet invasion of Afghanistan and its cosy relations with Iran, which was fighting Iraq and enjoyed the financial support of Saudi Arabia and the Gulf states. The secret trial and execution of Muti'a for 'unauthorized contacts' with Saudi intelligence officials could not have gone down well in Riyadh. There was a gradual thawing of relations after 1982, and Saudi Arabia provided emergency assistance to the PDRY to help cope with the 1982 floods. Relations were correct, not cordial.

Oman had long presented an obstacle to the PDRY's relations with regional states, notably Saudi Arabia and the Gulf shaikhdoms. Soon after coming to power, Ali Nasir told PFLO that the time had come for it to make its peace with Sultan Qaboos and return home.[18] In June 1982, Kuwait arranged meetings between officials that led later in the year to an agreement between the foreign ministers setting up a mechanism for dealing with future problems and establishing diplomatic relations. The Emir of Kuwait visited in February 1981, and there was then some increase in Kuwaiti aid for projects which, unlike some of the Soviet-backed ones, reached completion. This gave the Kuwaitis the opportunity to mediate in disputes between the PDRY and its close neighbours. The PDRY established diplomatic relations with the UAE only in 1981 and support from the UAE started to flow in greater quantities after 1982.

These moves have to be set against events in the wider region. The Ali Nasir years saw the Iran–Iraq war and the Israeli invasion of Lebanon, which eventually led to the deployment of several hundred PLO fighters to a base near Aden (enabling the PDRY to play a mediating role in Palestinian disputes in 1983 and 1986). Egypt's relations with the Arab states marginally improved after President Mubarak succeeded Anwar Sadat in 1981, but the PDRY was irritated by the presence in Cairo of a major opposition alliance now led by Muhammad Ali Haytham, who had once been a friend of Ali Nasir. The PDRY supported, though it was not formally a member of, the Rejection Front set up in 1978 by Iraq, Syria, Algeria and the PLO.

Iraq was clearly unhappy at the PDRY's friendship with Iran, which delivered some oil for refining in Aden. Ali Nasir recounts how he had as prime minister rejected a request from Saddam Hussein to build a naval base in Socotra in 1978. Relations had been badly damaged by the assassination of an Iraqi communist and subsequent PDRY action in Aden in 1979. An attempt at mediation was arranged, according to Ali Nasir, by Prince (later King) Fahd bin Abd al-Aziz at an Islamic summit in 1982; but relations remained strained, and in a private exchange with a prominent Ba'athist in Sana'a (which was pro-Iraqi), Ali Nasir was told that Iraq supported the PDRY opposition just as the PDRY supported the Iraqi opposition.[19] Relations with Syria were cordial but lacked content, while those with Libya had their ups (a tripartite alliance between Libya, the PDRY and Ethiopia) and their downs (Libyan disappointment that the PDRY stopped supporting the NDF in the YAR). Little of the money promised by Qadhafi reached Aden.

The relationship with Addis Ababa became more important under Ali Nasir, who by January 1986 had a strong personal rapport with the Ethiopian leader Mengistu Haile Mariam. This put the PDRY at odds with the Arab states supporting Mengistu's opponents and, of course, Somalia. There is evidence that Ali Nasir consulted Mengistu in December 1985 about how to deal with internal opponents, and received promises of support. Mengistu gave temporary refuge to Ali Nasir after the January 1986 attack.

The PDRY's difficulties with the USA continued under Ali Nasir, mostly over the issue of the presence of terrorist training camps in the country and suspicions of the PDRY's support for revolution in Saudi Arabia and elsewhere. The PDRY saw itself potentially threatened by the US military presence in Oman. Ali Nasir commented later that he had moved to close the camps down, or restrict the activities of the groups on the US list of terrorist organizations, but elements in the leadership believed they could be used to put pressure on some Arab and non-Arab governments. A court case in Aden in 1982 heard details of a plot to blow up oil storage facilities in Aden by south Yemenis who had received training from the CIA. Neither side showed any interest in restoring diplomatic relations, but Boeing was allowed to sell aircraft to Aden in 1985. France provided a loan tied to the building of a hotel in Aden by a French company, and there were improved relations with other European countries: the UK, for example, offered scholarships.

Ali Nasir was later criticized for downgrading the relationship with Moscow at the expense of better relations with its Arab neighbours and the West. Ali Nasir himself has spoken of the difficulties he faced in getting his policies agreed. The record, however, shows that Haydar al-Attas was right in saying that the broad direction of policy followed YSP guidelines. There were nuanced changes under Ali Nasir, but no major shifts in direction. It seems that the criticisms were a symptom of the tensions within the leadership, and not a cause of them. The relationship with Moscow remained at the centre, as it had done since the Corrective Move. Ali Nasir said that his policy was to move gradually – and he had done so. He probably could not have gone any faster. He was preoccupied after 1984 by the personality disputes within the leadership, which were widely discussed in the Arab media. Most governments were thus just as cautious as Ali Nasir, and the better informed may have been waiting for the outcome of what many believed was an inevitable and probably violent showdown.

PART D

FROM THE PDRY TO THE REPUBLIC OF YEMEN

10

FRACTURING THE REGIME: THE EVENTS OF JANUARY 1986

On Monday 13 January 1986, members of the Politburo and the YSP Secretariat gathered for the adjourned meeting to discuss the reallocation of responsibilities within the leadership of the party, due to start at 10 a.m. Ali Nasir's car had arrived, and he was thought to be conferring with a colleague. None of his supporters on the Politburo were in the room – they had been told the meeting had been postponed. At 10.20 a.m. two of his bodyguards entered, one carrying tea for those present. Instead of pouring tea they opened fire, killing Ali Antar, Salih Muslih and Ali Shaya Hadi, and then turning their guns on the others. In the confusion, Ali Salim al-Bidh, Salim Salih Muhammad and Abd al-Fattah Isma'il managed to get into an adjoining room.[1] Weapons were passed to them by their guards outside the building, and they used these to escape to the house of Sa'id Salih Salim (who became head of security in February 1986). There was firing on the Secretariat and other adjoining buildings. The three men remained in Salih's house until tanks came to their rescue later that day. As the tanks were ferrying them through Aden, they came under rocket fire from naval vessels. The tank carrying Abd al-Fattah Isma'il was blown up, incinerating him.[2] Al-Bidh suffered a minor injury when his was attacked, but he, Salim Salih and Sa'id Salih reached safety.

As the Politburo members were being killed, other supporters of Ali Nasir arrested or killed his opponents on the Central Committee. The Ministry of Defence came under attack and military, security and People's Militia units loyal to Ali Nasir started taking over parts of the city, supported by firing from naval vessels and attacks from some aircraft. It was claimed later that officers in the armed forces had been ordered to attend YSP meetings, where they were attacked and arrested by Ali Nasir's supporters, who had been supplied with arms earlier on the pretext of an expected Israeli attack on Aden.

In the early afternoon, Aden radio announced that 'elements of the opportunistic rightist grouping began to implement the coup by attempting to assassinate Ali Nasir Muhammad'. The leaders had been tried, sentenced to death and executed. Others were in custody and awaiting trial. It claimed that al-Bidh and Isma'il were among the dead.

It appeared by mid afternoon that Ali Nasir's supporters had eliminated many of their opponents, and might quickly have overcome the remaining opposition. However, al-Bidh, Salim Salih, Isma'il (still alive at the time) and others rallied their supporters in the armed forces – notably the armoured brigade located just outside Aden, and commanded by Haytham Qasim Tahir, an officer from Radfan who was close to Ali Antar and Salih Muslih. He linked up with other military units led by officers from Lahij province. The tanks moved into Aden in the late afternoon, and after fierce fighting they recaptured the Ministry of Defence and Operations Room and other key buildings, which had been seized by Ali Nasir's supporters in the morning. The heavy fighting, involving tanks, artillery, aircraft and naval vessels, continued in Aden on 14 and 15 January, inflicting major damage on public buildings, infrastructure and housing.

By the end of 15 January, it seemed that Ali Nasir's opponents were winning the day. A broadcast from Lahij claimed that Ali Nasir had failed to 'exterminate members of the Politburo and impose individual rule instead of collective leadership'. The Politburo had reconstituted itself and had ordered the armed forces to 'resolve the situation'. Fighting continued in and around Aden over the next few days as the collective leadership forced Ali Nasir's men to surrender or retreat towards Abyan.

On 18 January there were reports of fighting in all six provinces of the PDRY. By 19 January, Aden radio was under the control of the collective leadership, and accused Ali Nasir of trying to 'physically liquidate members of the Politburo and install individual rule'. Messages were transmitted from military units, mass organizations and YSP branches throughout the country supporting the collective leadership. Fighting continued in Abyan and Shabwa, but it died down elsewhere. On 20 January, the collective leadership announced the withdrawal of tanks and heavy weapons from Aden and referred to Ali Nasir's supporters as the 'misled' and promised lenient treatment to those who gave themselves up. By 22 January life was said to be returning to normal in Aden, and the collective leadership sent a message that day to President Ali Abdullah Salih to say that it was in full control.

Ali Nasir's precarious position was made worse on 23 January when he withdrew into the YAR. He may have been trying to persuade Salih and Mengistu, who knew of his intentions but not the precise timing of his strike, to provide support. Two of the senior military officers who had planned Ali Nasir's strike said that his departure dealt a fatal blow to the morale of his supporters.[3] There were attempts from Sana'a and Addis Ababa to start negotiations between the two sides, but by then the collective leadership was dominant. Though Ali Nasir was back in Abyan on 25 January 'with 40,000' men,[4] and threatening to march on Aden, the damage had been done. The military units that had remained neutral or were wavering had by then thrown in their lot with the collective leadership. Ali Nasir was forced to abandon attempts to rally forces in Abyan and Shabwa, and left with tens of thousands of his followers to the north. His naval supporters sailed their ships to Ethiopia.

The foregoing account, which is based on the official version and the trial testimony of the ringleaders, implies that Ali Nasir had staked all on a three-day campaign in Aden in which he would eliminate his opponents, who might otherwise have voted him out of one of his two offices, if not both. Details of the alleged plan drawn up by the commander of the navy, Ahmad Abdullah Muhammad Hassani, showed that the intention was to seize control of Aden, block the road from Lahij and open routes to Abyan, where militias loyal to Ali Nasir were waiting to move. Ali Nasir himself left for Abyan on the morning of 13 January, before the start of the Politburo meeting.

One former Politburo member said that Ali Nasir should have attended the Politburo meeting himself to make sure that all his opponents were killed, instead of leaving this to his bodyguards! There had been a plan to arrest or assassinate the commanders of leading military units. They had been summoned to a meeting at the Ministry of Defence by Abdullah Ali Ulaywa, the deputy minister and commander of the air force; but he did not act until he was certain that the minister, Salih Muslih, had been killed, and there was a delay in getting the message to him. As soon as news of the shooting reached the senior officers, they left the Ministry and went back to their units.

One of Ali Nasir's leading military supporters commented that the real problem was that 'we thought that the army would obey our commands. We had the top posts. But they had the middle-ranking positions and control of the key units.' He also blamed Ali Nasir for lacking the ruthless decisiveness that such a coup required. Salih Muslih, though dead, had been the victor, since he was largely responsible for placing people from Lahij in command of the armoured brigade and in the middle and junior ranks throughout the army.[5] Another of the principal instigators said that his opponents had won because they controlled the armoured brigade located near Aden. The units led by Abyan officers were more lightly armed, and were in positions on the PDRY's borders, not close to Aden. Ali Nasir had expected the air force to support him, but it had split down the middle.[6]

Haydar Abu Bakr al-Attas in Moscow

The prime minister, al-Attas, was on a visit to New Delhi on 13 January, and the foreign minister, Abd al-Aziz al-Dali, and 17 other Central Committee members were abroad. Ali Nasir's supporters claim that al-Attas had sent a message to him congratulating him on his victory. Al-Attas commented that there was so much confusion in the first three days that it was impossible to know which side would emerge as the victor.[7] On 17 January, al-Attas and al-Dali flew to Moscow, the place with the most influence on events in the PDRY. They found that the Russians had been caught off-guard. They were in communication with the Soviet ambassador in Aden, but 'he did not know what was happening'.[8] At first the Russian media referred to Ali Antar's supporters as 'putchists'. On 15 January the Soviet ambassador in Sana'a met President Salih to say that the Russians were not intervening, and strongly advised the president against doing so. Salih made a call for a ceasefire the following day. Two days later the Soviets had started to evacuate over 4,000 of their civilian advisers and dependents to Djibouti.[9] On 18 January there was a meeting at the Soviet embassy, arranged through the head of the PDFLP office in Aden, between representatives of the warring factions: Muhammad Abdullah al-Battani, minister of interior, and Sulaiman Nasir Mas'ud, commander of the People's Defence Committees, represented Ali Nasir, and Muhsin and Salih Abu Bakr bin Husainun attended on behalf of the collective leadership.[10] Bin Husainun, who was an old friend of Mas'ud, was prepared to negotiate, but Muhsin simply went through the motions. It was Muhsin who later reported to the collective leadership that Ali Nasir's forces were not interested in reaching an agreement.[11] Muhsin probably realized[12] that Ali Nasir was beaten, and saw no reason to compromise. On the same day, al-Attas and al-Dali rallied to the collective leadership. Their support – and presence in Moscow – helped persuade the neutral and uncertain that Ali Nasir had lost. On 21 January al-Attas affirmed that the new leadership had the backing of the YSP at a national and local level. They claimed that Abd al-Fattah Isma'il was still alive.

President Salih was aware of Ali Nasir's plans[13] and may have provided some support.[14] Salih was surprised that Ali Nasir waited until 18 January before trying to make contact with him by sending Abdullah Bukair, the minister of health, to meet him. President Salih and the Ethiopian leader Mengistu, who was also aware of Ali Nasir's plans, had not given up hope of trying to negotiate a settlement between the two warring sides. By 21 January, al-Attas was sending Salih messages from Moscow assuring him that the collective leadership was in full control. If the objective of Ali

Nasir's visit to Sanaʿa on 23 January was to win support from Ali Abdullah Salih, all that he got was an offer of help in reaching reconciliation with his opponents.

The new leadership summoned what remained of the Central Committee and Politburo to a meeting on 24 January. According to Ali Nasir, only 33 out of 118 members attended. It elected a new leadership and appointed a new government. Ali Salim al-Bidh became secretary general of the YSP, Haydar al-Attas chairman of the Presidium, and Salih Salim Muhammad deputy party secretary. Haytham Qasim Tahir was made chief of staff. Salih Ubayd Ahmad, from Lahij, was appointed defence minister, on the grounds that he had more political experience than Tahir, and Saʿid Salih Salim was the new head of state security. Al-Attas returned to Aden on 25 January with al-Dali and Fadhl Muhsin.

Ali Nasir's supporters do not dispute what happened on 13 January, but seek to justify what drove them to such desperate action.[15] They cite the tensions within the leadership over the preceding 18 months and admit that, by early 1986, it had become a matter of who would fire the first shot. In one interview, Ali Nasir said that he had in his possession tape recordings of a party meeting later in 1986 which showed that Ali Antar, Ali Salim al-Bidh and Abd al-Fattah Ismaʿil had formed a secret cabal within the YSP, later joined by al-Attas, to plot against him. On one of these tapes, al-Bidh spoke about how well their plan had worked on 13 January. In late December the armed forces had been placed on alert, and tank units moved close to Aden to avert a possible Israeli attack on Palestinian camps near Aden. They were thus deployed on 13 January around Aden, ready for action. Ali Nasir received intelligence that he would be assassinated on 13 January before or during the Politburo meeting, and had acted to pre-empt a strike against him. Ali Nasir says that he tried to settle his differences with his opponents through dialogue before, during and after the events of January 1986.

Both the official and Ali Nasir accounts accord with events at the time. The two sides had been arming for months, and the political situation had deteriorated sharply in the weeks before 13 January. There were military deployments around the end of 1985 to deal with a threat from Israel. It is not clear when Ali Nasir decided to make his move, but there is evidence that plans had been drawn up by the naval commander, Ahmad Abdullah al-Hassani, and that Ali Nasir had sought prior support from the YAR and Ethiopian leaders. He gambled on making a pre-emptive strike against his politically stronger opponents. He failed because they were strongly entrenched in the armed forces, and proved to be both well led and resilient.

Ali Nasir relied mostly on his supporters in Abyan and Shabwa. Muhammad Ali Ahmad was singled out by his opponents for playing the major role in raising funds, acquiring weapons, building up the People's Militia in Abyan, recruiting tribal fighters and urging Ali Nasir to action.[16]

The new collective leadership takes over

In early February the Central Committee and the SPC confirmed Haydar al-Attas as Chairman of the Presidium, Ali Salim al-Bidh as party secretary and Salim Salih Muhammad as deputy party secretary. These three were elected to the Politburo with Salih Munassir al-Siyayli, Yassin Sa'id Nu'man, a Subayhi from Lahij, Sa'id Salih Salim from Lahij and two northerners Abd al-Aziz al-Dali and Muhsin. There were three candidate members: Salih Ubayd Ahmad, defence minister, from Lahij; Abdulla al-Khamiri, an Adeni northerner; and Muhammad Haydarah Masdus, the new party secretary in Abyan, and virtually the only man from Abyan to remain in the higher reaches of the party. He had a PhD from eastern Europe, and had been ambassador in Bulgaria. He had been close to Abd al-Fattah Isma'il, though he was also a brother-in-law of Ali Nasir Muhammad, and had somehow managed win the trust of both. In addition, as always, there were the undeclared members of the northern branch of the YSP though at least one of them left for the YAR with Ali Nasir.

Twelve new people were elected to the Central Committee. Among them were the two main military victors – Haytham Qasim Tahir and Muhammad Haytham Qasim, both from Lahij – and Umar Ali al-Attas, a Hadhrami, who was the new deputy chief of staff. New party secretaries were appointed in Abyan, Aden, and Shabwa.

A new government was announced on 10 February with Yassin Sa'id Nu'man as Prime minister.[17] Dr Yassin was an able technocrat who had risen through the ranks of government and done his best to keep a low profile in the power struggles within the historical leadership. He was from a new generation of leaders who had been abroad studying in the pre-1967 period. In the 1986 cabinet, there were no ministers from Abyan or Shabwa, and only three from Aden (compared with six in the last Ali Nasir government).[18] This demonstrates clearly the regional, if not tribal, nature of Ali Nasir's core support. Yassin Sa'id Nu'man and others have said that the regime had little authority in Abyan and Shabwa in the late 1980s.[19]

The changes in 1986 also saw the expulsion of the communists and Ba'athists (who split into two factions). The leaders went with Ali Nasir to the north, but some of the secondary figures stayed behind and continued to work for the regime. They encountered extreme suspicion from al-Bidh, though others (such as Muhsin) were more accommodating.[20]

The impact of the 13 January events

The events of 13 January inflicted immense human, physical and psychological damage on the PDRY. Though it was not immediately apparent, the state had been mortally wounded and would not recover. Nearly three-quarters of the Central Committee of the YSP were gone, and there was only one of the historical leaders of the NF left in Aden. Four members of the Politburo and another nine members of the Central Committee were killed – all opponents of Ali Nasir – including Ali Asʿad Muthana and Mahmud Ushaysh.[21] Another 32 went into exile with Ali Nasir, and 26 were arrested by the new leadership. Among the dead were key party officials, ministers and senior government people, leaders of the mass organizations, and a 'large number of officers, NCOs and soldiers killed during ten days of fierce fighting'.[22] The official death toll was put at 4,330, but most observers believe the figure was much higher – with some estimates as high as 10,000. There are eyewitness accounts of the systematic killing by partisans on both sides. In addition, up to a further 30,000 (some reports say 40,000) people had left with Ali Nasir, taking their weapons to north Yemen, where there were reorganizing. Around 5,000 of Ali Nasir's supporters were in custody, and others had been purged from their positions in the YSP, the armed forces, civil service and the professions.

The events of 13 January were a virtual civil war that opened a chasm in the regime and undermined its legitimacy in the eyes of much of the population, particularly in Aden. It was a catastrophe for the YSP and for the PDRY. They had lost many of their leading figures, and their military and security forces had been damaged, and much equipment destroyed. The YSP conference of August 1987 admitted that it had failed to establish a stable state; it had allowed the quarrels among the leadership to lead to the neglect of the needs of the people. The collective leadership had defeated Ali Nasir because of the support it had received from the military officers and men from Lahij. Military representation on the Politburo was relatively limited, but had a disproportionate influence on decisions and policy, and it increased over the next four years.

Ali Nasir and his men were a constant menace to the new leadership. They were in 'refugee camps' according to Sanaʿa, and in 'bases' according to the PDRY. Ali Nasir continued to regard himself as the legal head of state and secretary general of the party, issuing documents in the name of the 'Central Committee of the YSP (Legitimate Leadership)'. He argued that there had not been a proper quorum within the YSP Central Committee, and that those present had been intimidated by the 'protection' provided by the tanks guarding the meeting hall. The Central Committee did not have the authority to 'announce the resignation of a president and the appointment of a new one' or for the election of a new Presidential Council. He called for fresh elections for the Central Committee, thus presenting himself as the legal authority for the PDRY – and he was given clear support by the Yemeni and Ethiopian regimes, while there were suspicions that he was receiving covert support from the Saudis. He continued to offer to negotiate with the new leadership, and put forward a plan for reconciliation.[23] He kept up his contacts with Arab leaders. Nayif Hawatmah – the PDFLP leader and the former MAN patron of the NLF, who never lost his interest in the PDRY – tried to bring about reconciliation between the two sides, and made a brief visit to Aden and Sana'a, but had given up by late February.[24]

There was immense damage in Aden, with many ministries, public buildings and facilities destroyed. The PDRY government assessed the damage at $120 million, the equivalent of one-fifth of the foreign assistance the PDRY had received since 1967.[25] Remittances dropped dramatically, with an immediate impact on living standards. Whatever money the PDRY could now raise would have to go towards repairing damage, and not expanding the economy. Meanwhile, the YAR economy, though it had problems, was overtaking that of the PDRY thanks to the increasing stability of the Salih regime and the onset of oil exports.

Regional and international impacts

The virtual civil war had attracted a great deal of media attention, not least because the foreign community, including Soviet and other military and civilian experts and workers, had been evacuated during the fighting. The British Royal Yacht *Britannia*, which happened to be passing, took on board many of those fleeing the violence. The reputation of the PDRY was seriously damaged in the eyes of its communist friends and regional neighbours. It was Fidel Castro who put the question all must have been asking: 'Why do you people kill each other?'

Moscow, as we have seen, was caught off-balance, but quickly decided not to intervene and that nobody else should do so, including the north Yemenis and Ethiopians.[26] Washington waited until 23 January before expressing the hope that the Russians would not intervene. The only military action was an offer to deploy aircraft to protect Oman from possible aggression. There was no immediate change in policy from Moscow. It reaffirmed the importance it attached to the PDRY and delivered substantial help towards repairing the damaged infrastructure. Soviet, East German and Cuban advisers started to return in February 1986 and the new PDRY leaders were soon in Moscow to reaffirm their commitment to the Soviet camp. The Russians had known al-Bidh and al-Attas for many years, and also had strong contacts with the military leaders behind the scenes. Even Ali Nasir continued to state how critical the Soviet relationship was to the PDRY. Gorbachev's period of *perestroika* and *glasnost*, and the pressures on the Soviet economy, contributed to a re-evaluation of Soviet support for the PDRY, though this did not become evident until 1989.

Regional powers were deeply suspicious of the new leadership. Most had long distrusted al-Bidh and some kept open their lines of communication with Ali Nasir in exile. Its neighbours also saw that the weakened PDRY government was no longer much of a threat, and would need their help in rebuilding its economy. They could approach the PDRY with much more confidence. Saudi Arabia soon tested the waters by making a claim to territory in Shabwa and Hadhramaut, where both the YAR and the PDRY were exploring for oil. However, following a visit by Ali Salim al-Bidh, Riyadh promised a substantial package of project aid. Oman was able to use this period to get close to an agreement on the disputed border with the PDRY. Relations with Ethiopia were gradually normalized; Mengistu now had to deal with the regime in power, and it was arranged for PDRY naval ships that had fled to Ethiopia to return, and for those Ali Nasir supporters in the Ethiopian embassy in Aden to leave.[27]

The coup gave encouragement to the regime's enemies in exile. Three of the opposition groups – National Congress, led by Ali Shaikh Omar, the People's Party of Muhsin Muhammad Farid, and the Democratic Union Party – started to put feelers out to Ali Nasir.[28]

Trying to put the pieces back together

The new leadership proved only a little less fractured than its predecessors, as divisions opened between civilians and military officers, the northerners and the southerners, and reformers and hardliner Marxists. One official who attended meetings in 1986 and 1987 said that 'members of the Politburo were uneasy and suspicious of each other. There was no dominant figure. The minutes of meetings did not reflect what had been discussed.'[29] Al-Bidh's supporters would speak openly about their differences with what they would call the 'tribal figures' from Lahij.[30] While leaders built patronage networks and manoeuvred against each other, there was a shared determination never to allow any differences to lead to the violence of 13 January; indeed, some argued that it showed the need for greater democracy, or at least pluralism.

Al-Bidh held the leadership together in the two years after the events of 13 January. He had shown considerable resourcefulness in rallying support for the collective leadership. He remained a moody man, and his colleagues could find him difficult to work with on a day-to-day basis.[31] Between 1986 and 1988 his socialism remained undimmed, and he believed that it was essential to rebuild the party and return to its core principles. Though he had a ruthless and unforgiving streak, combined with an unshakable belief in the correctness of his own views, he also had considerable charm and chose to exert it in 1986 and 1987 to try to retain the collective character of the leadership. He displayed a previously unseen pragmatism in his public statements, though he wrapped them in the YSP argot. He could sound like Abd al-Fattah Isma'il, but he soon started to pursue the policies of Ali Nasir. He was a Marxist, but at one stage had had two wives.

Al-Attas and al-Bidh had been friends since their student days 20 years earlier. In the 1970s they had worked together to look after the interests of many individual Hadhramis.[32] The apparently neutral and technocratic al-Attas appealed to government officials and those outside the YSP who had admired Ali Nasir's administrative and political skills. Al-Attas quickly showed himself to be more than a figurehead president, touring the country and the region to win support for the new leadership. His relationship with al-Bidh was sorely tested when al-Bidh proposed to the Politburo that he become chairman of the Presidium in place of al-Attas. However, the Politburo insisted that al-Attas should keep his post.[33]

Salim Salih Muhammad was the leading Yafi'i, and was a man with great confidence in his own abilities and judgement. He had not been quite in the top flight of PDRY leaders but was admired for his hard work and administrative abilities. His rivals said that his ego could get in the way of his political judgements and personal relationships; relations between him and al-Bidh grew increasingly difficult. Changes to the Central Committee made in November 1987, when the minister of housing, Muhammad Sulaiman, lost his position, were a result of manoeuvring by al-Bidh, who was trying to undermine Salim Salih.

The new prime minister, Yassin Sa'id Nu'man, who in 2010 was general secretary of the YSP, was seen as a technocrat not unlike Haydar al-Attas. He was from a newer generation of well-educated YSP figures, and had served in the fisheries and planning ministry before being made prime minister. He was a man who understood how government and party worked, and played a key role in steering the PDRY through the late 1980s. In 1986 and 1987 he was somewhat eclipsed by the influence of the military men from his own province of Lahij – Salih Ubayd Ahmad and Haytham Qasim Tahir. Relations between these two officers were said to be difficult as Tahir, who had been the key figure in securing victory against Ali Nasir, wanted a bigger role in the leadership, but al-Bidh and al-Attas felt that Ahmad's political skills and greater experience made him better qualified for the ministerial post. Tahir and Ahmad both had good relations with their former boss as chief of staff, Salih bin Husainun, who was also close to al-Attas and enjoyed wide respect and influence. He appears to have played an important role in preventing tensions between the two officers from causing serious problems for the regime.

The Adeni northerners had greatly improved their power and influence as a result of the 13 January events, and the most important was now Muhsin. He was one of the great survivors who had fallen out with both Salmin and Ali Nasir. In the 1980s he proved to be an effective member of the Politburo, but he remained dedicated to creating a united socialist Yemen.

Policies from 1986 to 1987

The overriding aim of the new leaders was to heal the PDRY's wounds and establish their own legitimacy, challenged by the menace of Ali Nasir in Yemen and undermined by the YSP's failure to improve the lives of ordinary people. Their priorities clearly lay in consolidating the regime, choking off support to Ali Nasir, rebuilding the economy, and reassuring the PDRY's communist friends that the country was stable. They also needed to persuade regional powers and international organizations to contribute to the costs of reconstruction and development. Unity with the north started to gather momentum after 1988 (see Chapter 11).

Choking off support for Ali Nasir

There was a relentless propaganda campaign against Ali Nasir and his associates, especially Muhammad Ali Ahmad.[34] The main leaders were put on trial in open court in the presence of television cameras and the media. For a while it was compulsive viewing, as hundreds of witnesses testified in a unique experiment. As the process dragged on, however, the leaders became increasingly uncomfortable. The desire for revenge in early 1986 had been replaced by a need by mid 1987 to heal wounds. They now wanted to persuade Ali Nasir's followers to return to the PDRY and cooperate with the new regime.[35] In March 1987, for example, al-Attas said that, of the 5,000 who had been arrested in early 1986, only 200 were still being held, of whom 94 were on trial in Aden and 48 were being tried in absentia.[36] Later in the year, a general amnesty was declared for people who returned to the PDRY by the end of the year – subsequently extended to July 1987. Throughout this period, Ali Nasir (by now living in Syria) offered negotiations, which were scorned, but also sent operatives over the border in Shabwa and Abyan to stir up trouble. There was also a steady stream of defections to his headquarters in Ta'izz, not far from the PDRY border.[37]

The trials were concluded in December 1987, and on 27 December the Politburo ratified death sentences on Ali Nasir, Muhammad Ali Ahmad, Ahmad Musa'id Husain, Abdullah Salih Ulaywa, Ahmad Abdullah al-Hassani, Abd Rabbuh Mansur Hadi (now president of the Republic of Yemen), Faruq Ali Ahmad, Alawi Husain Farhan (former deputy minister of state security), Hadi Ahmad Nasir (former YSP Secretary for Aden), Ahmad Husain Musa and Mubarak Salim Ahmad. It commuted sentences passed on another 24 to 15 years in prison (including Muhammad Abdullah al-Battani and Sulaiman Nasir Muhammad), and it reduced a sentence of 15 years imposed on al-Tali'a leader Anis Hassan Yahya to seven years. Others were given lengthy sentences. Five were executed on 29 December: Faruq Ali Ahmad, Hadi Ahmad Nasir, Alawi Husain Farhan, Ahmad Husain Musa (a former commander of the air force) and Mubarak Salim Ahmad (commander of Ali Nasir's bodyguards). The executions led to outrage in the north and parts of the PDRY, as well as the wider Arab world. A shocked al-Bidh remained firm, but al-Attas and others argued that the remaining prisoners should be treated with leniency. Over the next two years, many of those in prison were released or pardoned.

Finding a way forward

Despite the difficulties within the Politburo, the regime organized SPC elections in November 1986 to seek greater legitimacy for the new leadership and to demonstrate that it was in charge. It was claimed that 725,568 people had voted, out of a total electorate of 817,252 – a turnout of 89 per cent. This figure does not seem consistent with the lack of central authority in Abyan and Shabwa, or the frequently expressed concerns about apathy, but in the circumstances at the time it was quite an achievement to have organized the election.[38]

Policies were 'debated' at the Exceptional Party Conference, held in June 1987. This Conference considered an important document analysing developments since the events of January 1986, and set out a way forward.[39] All comparisons of progress were measured against 1967, as little success could be attributed to the Ali Nasir years. There was much criticism and self-criticism, made easier perhaps by the fact that Ali Nasir could be blamed for most of the problems. There was a need for greater party, organizational and ideological unity. Leadership had to be collective but operate on the principles of democratic centralism (which still meant obeying the leadership). The worldwide struggle between socialism and capitalism continued.

There was much else in the document that was reminiscent of Abd al-Fattah Isma'il, though expressed more clearly: the YSP had to go back to basics, to a programme of party and regime survival; the mistakes of the Ali Nasir period must not be repeated – that is, the opening of a gap between the interests of the party and those of some state officials and the 'exploitation classes hostile to the socialist path'; 'economic consciousness' must be restored and given a proletarian character; regional tendencies (that is, tribalism) had to be eliminated; the party had to root out corruption and commit itself to a more cooperative spirit in the drive for economic development; the PDRY would continue to build its relations with the communist countries, led by the Soviet Union, but also reach out to regional states as potential sources of support.

Party members were to inspire people to join the YSP, and motivate themselves and the people to work much harder to reach economic and social development goals, a theme repeated many times over the next two years. The state needed to improve its capacity to translate party policies into practical programmes. The economic policies agreed at the conference were also expressed in Marxist terms, but PDRY ministers, like Ali Nasir before them, took little notice, concentrating on finding practical solutions to the PDRY's problems. The YSP wanted the state and cooperative sectors to improve their performance by modernizing management, technology and marketing. It acknowledged the need to involve local and foreign capital, but under the supervision of the state sector. The economic relationships with the communist world were to continue.

The Presidium and Politburo were re-elected without changes (though Abd al-Aziz al-Dali lost his position a few months later). The dismissal of 26 associates of Ali Nasir from the Central Committee was confirmed, and replacements elected.[40] In December, Abdullah al-Khamiri, Salih Ubayd Ahmad and Muhammad Haydarah Masdus became full members of the Politburo, and there were three new candidate members: Dr Sayf Sayl Khalid, Haytham Qasim Tahir and Salim Muhammad Jubran. Sayf Sayl Khalid was an interesting figure from Lahij, who was leader of a radical group within the YSP known as the 'Fattahiyin', or followers of Abd al-Fattah Isma'il's brand of Marxism.

One significant change after 1986 was a greater show of interest by the YSP in Islam. For example, in May 1987 al-Bidh met a number of imams and thanked them for their support. There was more space in party documents and speeches given to Islam, though it was a relatively small shift in emphasis. It lacked conviction, and seemed like a device to reduce potential opposition rather than to mobilize Islam behind the regime. Some of this had started under Ali Nasir, and seemed linked to his attempts to persuade Saudi Arabia and other regional states to provide greater economic support for the PDRY, but it went further under al-Bidh.

Reconstruction

Once the immediate damage had been repaired, the main priority was to find sources of income to invest in modernizing the economy. Despite the resolutions of the 1987 Conference, ministers knew they could not rely on calls for harder work and greater sacrifice, but had to revert to some of Ali Nasir's ideas for decentralizing decision-making, encouraging foreign investment and improving the management of the economy. In mid 1987, the government admitted that there had been a serious shortfall of investment targets in the five-year plan ending in 1985. A new five-year plan was drawn up with modest aims: a growth in national income of 5.5 per cent in real terms between 1985 and 1990; exports and re-exports would grow by 40 per cent in the same period. Meetings of the Politburo and Central Committee spoke of the need to stimulate production and exports, curb government spending and regulate consumption, while retaining subsidies on basic foods. Ministers discussed the difficulties in increasing production, raising the morale of workers and fighting corruption. Problems were blamed on petty-bourgeois tendencies 'allied to parasitical layers of society'.[41] There were frequent references to shortages of foreign exchange and the growing burden of the PDRY's international debt. What distinguished what was said in public after 1986 was a willingness to admit frankly the scale of the economic problems and the difficulties the PDRY faced in trying to handle them.

The main hope was oil. The first significant discovery was by the Soviet Technoexport Company in Shabwa in 1986, and by the end of 1987 three small fields were producing up to 10,000 barrels per day, which were trucked to Aden. Contracts worth nearly $500 million and financed by the USSR were finally awarded in early 1988 for expanding production, and for the construction of a 150-km pipeline from Shabwa to Bir Ali. Exports were planned to start in 1989. But progress was very slow compared with the rapid development of adjoining fields in the Marib province of the YAR by US oil companies.

Relations with the YAR

PDRY leaders faced a dilemma in dealing with the YAR. On the one hand, they feared that President Salih might press for unity, given the weak legitimacy of the new leaders; on the other, they needed President Salih to restrain Ali Nasir, who was operating in the north with clear support from the regime. Salih himself appears to have been in no hurry for unity, but knew that Ali Nasir had presented him with a useful tool to put pressure on Aden even if he was concerned about the costs to the YAR government of supporting Ali Nasir's thousands of followers. In early 1988 President Salih commented that there would be no question of Ali Nasir leaving his 'homeland' of Yemen. In this period the US ambassador in Sana'a described the YAR's suspicion of the new regime and its desire to keep it off-balance.[42] Burrowes notes that in 1987 the YAR, when celebrating the 25th anniversary of its foundation seemed 'secure and comfortable in its separateness'.[43]

The events of 13 January had further weakened the northern branch of the YSP and the remnants of the NDF. It had split into three: one faction, led by Sultan Ahmad Umar, sided with Ali Nasir; another, led by the more politically shrewd Jarallah Umar, was working with the new leaders and playing a key part in the YSP. The third group was linked to the radical 'Fattahiyin' led by Sayf Sayl Khalid. There was also a growing faction within the southern regime wanting to see the role of the NDF reduced within the YSP.

The southern leaders were determined to resist any pressure from Sana'a, devoting their energies to restoring the physical and moral damage done by the events of January 1986.[44] Al-Attas recalls that he met Salih in Sana'a in 1987 with Mu'ammar al-Qadhafi, who was trying to persuade the two Yemeni leaders to unite immediately. Salih agreed, much to Qadhafi's delight. Al-Attas had to react quickly: he proposed instead that Libya and the two Yemens unite as a major step towards Arab unity. Qadhafi jumped at the idea, much to the chagrin of Salih.

Soviet and communist relations

The Soviet Union quickly decided to work with the new leadership, and may have entertained the hope that it could persuade al-Bidh, who went to Moscow in February 1986, to reach out to Ali Nasir. They kept their lines open to Ali Nasir, who used his PDU and al-Tali'a friends to talk to Moscow through the CPSU. When al-Bidh attacked Ali Nasir in a speech in Moscow in February 1986, his words were – by mutual agreement – not translated. A new Soviet ambassador was appointed with a

CPSU background, in an attempt by Moscow to build up the YSP party apparatus. There was no sign of any change in Soviet military policy, and arms supplies were quickly resumed, as were training courses, and Soviet military experts returned.

The Soviet Union appreciated the urgent need to improve the economy, if only to help the regime win more popular support, and thus legitimacy. This led to a series of new agreements and an effort to ensure that existing projects were completed. The Russians agreed in 1986 to send 600,000 tons of oil to the oil refinery in Aden, which it would repair and modernize. The CPSU paid for new YSP buildings in Aden, replacing those that had been destroyed in January 1986, and in January 1987 agreed to expand the Hiswa power station at a cost of 89 million roubles. Additional support was provided through the Council for Mutual Economic Assistance.

There were early signs that some in Moscow were having doubts about the reliability of the PDRY. Soviet watchers noticed that the Soviet delegations to the PDRY were led by more junior officials than had been the practice before 1986. Gorbachev, who had liked Ali Nasir, is said to have reminded al-Bidh that 'no revolution is guaranteed from the vanguard's striving to skip over unavoidable phases'. He urged a much greater dose of realism. Soviet commentators criticized the PDRY's economic policies for being too political. Soviet officials were saying in private that their support for the PDRY could not be guaranteed if there was another outbreak of factional fighting, with the two sides using Soviet weapons to kill each other, and putting shells – either by accident or design – into Soviet embassy buildings in January 1986.[45]

The region and the West

The 1987 party document was quite frank in discussing the PDRY's need for foreign assistance to ensure the survival of the regime and its lack of diplomatic capacity. Too much of the burden was placed on the president, which had in the past caused problems of a political nature. There was a need to train more diplomats. A series of visits to regional capitals took place, and relations with Egypt were restored in 1988. Saudi Arabia maintained links to both the regime and Ali Nasir, and provided some economic aid. A Saudi delegation arrived in August 1986 to discuss a soft loan for the development of Aden port and a housing project. Oman and the PDRY reached an agreement to open embassies in 1987, and Oman offered to provide assistance to the PDRY; they later agreed to demarcate their joint border. The other Gulf states, notably Kuwait, continued to provide some assistance. The PDRY shifted away from its neutral position on the

Iran–Iraq war to one more openly favouring Iraq. It maintained its links with the left-wing regimes in Syria and Algeria, as well as with the Palestinians. Correct relations were maintained with Ethiopia, as Mengistu was wooed away from Ali Nasir; but the relationship lacked the previous warmth and depth. There was talk of a possible opening of relations with the USA, but this did not occur until just before unity. Relations with other Western countries were correct, though several reduced their diplomatic missions after the 1986 events.

II

UNITY OR REFORM?

The economic problems and political divisions deepened in 1988 and 1989.[1] GDP per capita was 20 per cent lower in 1989 than in 1985.[2] Anxieties over the availability of foreign exchange and the scale of foreign debt ($5 billion) were compounded by demands from East Germany for the PDRY to adhere to repayment terms despite its economic difficulties. Remittances fell from the mid 1980s as the second oil boom ran out of steam.

Oil production had started by late 1989, but all that the PDRY had to show for it were '60 or so mostly non-functioning wells, a pipeline suspected of leaking, an outmoded oil processing complex, and a few barrels of crude oil trucked sporadically to Aden's decrepit refinery'.[3] The Western oil companies exploring the more promising areas in Hadhramaut had not yet made the discoveries that so benefited Yemen after unity. The technocrats in the ministry fully understood that the main prospects were in Hadhramaut, but the politicians would not listen to them.[4]

A new investment law was endorsed by the cabinet in September 1988 and in early October the Central Committee discussed radical economic reforms but a few weeks later Haydar al-Attas spoke of 'insufficient financing for projects' and of the weakness of the 'productive infrastructure'.[5] Salim Salih indicated that it had been a mistake to copy the models of some Arab and Communist states in building the PDRY's structures; but it simply got worse. Just before unity, for example, one observer noted, 'the economy had effectively broken down; farmers refused to deliver food for the miserable prices they could get, for weeks the only food available in Aden market was potatoes, bread and onions. The government's coffers were empty.'[6] A deputy minister in the period 1988–90 summed up the situation: 'there was no money for anything. Everyone suffered – ministries, local governments and even the security services'.[7] The PDRY was virtually bankrupt.

Glasnost and *perestroika*

The changes in the Soviet Union in the late 1980s had an accelerating impact on the PDRY. There was a subtle downgrading of relations, with more open criticism of its economic policies and of its limited achievements. Moscow began to suggest that the PDRY should study how *perestroika* was working in the Soviet Union, and learn lessons that might fit the PDRY. Articles appeared in the PDRY press in mid 1988 arguing for and against the adoption of a tailored version of *perestroika*. The Soviets also advised PDRY leaders to open up the debate about the future to other political forces.

In 1989 it was plain that the changes in the Soviet Union were so profound that it was unlikely that Moscow would back the PDRY much longer for strategic or military purposes – and that the USSR, in its parlous economic state, could no longer afford to support countries that were of marginal interest. It was allowing the regimes in Eastern Europe to drift away, even East Germany, which had been an important source of support for the PDRY. As Jarallah Umar put it, 'It is no longer anticipated that the Soviets will send their armies to defend their other allies once they face domestic turmoil.'[8] In October 1989, the PDRY foreign minister noted that – 'so far' – the Soviet Union was continuing to implement agreements, including that on oil exploration, but that Aden did not expect anything new from Moscow. When a secret delegation from the PDRY went to Moscow in mid December 1989 to inform the Soviet Union about its motives for agreeing to union with the north, it was told that the PDRY should stand on its own feet and reminded that its debt to the Soviet Union was $6 billion.[9] However, a senior figure in the PDRY finance ministry said that the debt to the Soviet Union in January 1986 had been $3.5 billion, showing that Soviet assistance was maintained at a high rate until the end of the PDRY.[10]

The PDRY realized late in the day that it would need to adjust its foreign relations, reverting to the policies of Ali Nasir and Salmin. The foreign minister, Abd al-Aziz al-Dali, for example, said that the PDRY had made 'faulty evaluations of foreign relations', and spoke of the need for more balanced and positive relations.[11]

Political divisions

The conflicts between personalities and over power continued. Ali Salim al-Bidh was increasingly less able to exert his authority over the Politburo, and could not persuade a majority of his colleagues to agree and then implement a coherent programme to address the PDRY's many problems. On the other hand, al-Bidh was able to exploit the divided nature of the Politburo to retain his position. Al-Bidh, the last of the historical leaders of the NLF to remain in power, lacked the support base that Salmin and Ali Nasir had developed in Abyan, and that Ali Antar and Salih Muslih had in Lahij. The Hadhramis in the Politburo, the government and the army did not act as a cohesive group, and often appeared to be competing with each other.[12] Abyan and Shabwa belonged to Ali Nasir politically, and could thus not function as a counterweight to the military leaders from Lahij now running the armed forces and the Ministry of State Security in the hands of Sa'id Salih Salim.[13] They continued to see Ali Nasir as a menace. In June 1988, Salih Ubayd Ahmad, the minister of defence, speaking at a conference of the YSP armed forces organization, stressed the need to strengthen political, ideological and military capacities to deal with 'dangerous practices of the opportunist right wing which are aimed at paralysing policy'.[14]

There were also divisions between what might be called the pragmatists such as Salim Salih Muhammad and Yassin Sa'id Nu'man, the prime minister, and the 'Fattahiyin' disciples of Abd al-Fattah Isma'il, who were not very numerous but had an effective leader in Sayf Sayl Khalid, and a solid base in Aden.[15] While the pragmatists and most ministers were arguing for profound economic and political reform, the Fattahiyin wanted to go back to the socialism of the 1970s.

Tensions between southerners and northerners grew worse. The northerners after 1986 were well entrenched within the YSP, now led by the highly experienced and politically skilful Muhsin and Fahdl Muhsin. Jarallah Umar, who remained the secretary for the northern branch and leader of the NDF, emerged in the late 1980s as one of the most influential politicians in the regime. Haydar al-Attas submitted a paper to the Politburo in 1987 in which he argued that it was no longer possible for the YSP to act as a governing party in the south and an opposition party in the north: the northern branch members of the Politburo should leave and organize a separate party. Al-Attas said that this produced a strong reaction from the northern contingent. Yassin Sa'id Nu'man, who was more sympathetic to the northerners, does not recall the paper, though at least two Hadhrami members of the Central Committee at the time say that there were some politicians arguing for a diminished role for the northern branch. Nu'man says that the northern branch did not interfere in what were purely southern issues though others in the YSP leadership at the time do not agree.

Jarallah Umar began to argue for greater pluralism and democracy in the south. Umar's intellectual capacity, his cultural achievements and his agreeable personality appealed to many in the south. He commented,

> In the aftermath of January 1986, I called for political pluralism inside the party. The leadership first rejected this suggestion, but events in the Soviet Union, the troubled economic situation in

the south, and the deleterious effects of the January events eventually worked to encourage the leadership to accept the call for political pluralism.[16]

Umar warned about the revival of Islam in both Yemens, and saw this as a threat to all that the YSP represented.[17] He thought that the socialist fervour of the 1970s had been throttled by bureaucracy in the 1980s. Other PDRY leaders were considering *perestroika*. Salim Salih Muhammad, for example, said in September 1989 that 'what is now happening in the Soviet Union and eastern bloc states reinforced what is now happening to us'. He later qualified this by saying that the PDRY would not 'mechanically copy' the changes in Eastern Europe, but work out what was right and practical for Aden.

The arguments about policy were reflected in the media as journalists discussed the relative merits of private enterprise and the restrictive rules that had strangled initiative and led to shortages of food and consumer goods in Aden in the late 1980s. There was much more open discussion in the foreign media, among diplomats, and increasingly among Adeni civil servants and businessmen, about the divisions in the leadership and its ability to deal with the PDRY's many problems. There were constant rumours about quarrels in the Politburo and a steady stream of defections to Ali Nasir, while others, including prominent officials, abandoned the regime for the north. Speaking 20 years after these events, Politburo and Central Committee members at the time thought that there was a possibility that al-Bidh could have been deposed in 1989 by a coalition of Lahij military officers, northerners and Fattahiyin. Al-Bidh showed skill in preventing his critics from uniting against him.

Liberalization or unity?

Leading figures in the PDRY concluded that, if the regime were to survive, it would have to undergo major reform or seek salvation in union with the YAR. Both options were considered, but in the end it was a third that was implemented: pursuing reform and unity simultaneously. YSP leaders had concluded that the 'totalitarian policies and directives would lead us only to a dead end, with political and organizational incompetence, a failure of the economic and social policies – even if the intentions were good'. It had to move away from 'static ideology' and recognize 'the variety of different movements that existed'.[18] A member of the Central Committee has described how a working party was set up in late 1988 to produce a document on reform.[19] Central Committee minutes in early 1989 showed that the document was being discussed at all levels of the YSP. In May 1989, for example, the Central Committee stressed that

> comprehensive political and economic reform was necessary in order to tackle the shortcomings in the structures of the authorities, organizations and other institutions, in the relationships between the different parts of the political organization including the vanguard role of the party – as well as in the relationship between the state authorities, one with the other, and the role of the mass organizations within the framework of the political organization, in addition to the imbalances and errors linked to the economic, social and administrative fields.[20]

On 21 June 1989, al-Bidh told the Central Committee that it was essential to prepare a plan for comprehensive political and economic reform. He wanted to escape from the leadership tensions of the previous 20 years that had caused the regime to adopt 'abortive and ineffective policies'. It was now necessary to harness the energies of the people within a broad social base. Democracy was to be the 'essence of the entire process'.[21] It took another nine months of internal discussion before the full details of the plan were agreed – three months after the signing of the unity agreement.

One sign that the regime meant what it said about reform was the televising of a session of the SPC held in June 1989, where members were encouraged to speak freely (within limits that most understood) about the issues facing the PDRY. For the first time, viewers could see some SPC members arguing for closer relations with the West and the adoption of Western economic policies, and others claiming that the party should return to its Marxist roots. SPC members criticized ministers and ministries.

This was taken a step further in elections for the SPC held in November 1989. Under a new law, candidates who were not members of the YSP were able to compete without restrictions. The 354 seats were contested by 809 candidates, and 40 of those elected were not YSP members as required by the constitution. There was a gradual relaxation of controls on the media in late 1989. Newspapers began to test the new limits, contributing to a growing political ferment that welcomed the prospect of unity with the YAR but also wanted to criticize the regime. There was an even bigger change in December 1989, when – perhaps driven on by the prospect of unity – the Politburo agreed that other political parties should be legalized providing they were formed by people who had fought colonization and remained loyal to the principles of the revolution. Towards the end of 1989, the YSP bureaus dealing with foreign affairs, economics and security issues were closed, and the functions taken into government. The final meeting of the SPC at the end of February 1990 approved a number of laws that liberalized the press and opened up political life. In March 1990, the YSP finally issued a document for wholesale economic and political reform. It came rather late in the day for the PDRY to take action, but was used by the YSP in political campaigns after unity.

In the late 1980s the regime tried to broaden its Islamic credentials. Jarallah Umar wrote at the time that 'religious groups have, within a decade and half, been transformed into a major power centre exercising extensive political and ideological influence'.[22] At the end of the Ali Nasir period, there was an attempt to revive Islamic dress for women at Aden University. In April 1989, a Council of Islamic Scholars was set up to provide religious guidance and deal with religious affairs. Six months later, the cabinet discussed the financial problems facing mosques, and agreed on steps to rehabilitate them. The government said that 'it is essential to preserve the militant roles played by true Islamic religion and the contribution of adherents in kindling the flame of the revolution'.[23] As unity approached, the SPC called in February 1990 for the establishment of a religious institute, and requested that permission be granted for a magazine for Islamic matters, as well as seeking the expansion of the time allocated to religious broadcasting on state TV and radio. The SPC members were perhaps more conscious than party leaders that ordinary people had never abandoned Islam.

Unity becomes inevitable

Haydar al-Attas put a paper to the Central Committee in late 1987 arguing that unity was not possible for at least ten years. There were too many differences between the two political, social and economic systems. Al-Attas and Salim Salih Muhammad spoke in public about the need for greater joint efforts for unity, but in private argued that the PDRY should concentrate on reform. Salih Munassir al-Siyayli, and even Jarallah Umar, were cautious about unity without a clear vision of how it would work in practice.

In early 1988, the YSP set up two committees to study the question of unity. One considered how to keep a peaceful balance between the two Yemens without unity, and the second, and much more important, was tasked to make recommendations on the practical steps that could be taken towards achieving unity at some time in the future. The latter was set up under the auspices of Salim Salih Muhammad, with membership drawn from the Politburo (both pragmatists and ideologues), the Central Committee, and experts from government and the University of Aden.[24] After six months work, it recommended a 'confederal' system. The report was discussed in the Politburo once only, and then deposited in the office of al-Bidh and not referred to again.[25] Separately, the YSP's northern branch was asked to examine how it could contribute to a greater democratization of the north, and play a role within it.

Tension on the YAR–PDRY borders flared up in 1987 and early 1988 over several issues, the most critical being the close proximity of oil exploration by Soviet and Western companies to the un-demarcated frontier between Shabwa and Marib. Troops were sent to the border by both sides, and meetings were held by the two chiefs of staff to defuse tension. Ali Nasir and President Salih thought they had dealt with the issue in 1985, but their agreement was never implemented. Some in Aden feared that the YAR might launch a military strike. Urgent action was needed.

President Ali Abdullah Salih and al-Bidh met in Taiz between 16 and 18 April 1988, and again on 4 May in Sana'a. President Salih pressed more strongly for unity than he had previously. The two sides agreed to the following, based on unity accords of the past:

1) a revival of the Supreme Yemeni Council, which had not met since the downfall of Ali Nasir, and the resumption of the work of its various sub-committees;
2) the setting up of a joint committee to work on creating a unified political organization;
3) a timetable for discussions on the constitution for a united Yemen, which would be placed before the two legislatures for endorsement;
4) the establishment of a demilitarized zone between Shabwa and Marib, and the setting up of a team to demarcate the precise border;
5) the establishment of a joint corporation to explore for oil and minerals in the region;
6) new joint investment projects, including the connection of the two electricity grids;
7) the setting up of joint border posts as a step towards permitting citizens of the one state to cross into the other using only an identity card.

There was speedy implementation of the agreed measures. Teams of senior officers arranged for the demilitarization. The Yemen Company for Investment in Oil and Mineral Resources was up and running in early 1989, and could start negotiating with a consortium made up of Western, Arab and

Russian companies. The teams put into it were composed of technocrats like Rashid al-Kaff (deputy minister of oil before unity in the PDRY, and in the Yemen government afterwards) from the PDRY, in place of politicians. There was prompt ratification by the PDRY cabinet of the follow-up steps.

The decision to allow free movement over the borders with ID cards proved to be extremely popular, and over 250,000 PDRY citizens visited the north. During the 1980s, the YAR economy, in contrast to the PDRY's critical position, had experienced growth of 5–10 per cent – leaping to 14 per cent after the commencement of oil exports in 1988, a factor that some in Sana'a saw as part of a pressure for unity.[26] The visitors from the PDRY found, to their surprise, that the YAR was now relatively prosperous and stable. It showed them how depressed the south had become. This had an important impact on the PDRY population, and changed popular attitudes towards the YSP regime, which portrayed the YAR as primitive compared with the modernized south. Tens of thousands moved permanently to the north over the next two years. According to Abd al-Qadir Ba Jamal, who had been jailed for a period because of his sympathy for Ali Nasir and was later a prime minister in the united Yemen, the scale of the exodus caused serious alarm among the PDRY's leadership, and helped to convince them of the need for unification.[27]

A few days after the May meeting between Ali Abdullah Salih and al-Bidh, King Fahd sent a message to al-Attas offering improved economic, technical and cultural relations. Aden interpreted this – incorrectly – as a signal that there was no objection from Riyadh to the renewed moves towards unity. The Saudis continued to claim parts of Shabwa and Hadhramaut, but an incident on the border in 1989 was solved without difficulty, and relations were cordial up to unity. A Saudi at the heart of his country's policy saw it differently. The PDRY 'was in dire straits and had little choice but to unite with the north. There was nothing we could do about it'. Their assessment was that unity would end in grief.[28]

Charles Dunbar, who was US ambassador in Sana'a in this period, found that many in the north were distrustful of the PDRY leadership.[29] Despite the May agreement, the YAR did not give a very high priority to unity negotiations in the second half of 1988 and early 1989, because attention had switched to the wider region after Sana'a joined the new Arab Cooperation Council (ACC) with Egypt, Jordan and Iraq. There were frequent statements about the desirability of unity, but nothing more than routine language. However, relations between the two parts of Yemen were better than at any time since the early 1980s.

In March 1989 a joint ministerial meeting took place, chaired by the two prime ministers and attended by the two chiefs of staff. They committed the governments to completing the implementation of what had been agreed the previous May, and set up a group of ministers to oversee this, under the chairmanship on the PDRY side of Salim Salih Muhammad. Both Yemens could see the benefits of jointly developing oilfields straddling their borders for export and for processing at the Aden refinery. They reaffirmed the need to arrange for the two legislatures to review the constitutions, and agreed on a process to tackle problems between governorates on either side of the border.[30]

Dunbar noted that the YAR was by the summer of 1989 ready for further unity talks. Its leaders could see that the PDRY was in bad shape, and there was an opportunity to put pressure on Aden over its foot-dragging on unity and keep its weakening regime off-balance. Salih had spotted that the changes in the Soviet attitude could only add to the PDRY's problems just as shortages of subsidized food and consumer goods were undermining its popularity and legitimacy.

There were also good domestic reasons for President Salih to push for unity. He had successfully consolidated the regime and strengthened his ability to deal with the powerful tribal leaders. He had had a much freer political hand to negotiate with the south than at any time in the previous 12 years.[31] The addition of nearly 3 million partly detribalized southerners to the YAR would help counter-balance the power of the Hashid and Bakil tribal confederations. He was in need of a success to divert public attention away from the failure of policies in the Arab world. The flow of oil exports had contributed to a higher rate of growth in the YAR, but had not led to any significant improvement in government services. As in the south, remittances were hit in the late 1980s by the fall in the price of oil. Some in Sana'a may have noticed that the oilfields in Hadhramaut looked more promising than those in Marib. The time was right, given the PDRY's obvious weakness.

In the PDRY, public references in the summer of 1989 were mostly about the detailed work going on between ministries to coordinate policies, but there was nothing to suggest a change in pace. Many in the YSP and the regime had come to regard unity as inevitable but believed it should be a gradual process that might build in steps on the success of the arrangements over the handling of oil exploration. There would first need to be changes in the political systems of the south and the north. Al-Bidh, addressing the Central Committee, said:

We do not envisage the establishment of a single Yemeni state except on a democratic basis and within the framework of a comprehensive construction process that takes the Yemeni people out of the circumstances of backwardness through which they are living ... We call for comprehensive reform measures which will correct the course of the entire Yemeni revolution in the north and south and rid it of all forms of rightist and leftist actions.[32]

Within the PDRY there was by late 1989 a consensus for some form of federation that would allow the YSP to remain in control of the south while it implemented its strategy for radical economic and political reform.[33] A Central Committee meeting as late as 23 November repeated the mantra of the need for a realistic and feasible course for unity based on current possibilities.[34] But by this time people working closely with al-Bidh believed that he had come to the conclusion that unity was the only viable solution for the PDRY's growing difficulties, even though he knew that many in the Politburo and Central Committee were not in favour.[35] One senior official said that he carried a private message from Ali Salim al-Bidh to President Salih, in either late 1988 or early 1989, in which al-Bidh said he wanted union, not confederation.[36] Two members of the Politburo and a member of the Central Committee (who was also a deputy minister) believe that al-Bidh's position was precarious, and that a move to unseat him was possible.[37] The northerners and their allies from Lahij in the party and the army had become too strong for the Hadhramis and Adeni pragmatists, bureaucrats and technocrats. The northerners wanted a loose form of unity that they could use as a platform for taking power in the north.

The Berlin Wall fell on 9 November 1989. Leading figures in both regimes immediately appreciated the psychological damage this did to the PDRY.[38]

Aden Agreement on Unity

The final stages of the process for unity started with the first meeting of the Joint Committee for a Unified Political Organization, which took place in October 1989. At about this time, Sana'a proposed publicly merging five ministries, including defence and foreign affairs.[39] The joining together of such critically important ministries was rather more than gesture politics. The PDRY leaders felt under great pressure to agree or make a constructive counter-proposal. Some sources say that the leaders feared a possible northern military strike perhaps to grab the southern oilfields after the fall of the Berlin Wall although there is no evidence to suggest that the regime in Sana'a was considering this.

The YAR government created an expectation of dramatic results at a meeting between the PDRY and YAR leaders scheduled for Aden on 29 November. On 23 November the information minister said new steps towards union would be announced, and referred to the merging of the ministries of foreign affairs and defence.[40] A Central Committee statement on 23 November said that it had examined 'two drafts for a transitional federal formula, which had been submitted by the leaderships of the two parts'.[41] The Yemeni Consultative Council followed up by urging its southern counterpart to discuss unity as a matter of urgency. Sinan Abu Luhum recalls that Ali Abdullah Salih wanted a gradual federal solution, and that he knew that there was disagreement within the PDRY leadership about the form unity might take.[42]

There are conflicting accounts of the dynamics of the Aden discussions.[43] Al-Attas and Salim Salih Muhammad both expected that there would be an agreement on a confederation or federation, starting with the merger of the two ministries, albeit very important ones. At the talks, the two sides presented their visions for unity. The north wanted the merger of the ministries, while preserving the separate governments, whereas the south proposed confederation. The northern delegation made it clear that their proposal was the minimum acceptable to them. Several of those present at the meetings said that the atmosphere was quite tense, and some even felt that the likely failure might lead to armed conflict.[44] President Salih expressed his disappointment at the outcome of the discussions on 29 November, and early on 30 November threatened to return to Sana'a.

The deadlock was broken when, during a car journey the two presidents took together without advisers, al-Bidh suggested that they should disregard the earlier proposals and instead agree to unite on the basis of the constitution agreed in Kuwait in 1980 – that is, through union, rather than federation or confederation. A surprised Salih immediately agreed. At the end of the journey, the presidents instructed their ministers of unity affairs to draw up an agreement on this basis. The two presidents went to al-Bidh's residence to await the outcome. Jarallah Umar has related how he and Yahya al-Shami (secretary general of the NDF and a member of the YSP Politburo) were summoned to meet them for a lengthy discussion on democratization in the new Yemen. While they were there, the ministers of unity affairs arrived with the draft agreement. Umar and Shami were told that they could stay, but not interject in the discussions between the two presidents on the draft. It did not take long for them to agree.[45] They agreed to make an announcement at a news conference at 7 p.m.

Salim Salih Muhammad and al-Attas were astounded when they were told.[46] They and other Politburo members objected. An angry Ali Abdullah Salih wanted to return to Sana'a immediately, but, according to Sinan Abu Luhum, changed his mind when al-Attas, Yassin Sa'id Nu'man and Salim Salih told him a little later that the YSP leadership accepted what the two Alis had agreed. When the news conference was eventually held, after midnight, a journalist present noted that the faces of al-Bidh's Politburo colleagues looked either grim or resigned.[47]

Twenty years after the event, al-Bidh had still not told them why he had made his proposal. He implied in later interviews that the pressure for a swift union had come from President Salih, who was worried about unrest in the north and feared Saudi interference.[48] Once the announcement had been made by the two presidents, there was no going back. The news was greeted with jubilation in the south. There were very difficult meetings of the Politburo in early December, which demanded to know how al-Bidh could sign an agreement without first obtaining the consent of the Politburo and Central Committee.[49] Some argued (and argue today) that the agreement was not legal, and therefore could not be implemented. In the end al-Bidh challenged his colleagues: vote for unity, the declared aim of the YSP, or face a public that had welcomed the Aden agreements, and saw unity as the panacea for all their ills. He said he would accept full responsibility for the decision. The Politburo endorsed the agreement without demanding any changes: they knew the game was up. At a later meeting of the Central Committee, which also endorsed the agreement, Salih Munassir al-Siyayli was alone in registering his reservations, but he did not resign from the Politburo or as minister of interior.[50]

The YSP insisted that none of Ali Nasir's men should be appointed ministers in the unity government, but they were allowed to be nominated to the Consultative Council. It also insisted that Ali Nasir should not return to Yemen but remain in Damascus, where he was now living.

Despite the way in which the deal had been done, it looked quite favourable to the PDRY. It gave a stronger weighting to the much smaller and weaker south than its population, economy and power warranted. The GPC and YSP would be treated as equals, at least in the transition period. The agreement required that the draft constitution would be put to the two legislatures, followed by a popular referendum within six months. This would lead to the proclamation of the Republic of Yemen (ROY), with its legislative capital at Sana'a and its economic capital at Aden, in November 1990. A new government would be formed on unity, pending elections scheduled for November 1992. The GPC and

YSP would set up a joint organizing committee for unity to produce a plan laying out the country's political path of the future. This was followed up swiftly with a plethora of meetings in early 1990 to work out the details of unity.

Though there was a great deal of action in following up the Aden agreement, Dunbar believed from his contacts in Sana'a at the time that the agreement would be a dead letter. In the several meetings between al-Bidh and President Salih in early 1990, it appeared that the PDRY wanted to extend the transitional period.[51] Al-Bidh was still under great pressure from his colleagues on the Politburo, who wanted to slow down the process. Negotiations between the two sides were often heated and difficult.

The last few months of PDRY politics were devoted to taking steps to implement union and to complete the political reform programme. Laws were passed granting new freedom to the media, for the legalization of new political parties and for removing many of the restrictions on freedom of expression. There was a parallel process in the north, and both governments agreed that there should be multi-party elections for the new political institutions. The YSP continued to examine how democracy could be deepened further in both the south and the north.

Cabinet discussions in the PDRY were taken up by such issues as merging ministries and the education systems, unifying the civil services, standardizing tariffs, tax and bank regulations, and preparing what was called fundamental legislation to guarantee the new freedoms. In early March the two Yemens agreed the measures to merge a number of ministries the tax authorities, their airlines, news agencies, and broadcasting organizations. Significantly, they agreed that Aden would continue to 'carry out its economic, financial and trade role with its historic status and the geographic characteristics it enjoys'.[52]

Despite this progress, there were signs of opposition to the union in both parts of Yemen. In the south it came mainly from within the YSP and parts of the armed forces but the powerful chief of staff, Haytham Qasim Tahir, was unwavering in his backing for unity. In the north some important conservative, tribal and Islamic figures expressed opposition. For example, in mid April, Shaikh Abd al-Majid Zindani, a leading figure in Islah (the Yemeni Congregation for Reform - see p. 184), objected to the phrase in the draft constitution that spoke of the shariah as being 'the main source' of law, and not 'the sole source'. He called the YSP leadership a 'tiny group of pagans'.[53] The PDRY leaders responded in measured tones, asking Zindani to present his political and economic programme, and protesting about 'obscurantist forces seeking to cast doubts ... about unification'.[54]

Ali Nasir, according to one of his close associates, had written to al-Bidh and other leaders in late 1989 arguing that there should first be reconciliation between his supporters and those of the collective leadership, before any negotiations on unity. To show his sincerity, he said that he and up to 50 of his supporters would stay out of Yemen. Many of his supporters after unity joined President Salih's GPC, and did not return to the YSP. Others remained silent: they had wanted unity, but not on the terms agreed.

It was against this background that Salih and al-Bidh met in April 1990 to hammer out what became known as the Sana'a Accord. Its key features included the following:

1) The date for the union was brought forward six months, to May 1990.
2) It would take the form of a full merger into a unitary state with a 30-month transition period to enable ministries and other institutions to complete their mergers.
3) The elections would take place in November 1992. The elections would produce a parliament that would elect a new five-person presidential council, which would invite a new prime minister to form a government. Popular referenda in the two states were judged to be unnecessary; it would be sufficient for the two peoples to vote on the new constitution in May 1991.
4) There would be a Chamber of Deputies, made up of members of the YAR Consultative Council and the SPC, as well as 31 appointed members.
5) The current cabinets would in effect be merged into an inevitably unwieldy 39-member cabinet, and there was a division of posts at lower levels, greatly in favour of the PDRY, given that its population was only a fifth of that of the ROY.

Al-Bidh's colleagues have said that he had not told them before this meeting that he would agree to bringing forward the date of unity by six months. They are not sure why he did so, but speculate that he was worried about growing resistance to the unity accords within the YSP, parts of the YAR and in Saudi Arabia. There had also been difficulties and some dislocation in the south over the merging ministries, leading to problems over paying civil servants and over handling claims for land confiscated in the early days of PDRY, leading to some small demonstrations in Aden.

On 23 April it was reported that al-Bidh attended what was called the first full meeting of the political leadership of the united homeland. On 4 May the two prime ministers met in Sanaʻa to agree the process for the unification of the currency, a budget for a united Yemen, and a range of other measures. There was also what was said to be a key meeting of a group working on the unification of the military and security organizations. The Political Organizations Committee, which had been set up to define relations between the political parties, issued its report on 15 May. It also drafted a joint agreement between the GPC and the YSP. An agreement was reached to remove military units from the two capitals to prevent the military from interfering in politics. On 15 May it was announced that there would be a joint security organization, and a new head was proposed.

Voting took place on 15 and 16 May to ratify the new Constitution. Registration and turnout were disappointing, but were significantly higher in the south than the north. The vote in favour of the Constitution was 98 per cent of those taking part. On 21 May the SPC in Aden and the Consultative Council in Sanaʻa ratified the unity agreement by an overwhelming majority.

Unity proclaimed

On 22 May 1990 unity took place, and the Republic of Yemen was formed, with President Ali Abdullah Salih and Vice President Ali Salim al-Bidh making speeches. Soon afterwards, a new cabinet was announced with al-Attas as prime minister and half of the ministers from the south.[55] A new chief of staff from the north was appointed, and a number of leading south Yemenis were appointed to the House of Representatives and the Advisory Council. These arrangements were not reached easily; there were long and difficult discussions as individual leaders bargained for positions in the new regime.

On 16 June the new government made its policy statement. It set its first objective as the 'completion of the merger of organs and the building of the basis for a modern state'.[56] It was clear from the statement that much work had still to be done.

It was also agreed that all political prisoners would be released. All remaining Ali Nasir supporters were freed by early March. An amnesty was granted to military personnel who had deserted for political reasons, referring to the many PDRY soldiers who had gone to the north. The deceased Qahtan al-Shaʻbi, Faysal al-Shaʻbi, Salmin, Jaʻam Salih Muhammad and Ali Salim Lawʻar were among other former southern leaders who were formally rehabilitated.

12

UNION WITHOUT UNITY

Unity was immensely popular in both countries.[1] The president and vice president were lauded as true Yemeni heroes. There were celebrations and scenes of spontaneous joy. Unity was to be the panacea for the ills of the two societies. The new constitution was probably the most democratic in the Arab world, with universal adult suffrage, freedom of expression and association, and legal rights for defendants.

In the headlong rush to unity, problems were ignored and solutions postponed. The political leaderships' individual motives for unity were rooted in their insecurities. Each thought it could impose its system, and use the strength of a united regime to solve the problems in its own part of the country. It was inevitable that popular hopes and the wishes of the regime would come up against the realities of political power, the interests of groups within the ruling elites, and a belief that it was the other side that should compromise. Unity proved to be an agreement to cooperate: amalgamation or marriage. The southern leaders were aware of the disparity in power between the two regimes, and of the influence of tribal and Islamic forces in the northern system. They felt that their superior organization, system, ideas, and perhaps their record of giving rights to women, would attract the support of northerners. How wrong they were! They were unable to match the political guile, determination and ruthlessness of President Ali Abdullah Salih.

President Salih had by 1990 built up a regime based on a military and security system dominated by family and tribal relatives personally loyal to him.[2] He had used the strengthened regime to reach out to tribal and regional interests that accepted his authority in exchange for degrees of autonomy in pursuing their interests. It was a patronage system, and the formal political party, the General People's Congress (GPC), supposedly a party including all political views, was a key vehicle for arranging local deals. Ministers, businessmen, national and local leaders, all having a vested interest in the system, were in the GPC, which rarely pretended to have an ideology.

Shaikh Abdullah al-Ahmar, leader of the powerful Hashid tribal confederation (of which Salih's Sanhan tribe was a minor part) might oppose the president on some issues and be Saudi Arabia's close friend (while Salih was often seen as its enemy), but he had a vested interest in maintaining the system to a point where Salih did not become too dominant. From the 1970s, the YAR gave sanctuary to the Muslim Brothers, among other Islamists from Egypt and Syria, who brought their ideas to Islamic institutes and schools in the country. Wahhabi and Salafi influences from Saudi Arabia were also spreading in the north, brought back by Yemenis trained in Saudi Islamic schools. Many Yemenis fought in the Afghan war and started to return to Yemen at the end of the 1980s. Al-Ahmar helped establish the Yemeni Congregation for Reform, known as Islah, which embraced the traditional tribal politics of the Hashid and allied tribes, plus several trends of political Islam, including a relatively moderate stream of Muslim Brothers, and Salafis associated with Muqbil al-Wadi'i, and a less moderate group influenced by one of Yemen's leading figures, Abd al-Majid al-Zindani. There were also links to the Afghan veterans. Islah had recruited many members from those parts of the YAR where the NDF had been active in the 1980s. Al-Ahmar was able to prevent the Muslim Brotherhood from challenging the regime, and went along with Salih's tactic of using tribal and Islamic militias to confront the NDF. Muqbil al-Wadi'i argued against fighting in Afghanistan, but supported fighting the regime in the PDRY.[3] Islah was a far from stable grouping, and needed someone of al-Ahmar's stature to hold it together. The Yemeni parliament was dominated by the GPC.

There was little pluralism in Yemeni society before unification. There had been serious problems in the YAR in 1989 that appeared to weaken the regime, despite the promise of oil revenues. Like the PDRY in late 1989, it needed a dramatic gesture to transform its domestic situation. Despite these difficulties, the YAR just before unity was in a stronger domestic political and economic situation than the PDRY. Some southern leaders must have understood this (al-Attas, for one), but their doubts were brushed aside by al-Bidh.

Failures in negotiation

The key documents were the unity accords signed in Aden in 1989, the Constitution agreed in 1991, and the laws governing political parties (1991) and elections (1992). These were important in allowing a freedom of debate that was unprecedented. The YSP leaders believed they could use the new freedoms to take their message into the north, but the GPC and the Sana'a regime saw these freedoms as a way of marginalizing a YSP that was forced into unity by its own inadequacies. The freedoms were not granted because of their objective value, but because they could be used for party advantage. Nevertheless, leaders referred to the benefits of freedom and spoke of democracy providing the stable foundation of unity.

Within months of unification there were over 40 political parties and a hundred new publications. In the south, two new political parties emerged: the return of part of the old South Arabian League under the title 'League of the Sons of Yemen', led by Abd al-Rahman al-Jifri, and the 'Yemen Unity Gathering', made up mostly of intellectuals based in Aden. The media was much freer, and there was an upsurge in the activities of civil society. Carapico summed up the situation in the early 1990s:

> The expansion of the civil space was palpable as the many barriers to assembly, publication, speech, travel, investment and open partisanship were lifted. A discernible, diverse realm of public opinion dealing with broad issues concerning the constitution, the judiciary, education, the very conception of the public arena, was debated in the press, symposia and conferences, replete with references to the full range of recent political experiences.[4]

Al-Attas and other PDRY leaders were concerned about the different levels of social development between the south and the north. They may have hoped to impose the organization and discipline of PDRY government systems to end the inadequacies of the northern civil service, but in reality they were unable to make much headway against the traditional tribal way of doing things, the patronage systems within the GPC, and the evident corruption. The GPC and Islah appear to have seen the unpopularity of the YSP in parts of the country as an opportunity to establish themselves in the south.

Economic problems

Hopes generated by unity were brought crashing down by the expulsion of around 800,000 Yemenis from Saudi Arabia and Kuwait as a result of Sana'a's equivocation over Saddam Hussein's occupation of Kuwait on 2 August 1990.[5] The arrival of the migrants added to the burdens of the state and at once cut off a major source of income, all but destroying the economic dividend of unity and of the promised riches from oil exports. It did not end with the 800,000: the number of returnees had reached 1.42 million by the end of 1992, according to the Yemeni government, and Somalia's internal problems added another 120,000 refugees.

In 1993, per capita income in Yemen was 10 per cent lower than in 1989; unemployment was 25 per cent, and inflation in the 30–50 per cent range. Central Bank reserves were the equivalent of one month's imports, and external debt was estimated at 200 per cent of GDP. The dinar and riyal (there was as yet no joint currency, but a fixed rate of exchange between the old PDRY dinar and the YAR riyal) collapsed, and by 1994 were worth 10 per cent of the pre-unity value. One-third of the population were thought to be living below the poverty line. Up to 1990, net remittances flowed in at a rate of over $730 million, mostly directly into the hands of families and individuals. Oil revenues, on the other hand, from by now mostly southern fields, went to state coffers and often benefited northern businessmen connected to the power structures. These revenues generated great expectations of imminent prosperity but Yemen's oil deposits were disappointingly small. The foreign donors that had come to the aid of both countries before unity did not show up in the early 1990s. The Soviet Union had collapsed, and the West for a time lost interest in an isolated Yemen. Another significant drought in 1990–91 added to Yemen's woes as did the costs of merging ministries.

The government under Haydar al-Attas found it difficult to agree a programme to deal with the economic problems, as the GPC and YSP were still steeped in the economic thinking of the previous regimes. Government spending plans were disorganized because of a lack of funds, and there was a certain haphazardness in how the limited money available was allocated – perhaps normal in the north, but not in the organized south. Southerners found that they had lost access to the subsidized food of the PDRY and were faced with sharp rises in prices. The problems reached crisis level at the end of 1992, when there were serious demonstrations and rioting in major cities (mostly in the north).

Through these years, the economic difficulties in the south were exacerbated by disputes over land. The nationalizations and sequestrations in the PDRY from the late 1960s had been reversed in the last months of independence, with the result that previous owners were able to make claims on land now occupied by others.[6] Because of the complexity of what had taken place, there were multiple claimants for some properties. Disputes over the ownership of land and property became part of the current of daily life, and were exploited by politicians. For example, Dresch notes that Islah tried to side with the poorer claimants as a means of extending its influence to the south.[7]

There were efforts to give special attention to the problems of the south. In January 1991, for example, a joint meeting of the Presidency Council and the cabinet was held in Aden 'relating to the vestiges of fragmentation and its effects'.[8] In October there was a large meeting of government and party officials in Aden to discuss the unstable availability of basic commodities, large price rises and a lack of medicines. However, the whole of Yemen suffered, and spending had to be cut everywhere. In early 1992, President Salih faced demonstrations on a visit to Aden calling for Zaydis to go home and Ali Nasir to return.[9]

The flaws exposed

The unity agreement gave roughly equal power to the two ruling parties – a highly significant concession on the part of the YAR. The 1995 census showed that the population of the former YAR was 15.8 million, and that of the PDRY 2.9 million. The PDRY economy was about one-fifth the size of the YAR's. While the PDRY had a much better-organized civil service, good state capacity and effective armed forces, these had been weakened by the January 1986 events, whereas the competence of the YAR regime had improved, albeit marginally, in the 1980s. The constitutional arrangements might give the YSP a disproportionate presence in the key institutions, but Sana'a would always have the upper hand. President Salih also had a useful tool: Ali Nasir's followers. Ali Nasir himself had to leave for Syria as a part of the unity deal, but the former military and political leaders from Abyan and Shabwa stayed behind. None were appointed as ministers, but some were put on the Consultative Council. Some of Ali Nasir's men were close to President Salih and worked to place people sympathetic to their cause in key positions in ministries. One of those involved claims that five of the ministers in the 1990 government were covert supporters of Ali Nasir.[10]

The southern leaders understood within a year of unity that they had miscalculated. More northern officials had moved into government positions in the south than vice versa, despite the balance within the cabinet. Within ministries it was often the case that powerful northern deputy ministers had more influence than southern ministers. In the military, northern units were moved to the south and vice versa, but the two armies remained virtually separate. Haytham Qasim Tahir, as minister of defence, found that the northern chief of staff often ignored his orders. There were problems over whether or not former PDRY officers should resign from the YSP, as was required under the Political Parties Law. In the PDRY all officers of the rank of major and above had to be members of the YSP, and the military influence in the YSP was strong after 1986. Many senior officers in the northern army were connected to President Salih through tribal and other links, and were part of the patronage system or members of the GPC. The security services were united in the Public Security Organization, but continued to function as separate organizations. Right up to the 1993 elections, there were signs that the mergers between ministries and institutions were taking place very slowly, despite some successes and many announcements that integration had been completed.

There were also concerns about the potential influence in the south of Islah and political Islam, forces that President Salih could not afford to alienate. There had been demonstrations in the north (one led by al-Ahmar and another as noted in Chapter 11 by Zindani) against the wording of the new Constitution in 1990 on Shariah law. The Presidential Council responded by stating that 'not only was the shariah the source and basis of all legislation in the entire Republic of Yemen', but that the endorsement of the referendum 'definitively and categorically invalidated all laws made by the two parts of Yemen which contradict the shariah'.[11]

Al-Bidh, in public statements in 1991, did not appear to lose faith in unity whatever he may have felt in private. He spoke of the need for greater sacrifices to ensure true democracy, and of the dangers of leftist and rightist deviations and the exploitation of religious feelings. Despite the difficulties, the new government passed a whole raft of laws. Charles Dunbar, who was US ambassador in this period, assessed that unity would survive despite the difficulties. He believed that the YSP was weak in both the north and the south and that it had no option but to work with the regime to improve its prospects in the elections then scheduled for November 1992.[12]

In 1991 there was the first of a series of assassinations that carried on intermittently for almost two years, in what looked to the YSP leaders like a campaign directed against them. Later evidence suggests that they were carried out by Afghan veterans, though there were suspicions of links between them and the security services.[13] One of those suspected of being involved was Shaikh Tariq al-Fadhli, who on his return from Afghanistan had formed a group of veterans and based himself for a time in his home tribal area in Abyan. At the time, however, it was not clear who was responsible, and as relations between the GPC and YSP deteriorated, PDRY politicians spoke of a conspiracy being directed against them. Even today, the former southern leaders believe the regime was responsible for many of these attacks, and cite examples of the involvement of northern military and security officials. Al-Bidh warned of 'vendettas' that could only cause instability and insecurity. Abd al-Wasi Sallam, the minister of justice, was wounded in an attack in April 1992. There was an attack on the house of al-Attas in May, and in June al-Attas's brother was killed in Aden. Al-Attas believes that there was an unrelated attempt to assassinate him.[14] There were frequent meetings at a high level to try to prevent such attacks and arrest the perpetrators, but these actions did not convince the southern leaders of the north's sincerity. Sceptics in the north blamed the killings on the vendettas within the YSP.[15]

The economic situation and the assassinations led to an accelerating deterioration in relations between the YSP and GPC leaders in 1992. Leaders avoided attacking each other in public. Al-Bidh, in typical language, described relations between the GPC and YSP as improving continuously, while noting that unity still had to confront objective difficulties. Northern and southern leaders would condemn campaigns of vituperation and slander in each other's media. However, al-Attas, in a remarkable report to the president, summed up 1992 – following a series of violent demonstrations against economic failings mostly in the north – as a year of crisis and instability:

> The deterioration of the economic situation reached a climax when differences between the GPC and YSP contributed towards the splitting of political parties and organizations into two groups, each of which held its own congress. This is a direct reflection of the differences between the GPC and YSP and not a true expression of pluralism. This has weakened national unity.[16]

He added that these developments had reflected 'negatively on the government's performance, and weakened its movement and ability to fulfil programmes'. He asked on behalf of the Yemeni people:

> Will the historical leadership, which willingly created Yemen's new dawn on 22 May 1990, enter the year 1993 with the spirit of fragmentation and division which will result in mistrust and the retreat of unity? Will it sacrifice the future of Yemen defined on 22 May 1990?

The YSP at this stage was starting to threaten, albeit in private, that it might revert to a PDRY if it did not get its way, and if the campaigns of assassination did not cease. The YSP was in favour of unity on its terms, but if this was not attainable it preferred to go back to running the south.[17] The problem was exacerbated when Ali Salim al-Bidh spent three months in the south from August 1992, absenting himself from meetings in Sana'a. In Aden he often operated as if the PDRY still existed. When he eventually returned to Sana'a, he demanded that moves to unify the armed forces should be speeded up, that the military units should be removed from the cities, and that there should be a national conference to try to resolve the difficulties facing the unity government.

An upsurge in Islamic militancy in early 1993 complicated the situation, and a brother of a YSP leader, 'Muqbil', was attacked in Aden. The government responded by trying to arrest Tariq al-Fadhli, but he evaded a siege of his compound in Abyan, and was given protection by Shaikh Abdullah al-Ahmar, whose Islah party al-Fadhli now supported. Relations between the leaders were getting worse by the week, amid deepening mutual suspicion as the date for elections neared.

The 1993 elections

These problems forced the leaders to agree to the postponement of elections twice, and after much arguing about how the elections should be organized and the votes counted, the main parties agreed to put the matter in the hands of the Supreme Election Commission, and that the polling day would be 27 April 1993.

The YSP entered the elections in some disarray. The broad stance of the party had evolved and it was now for decentralization, social democracy and the policies of the left, but without the extremism of the past. Underneath, the divisions of the 1986–90 periods remained. Ali Abdullah Salih may have found al-Bidh difficult to deal with, but so did his divided southern colleagues. People like Salim Salih Muhammad and Yassin Sa'id Nu'man wanted to try to work with the GPC, while the old northern branch, including Jarallah Umar, wanted to make the YSP as distinct as possible from the GPC, believing this would help the party in the NDF strongholds in the provinces of al-Bayda, Ta'izz and Ibb and among the disaffected tribes in the Bakil confederation. Al-Attas noted that the YSP was again starting to operate almost as two different parties: one used to being in government in the south, and another that saw itself as the opposition to the regime in the north.[18] The Ali Nasir faction remained important, especially in Abyan, and was used by the north's political leaders to put pressure on the main YSP leadership. Some Ali Nasir supporters and other exiles from the former PDRY stood in the election as candidates for the GPC.

Under the electoral system, there were to be 301 constituencies of roughly equal size. Despite the proliferation of parties, the main contestants were the GPC, YSP and Islah. The campaign was hard-fought and often bitter. The results were a major disappointment to the YSP:[19]

1) The GPC, with 28 per cent of the vote, won 123 seats. The YSP got only 18 per cent, taking 56 seats, and Islah 17 per cent and 62 seats. There were 47 independents taking 29 per cent of the vote – mostly people supporting the GPC, or local leaders whose interests could be satisfied by linking up with the GPC. The Ba'ath took seven seats, the Nasserists three, and al-Haqq two.
2) In the south, the YSP received 44 per cent of the votes (41 seats) compared with 12 per cent for the GPC (3 seats – one each in Hadhramaut, Abyan and Shabwa). Islah got 7 per cent (no seats).
3) In the north, the GPC got 32 per cent (117 seats), the YSP 11 per cent (15 seats) and Islah 19 per cent (62 seats). Most of the YSP seats were in Ta'izz, Ibb and al-Bayda, though it got one in Sana'a and another in Marib. Though the GPC had clearly won, its share of the vote indicated its lack of popularity compared with the YSP in the south.

Though some sources give slightly different figures, the results undermined the claim of the YSP to be an equal of the GPC. It remained a southern party with some support in the old NDF strongholds and its vote was thus about the same in percentage terms as its contribution to Yemen's population and GDP. Neither the GPC nor Islah did well in the south (though Islah won 17 per cent of the vote in Hadhramaut). The election results showed that the northern and southern parties remained virtually separate, and that in a united state the YSP would now be at a serious disadvantage – though it could legitimately claim that it spoke for the people of the south.

The post-election settlement

Speaking in December 1993, Salih gave his view of the post-election situation:

> the two entities were merged into one governmental entity. The share of the government had been 50 per cent for each party. When elections took place, new parties were released onto the political scene. Some brothers in the YSP believed that we must continue the 50 per cent share. This is what I believe caused the difference of opinion ... They insisted on maintaining the status quo of 50 per cent while we all declared that we would accept the election results and a peaceful transfer of authority.[20]

The new parliament, in which the YSP had only 20 per cent of the seats, would now have to elect a new five-person Presidential Council. The vote was postponed until October as fruitless discussions were held between the GPC and YSP about a possible merger. The YSP put forward a series of demands: a Presidential Council of only two (the president and vice president); an upper house of parliament of which two-thirds would be elected, with each of the country's provinces having the same number of seats; provincial governors to be elected and not appointed by the president; and the decentralization of decision-making.[21] Although these proposals were rejected by the GPC, the two parties agreed to enter a coalition government, and some days later Islah also signalled that it was willing to join. This paved the way for the election of Abdullah al-Ahmar as speaker of parliament, replacing the southerner Yassin Sa'id Nu'man. A coalition government was appointed by President Salih when he gave the appearance of losing patience with what seemed to be an endless round of bickering among the three parties over the allocation of ministerial posts.

Al-Attas remained prime minister, with a cabinet consisting of 15 from the GPC, nine from the YSP and four from Islah. One of the new ministers representing the GPC was Muhammad Ali Haytham, the former prime minister of the PDRY who had been in exile opposing the PDRY regime since 1971.[22] He was just as surprised to be appointed out of the blue as Jarallah Umar, a man who never expected a post in cabinet, though he was obviously well qualified to be minister of culture.[23] There were deputy prime ministers from all three parties, with Muhammad Haydarah Masdus representing the YSP, which retained the portfolios of defence, fish, minerals, industry, electricity, transport and housing. The three parties signed a joint political programme.

These arrangements solved nothing. Discontent spread rapidly in the south as the unified state failed to provide the jobs or the level of social services made available by the PDRY. The demonstrations that had started in the north at the end of 1992 spread to the south in mid 1993, driven by rising prices. Civil society groups associated with the GPC and Islah stepped into the breach and provided direct support to families, presumably to undermine the YSP's position. Other changes were taking place as the families of the old South Arabian elite returned to try to claim back land confiscated by the PDRY, or to reassert their influence in tribal areas in Abyan and Lahij. Others took land by force. Tribalism and political Islam were returning to the south, encouraged by Ali Abdullah Salih and leaders of Islah.

The deterioration in relations between the GPC and the YSP was no longer being hidden, though the leaders were still careful in public to avoid exacerbating the situation. They spoke, as President Salih did on 15 July, of the 'negative tendencies that exceeded our expectations', which included 'apportioning blame to others'.[24] In October the YSP, while proclaiming its adherence to the coalition and policy of unity, spoke of difficulties caused by 'what was left over from the era of fragmentation; the complications in the country; the conspiracies hatched by forces hostile to unity and what remained of a tendency to force annexations'.[25]

In August 1993 al-Bidh departed for Washington for medical treatment, but arranged while there a meeting with the US vice president without informing President Salih or Mohsen Alaini, then Yemeni ambassador in Washington.[26] He travelled direct from the US to Aden, and never again visited Sanaʻa. In Aden he behaved as if the PDRY government still existed. The situation was made worse by attacks on al-Bidh's family.[27]

The postponed elections for the Presidential Council had to be held in October. After the now usual brinkmanship, a compromise was agreed whereby the Council would have two members each from the GPC and YSP, and one from Islah replacing the former GPC member. In the voting, Salih got 263 votes, Abd al-Aziz Abd al-Ghani 244, Ali Salim al-Bidh 207, Abd al-Majid al-Zindani of Islah 203, and Salim Salih Muhammad 172. This created two problems. Firstly, Salim Salih did not have enough votes to qualify for election. As the YSP prepared to walk out in protest, the speaker, Abdullah al-Ahmar, ruled that Salim Salih had been elected by acclamation. Secondly, al-Bidh had finished third, and could not be vice president. President Salih stepped in to nominate al-Bidh, who now understood from his self-imposed exile in Aden that his position would depend on the good will of Salih. Unlike Salim Salih, he did not take the oath of allegiance after his 'election'. A few days later, al-Attas spoke of Yemeni unity going through a severe test.[28] Al-Bidh spoke of his disillusion with unity:

> I cannot go to a capital that is not the capital of the united country. Sanaʻa has insisted on maintaining the mentality and conditions of the Yemen Arab Republic. We have agreements that say something else, but the other side is refusing ...[29]

In November, the assistant chief of staff (operations) spoke of 'the military manifestations generated recently as a result of the political crises', though no clashes were reported.[30] He could have repeated this statement several times over the next three months. There were redeployments of northern military units. In December the Yemeni foreign minister spoke of an 'unannounced split', adding that 'the only thing left is to declare the split'.[31] A few days later, al-Bidh said, 'I tell you that Yemen has not yet reached a union. The army is still two armies and we still have two of everything'. He again referred to the 'mentality of annexation'.[32] The economic crisis grew even worse at the end of 1993, adding to the tensions. The currency lost 12 per cent of its value in a single day, sparking further demonstrations and riots in Aden and Mukalla. Most people in the south were by now blaming unity and the north.

Towards the end of 1993 there were energetic attempts by internal and external actors to try to stop the rot.[33] The most significant was organized by the Political Forces Dialogue Committee, made up of distinguished northern personalities. It showed a remarkable degree of patience and persistence in negotiating, sometimes with some external assistance from Jordan, Oman and others, a Document of Pledge and Accord.[34] This balanced the demands made by the two parties and conceded a significant degree of decentralization in favour of the south. The two Alis came close to signing in January, but did not do so.

There were signs in early 1994 that the south was preparing for secession and the north for war. Much of the activity was centred in Abyan. Al-Attas appointed Muhammad Ali Ahmad as governor of Abyan, a position he had held in the days of Ali Nasir. Muhammad Ali Ahmad was no longer close to Ali Nasir, and was one of those calling in private for secession. At the same time, other associates of Ali Nasir were contacting former comrades in the southern military units, in what proved to be the first steps in a campaign to persuade them to support Sana'a and not Aden in the now expected military confrontation. The aim was to weaken the southern military capability in Abyan so that a northern thrust through that province could cut off Aden from Hadhramaut.[35]

Ali Salim al-Bidh and Ali Abdullah Salih were invited to Amman where, on 22 February, they signed the Document of Pledge and Accord in front of King Hussain. It was clear from their body language that it would not be implemented: King Hussain had to force the two Alis to shake hands in front of television cameras. Al-Bidh said that he saw the agreement as leading to reform; Salih believed it maintained the existing basis for unity. Salih consciously gave a national leader's speech. He talked of 'hands stretched outwards to your hands'. He rather undermined this by publicly receiving Ali Nasir Muhammad. Al-Bidh and Salim Salih Muhammad did not return directly to Yemen, but spent time in Saudi Arabia and the Gulf – fuelling the suspicion that they were planning secession. Salih bin Husainun, the minister of oil, told a foreign official shortly after the signing that 'the north and south were in an unannounced separation' and that relations between Ali Abdullah Salih and Ali al-Salim al-Bidh were 'below zero'. He added that neither side wanted separation and that a complete breakup of the country was out of the question. The south still wanted the confederation proposed by the southern side at the 1989 unity discussions in Aden.[36]

The civil war

The opening shots of what proved to be the civil war took place on the very day that the document was signed.[37] There was a clash in Abyan between southern and northern military units that left four dead and 20 wounded. The defence minister, Haytham Qasim Tahir, spoke of an 'undeclared state of war'.[38] Sana'a now portrayed itself as a unifying force that was ready to impose union if necessary on the whole of Yemen. The south woke up to the fact, belatedly, that Salih had ordered troop movements in late 1993 that gave the YAR's armed forces an early initiative. The south remained inactive while the north increased the size of some of its units and brought parts of Ali Nasir's forces under its command.

When the war started on 27 April, the YAR forces quickly established their superiority in Abyan and Shabwa, while the southern brigades located in the north were neutralized. The YAR army was better prepared and better positioned, and within a week clearly had the upper hand. The YSP leaders believed that the war would be confined to some limited fighting along border areas that would not threaten Aden or the major cities. They thought that it would be seen as sufficiently destabilizing to persuade Arab mediators to intervene, as they had done in 1993 in moves to prevent war.[39] The north subverted some of the southern units as money changed hands and people changed sides. Thus, in parts of Abyan, Shabwa and Yafi'i local militias stood aside and let northern troops pass through. President Salih, in justifying the attacks, spoke of a nine-month-long 'suffocating and cruel crisis' for which 'some had paid filthy money – the same money that once tried to abort the revolution and now tries to abort unity' (presumably a reference to the Saudis).[40] He called on the people of the south to turn against the separatists. He spoke of parties holding 'more power than their real size', and accused the YSP of being merely a regional party, not a party of unity. The YSP said it was committed to unity and to the Document of Pledge and Accord. It hinted that it was seeking the backing of regional governments.

The full-scale offensive started on 4 May. Northern units launched attacks that were directed at isolating Aden and then threatening it. A southern counterattack against the Marib oil fields was blocked, and southern forces were then forced to regroup to defend Aden and the Hadhramaut, which was soon virtually cut off from the former capital of the PDRY. The north had the initiative throughout the fighting, which continued for several weeks with the intervention of air forces and the use of Scud missiles; there were heavy casualties.

Saudi Arabia and some of the GCC states openly sided with the south, and there were reports of money and arms reaching Aden from these sources': it was a time for revenge for Yemen's attitude towards Saddam Hussein in 1990. Formally, Saudi Arabia called for a ceasefire and truce.

The brief life of the DRY

On 21 May 1994 al-Bidh announced the following on Aden radio: 'I proclaim the creation of the Democratic Republic of Yemen (DRY) as an independent state with its capital at Aden.'[41] In justifying this move, al-Bidh asserted that the DRY was the 'nucleus for a unified Yemen, because it was erected on the firm foundations of the Document of Pledge and Accord, this being a document of national consensus'. The DRY was thus not a secessionist state, but an alternative regime for Yemen. Other south Yemeni and south Arabian groups were brought into the alliance forming the new republic.[42] There would be a 'council of national salvation' consisting of the elected members of the Yemeni parliament, representatives of political parties, and religious leaders, which would select a Presidential Council and arrange for multi-party elections within a year.

Al-Bidh was head of state in a presidential council composed of Abd al-Qawi Makkawi, the former leader of FLOSY; Abd al-Rahman al-Jifri; Sulaiman Nasir Muhammad; and Salim Salih Muhammad. A government was announced on 2 June with Haydar al-Attas (who had left Sana'a a few days before the war) as prime minister and minister of finance. He was joined by five deputy prime ministers, including Muhammad Haydarah Masdus and Salih Ubayd Ahmad. Haytham Qasim Tahir was minister of defence, and other prominent YSP ministers were Muhsin, Fadhl Muhsin Abdullah, Abu Bakr Abd al-Razzaq Ba Dhib, Muhammad Sulaiman Nasir, Ahmad al-Sallami and Salih Abu Bakr bin Husainun. Each retained the portfolio he had held in the Yemeni government set up after the 1993 elections. Muhammad Ali Ahmad joined them as minister of interior.

Abdullah al-Asnaj, the former head of FLOSY and the PSP, who had served in northern cabinets in the 1970s, was made a deputy prime minister and minister for foreign affairs. Muhsin Muhammad Abu Bakr bin Farid was another deputy prime minister. He was a scion of the family that had been shaikhs of Upper Awlaqi before 1967, who had led one of the more effective armed opposition groups against the PDRY in the 1970s. Other ministers and ministers of state were drawn from outside the ranks of the YSP. Al-Attas insisted that the whole YSP leadership supported this move, but a majority of the YSP Politburo had voted against secession in early May. Several members of the Central Committee issued a statement condemning al-Bidh's declaration. Jarallah Umar went abroad claiming that al-Bidh had threatened his life. Some leaders of the YSP remained in Aden but did not declare their public support for the DRY. There was also uncertainty about the status of those appointed to the Presidential Council and cabinet. Salim Salih Muhammad was in London when the DRY was set up, and remained there – and he was not removed at the time from the Presidential Council in Sana'a. Makkawi and others were not in Yemen.

Somalia was the only state to recognize the DRY, though the GCC states (except Qatar) issued a statement that implied recognition as well as support for the new state. The Yemeni government said that it had evidence that Saudi Arabia was supplying arms to the breakaway regime – the evidence was manifest and manifold – and implied that Riyadh had had foreknowledge of al-Bidh's intentions. Salih denounced the action and lambasted the motives of the southern leaders. The accusations went back some way:

1) The YSP had sought unity because of the collapse of the Soviet Union and the impact of the suffering of its people from 25 years of tyrannical rule.
2) The north paid a price for unity in giving half of the components of power to the YSP.
3) From the day that it got that power, the YSP started to weave plots involving 'sectarianism, tribalism and racism'.
4) The YSP sabotaged the national economy, and the institutions of the unified state had been destroyed under the 'hammer of al-Attas'.
5) Al-Bidh had fabricated the crisis, and the YSP had stockpiled weapons.[43]

He announced changes to the Yemeni government on 26 May, with Abd al-Qadir Ba Jamal appointed as deputy prime minister and two other southerners being given posts: Faysal bin Shamlan and Ahmad Musa'id Husain. He appointed new governors for Lahij and Shabwa. All these figures were linked to Ali Nasir.

Al-Bidh left with many of his colleagues for Mukalla shortly after announcing the DRY, leaving Abd al-Rahman al-Jifri and Haytham Qasim Tahir to run the government from Aden. The northern military stranglehold on Aden was gradually tightened, and Aden came under siege in late June before it finally fell to northern forces on 7 July, two days after Mukalla had been captured. Al-Bidh and other DRY leaders had by then fled to Oman. A few days later, Sana'a issued a statement charging most of this government and other leaders of the former PDRY with various crimes. Aden was sacked by the army and militias from Islah led by Tariq al-Fadhli. However, Salih moved quickly to try to bring about reconciliation. There was a general amnesty for all except the 16 government members, and only three survivors were to face trial (al-Bidh, al-Attas and al-Jifri). A ten-day cabinet meeting was held in Aden to try to repair the damage done by the civil war and the looting that followed it.

The war destroyed the remnant of the PDRY regime, and forced many of the YSP leaders into exile. Others, such as Salih bin Husainun, were killed or, like Salih Munassir al-Siyayli, died in the aftermath. Salih, always a skilful if ruthless politician, understood the need to entice many of the YSP leaders back into Yemen and government positions. He was also content to live with the YSP representing parts of the south without challenging the idea of unity, which had always been a central plank in the YSP programme. He could now extend his well-tried system of co-option and patronage to take control of the south, and use his strength to marginalize the YSP and others wanting to challenge him.

The YSP had sought a solution in unity to the problems of the late 1980s, which had largely been created by the actions of some of its leaders. Ali Nasir Muhammad has said it had fled into unity in 1990 and fled from it in 1994. This is too harsh a judgment: the real problem was that the southern leaders overestimated their ability to shape a united Yemen and underestimated the cunning and ruthlessness of Ali Abdullah Salih, who constantly took the initiative and comprehensively outmaneuvered al-Bidh and his colleagues. From the outset, the southern leaders were divided and forced on to the defensive. They were too weak to impose the well-developed southern administrative systems and financial control mechanism on the north. Salih adapted the divide-and-rule tactics that had served him well in the YAR to extend his control to the south, and when peaceful means failed to work he was able to use his now stronger armed forces to take over the south.

PART E

DID THE PDRY FAIL?

13

COULD AN INDEPENDENT SOUTH YEMEN RETURN?

The PDRY survived for just over twenty-two years, a mere interlude in the long his tory of Yemen, and somewhat shorter than President Ali Abdullah Salih's time in power. It was created by a small group of Marxist Arab nationalists in Aden and on lands that had been loosely protected by the British since the nineteenth century. South Arabia by 1967 had not been fashioned into a single country with a clear national identity. Its people saw themselves as Yemenis, but did not feel compelled to live together in a single Yemeni state. For centuries, the authority of imams based in the highlands of the north expanded into the south, and then retreated, leaving behind a shifting pattern of local potentates until the next expansion. The PDRY was a larger-than-usual local state created during a period of weakness in the north, and reabsorbed by a powerful, now republican, authority in Sanaʻa. This, of course, implies that a new southern state or states could re-emerge if the strength and determination of the Republic of Yemen diminished. Could this happen? Are there any conclusions to be drawn from the PDRY's experience that might be relevant to the future? Did the PDRY fail as a state or as a regime?

The Southern Mobility Movement, known in the south as al-Hiraak, or 'the movement', calls for self-determination for the south leading to a federal Yemen or secession through non-violent protest. There is no clear overall leadership and, as so often in south Yemen, there are several leaders of local groups, most visibly in the provinces of Dhala, Lahij and Abyan,[1] as well as Aden, and several umbrella organizations claiming to represent the southern population. These divisions are undermining the ability of the south to make its voice heard in the inclusive national dialogue that starts in November 2012, which will lead to a new constitution and prepare the way for parliamentary and presidential elections in 2014. A new generation of southern politicians has come to the fore; Ali Salim al-Bidh, Haydar al-Attas and Ali

Nasir Muhammad remain active in exile politics, and are in touch with al-Hiraak. Al-Bidh regards himself as the president of the DRY, and wants the south to be independent. The two former presidents of the PDRY speak of a solution within unity, but demand that south Yemenis be given the choice of opting for decentralization, federation or independence.

There are many south Yemenis that want to remain in a united but reformed Yemen. They include Abd Rabbuh Mansur Hadi, who was elected president of Yemen in February 2012 (he is a Fadhli who moved to the north with Ali Nasir in 1986). Most Yemeni prime ministers since 1994 have been southerners. In 2012 the minister of defence and several others ministers were from the south. A son of Ali Antar commanded a Yemeni army brigade in 2010. Former PDRY leaders, such as Salim Salih Muhammad, have returned to Yemen after being active in exile politics. Others prominent in the past, such as 'Muhsin' and Fadhl Muhsin Abdullah, live in retirement in Yemen. The late Faysal bin Shamlan, a minister in the first PRSY government under Qahtan al-Sha'bi, and Najib al-Sha'bi, Qahtan's son, fought against Ali Abdullah Salih for the opposition in presidential elections in a unified Yemen. A reduced YSP, led by its secretary general, Yassin Sa'id Nu'man, has been in alliance with Islah (whose secretary general, Dr Muhammad al-Sadi, is a Yafi'i) to form with other political parties the Joint Meeting Parties (JMP), since 2005. These opposition groups were deeply critical of Salih's policies and of the repression of southern protest. The YSP seeks to persuade the northern political establishment of the need to win the support of the south for a united Yemen. They do not want a return to a PDRY, but seek recognition of what they call the 'southern personality' within a united but reformed Republic of Yemen.

The grievances voiced by southerners are shared by Yemenis in all parts of the country. Yemeni ministers acknowledge the problems and their inability to solve them. The patronage networks of the Salih regime remain in place, and continue to breed corruption, distort the allocation of resources, and deter investors. Yemen has coped since the early 1990s thanks to revenues from oil exports, even though too much has been invested in maintaining the patronage networks rather than developing the economy, so that well over 40 per cent of Yemenis live below poverty levels and cannot get enough to eat. Income from oil revenues will fall rapidly, and the new liquid natural gas exports will not cover the gap. There are few other viable resources. Ministers point to the poor capacity of the civil service, the extreme youth of the Yemeni population, and its dispersal in over 120,000 settlements. To quote a deputy minister of finance, no matter how much money is put into the civil service, bloated by being the employer of last resort, and government, the output remains the same. Yemen is high on lists of potentially failing states. Intermittent uprisings of Zaydi revivalists (known as al-Huthi) have taken place in the Sa'ada and adjoining provinces in the north, and al-Qa'ida in the Arabian Peninsula will be difficult to eradicate. The state is fragile, but it is still some way from failing, and the transition deal provides the best opportunity to reverse the downward trajectory. The international community and the GCC are willing to help. But options are narrowing, and the time available is fast diminishing.

The Yemen government argues that, if its economic problems can be solved with international assistance, then issues such as southern discontent will fade away. There is no doubt that the southern grievances are exacerbated by poverty, inadequate social services and governance, a lack of trust in the rule of law, and the many other difficulties of life in Yemen. But the southerners have a number of specific complaints that go back to the 1990–94 period, and especially to the few years following the end of the civil war. Some are real and others imagined, though the political effects are the same. Most of the south had not been subject to the authority of a regime based in the north for nearly 250 years before 1990. There is a southern identity based on the shared experiences of the PDRY, and a feeling that the grievances that all Yemenis suffer are particularly severe in the south. It was reinforced by the Salih regime's repression of al-Hiraak, even if Yemenis unsympathetic to al-Hiraak comment that the PDRY was hardly a shining example of a state that succeeded.

What did the PDRY achieve? Where did it fail?

The PDRY's decision to end its existence was a voluntary act by its leaders, who did not view their move as a form of state suicide but as the achievement of a long-desired unified Yemen, in which they would play a leading role. Despite their doubts about the type of unification agreed by President Ali Abdullah Salih and Ali Salim al-Bidh, the YSP leaders tried to make it work, believing that the PDRY's superior system of government and of law and order, its social policies and relative lack of corruption would persuade all Yemenis to vote for the YSP in the free elections that were to follow unity. There was clearly a large element of self-deception in this assessment, which contrasted with the feelings of many ordinary south Yemenis, who had experienced the bloodletting of 1986, four years of weak government since then, a shattered economy, and shortages of basic subsidized commodities in Aden. The people wanted unification and were not too concerned about how it was achieved.

The story of the PDRY shows that the NLF and the YSP created a viable and progressive state from some very unpromising material. Part of the NLF mythology was that it won independence by driving out the British colonial occupiers. In reality, the main battle was not with the imperialists but with other south Yemenis, for control of a postcolonial south Yemen. This is not to belittle the NLF's role in the independence struggle: it had only been in existence for four and half years before taking power – by any standards a considerable triumph, even though Egyptian and north Yemeni support played an important role. However, it developed a legend that endowed its historical leaders with heroic qualities that gave them undue influence in the PDRY.

The NLF took power without a settled ideology, an agreed programme or a united leadership. The pragmatic Qahtan al-Sha'bi and his allies believed that they would have to make do with what they inherited, but they were forced out from power by the left-wing majority, who, egged on by Nayif Hawatmah, wanted to rebuild society from the bottom.

If the Suez Canal had not been closed in June 1967, an independent PRSY/PDRY would have inherited a prosperous Adeni economy built around the port, ideally placed to attract the shipping trade now largely in the hands of Salalah, Djibouti and other regional ports. After 1990, the rapid development of the Hadhrami oilfields would have helped raise an independent south out of poverty. The NLF and YSP had the misfortune to be in power between these peaks of potential prosperity. Admittedly, the regime's policies did not help. It failed to develop the port, seeing it in the first years as an asset to be stripped, and not one to be nourished. The PDRY might well have found oil much sooner if it had not awarded the exploration contracts to Soviet companies lacking the technologies that only Western oil companies then possessed.

The PDRY could not generate investment income from internal resources, and thus had to rely on the export of people to produce remittances, and on its ability to attract foreign assistance and investment. In the early years, its policies were aimed at redistributing income through improved government services. South Yemenis were given decent levels of employment, education, health and support services, putting previous colonial neglect outside Aden to shame. Moreover, the regime enforced law and order in most parts of the PDRY and established a good level of government administration. Any corruption was on a limited scale. To those south Yemenis who remember the PDRY before 1986, these can seem like halcyon days compared with their current lives. Others remember the more brutal state of the 1970s and the fighting and instability of the 1980s.

The PDRY was plagued by violent confrontations within its historical leadership. Former PDRY leaders disagree even today about the causes of their disputes: were they about power or policies. There were differences in approach over the role of the state and the private sector in the economy, and over the balance in relations with the communist and Arab worlds in external policies. There were more substantive differences over Yemen. Though these disagreements were real, they were used as weapons in the wars between personalities and factions, and were less often the causes of the rivalry.

The PDRY set out in its early days to eradicate tribalism through edict and education. It achieved considerable success in the first ten years, but tribalism crept back in the late 1970s. The bulk of the NLF's recruits were in the Dhala region of Lahij and Abyan, and leaders from these areas dominated the regime after independence. The NLF arrived in Hadhramaut late, and had a less well developed organization in that governorate, which may explain why the Hadhramis in the leadership, government and armed forces mostly behaved as technocrats in the mould of Haydar al-Attas, and were loyal to the PDRY and the party as individuals. They did not coalesce into a regional force even after 1986, when there were more of them at the top of the regime. The record shows clearly that leaders such as Ali Nasir Muhammad, Salim Rubayya Ali, Ali Antar and Salih Muslih drew their friends, staff and supporters either from among fellow tribesmen or from the traditional tribal alliances of their home region. This was most clearly seen in the 1986 fighting, which witnessed Ali Nasir's supporters from Abyan fighting opponents from Lahij and Dhala, and again in the civil war of 1994.

In the early days Adenis, mainly of northern origin, wanted to create a party based on the Soviet system. They aimed to develop a new identity, a new ideology and a new method of governing by a 'vanguard party' in which the individual would sublimate his or her aims to achieve a better society for all. A powerful party could overcome tribal and regional loyalties and interests and define policy goals for a government, which would then be accountable to the party as well as to the people in meeting those tasks. Through the Central Committee and the Politburo, the YSP could provide a means of rallying what was called the 'collective leadership' to challenge the power of a president, as it did in 1978, 1980 and 1986.

The party set out to control the Popular Defence Forces and the People's Militia, as well as State Security. However, this goal was subverted by politicians from Abyan and Dhala, who placed loyalists in key units and recruited from their own regions whenever they had the chance. In 1986 the armed forces fractured, and Ali Nasir took part of them with him to the north.

The party would confine religion to the home as it built a secular society in which women were guaranteed rights not then available to others in the Arab world outside Tunisia. Abd al-Fattah Isma'il understood the need to create a cadre of younger leaders, and helped set up what eventually became the Abdullah Ba Dhib School of Socialism to achieve this. It drew heavily on support from the CPSU, and was a brave concept for such a poorly developed tribal society. The graduates played a significant role in the latter days of the PDRY, but only a few had reached senior positions in the Politburo by 1990. Many of them were 'de-tribalized', and some can be seen today within the YSP operating as social democrats.

The PDRY remained remarkably faithful to the Soviet Union and its allies throughout its life. Moscow provided strategic and political support to the PDRY, though it was never clear whether the USSR would come to its defence if it was seriously challenged. The facilities offered by Aden were of undoubted importance to the Soviet Union in the Cold War, but there was always a limit to what Moscow would pay. The PDRY was merely one pawn in a much bigger game, but the Soviet Union provided weapons, training and experts, and encouraged the East Germans to do the same for the security services, and the Cubans for the People's Militia. The PDRY, it can be argued, invested too much in its relationship with Moscow, and quickly became so dependent on its strategic and security support that it could not diversify its relations to take advantage of the oil boom that benefited other regional non-oil states like Jordan. When there were good relations with Saudi Arabia, they were often confined to the head of state and the foreign minister, and did not extend deep enough into the regime to persuade the Saudis to be more generous. The Saudis abhorred communism and many regarded the PDRY as a Soviet stooge. Riyadh's policies to the south were clearly linked to its relations with the YAR, where throughout the 1970s and 1980s its main aim was to prevent Yemen posing a threat to the Saudi regime or becoming strong enough to take back the Yemeni provinces of Jizan and Najran that had been conquered by King Abd al-Aziz in the 1930s. The PDRY's support for revolutionary movements in the Arab world until the early 1980s sowed mistrust among its rich neighbours, who were prepared to help when the PDRY was faced with flood or drought, but otherwise provided only enough to keep the regime alive, but weak. The result was that the PDRY remained dependent on the Soviet Union throughout its existence.

The profound changes in the Soviet Union in the late 1980s thus had an enormous impact on the PDRY. The Russians maintained their support until well into 1989, but had for the previous two years been advising Aden to consider a local version of *glasnost* and *perestroika*. The process got underway, but was overtaken by the dramatic acceleration of Soviet decline in 1989. It was then clear that Aden would lose its main ally and source of support, and had not done enough to find replacements. It proved to be the final blow to a regime weakened by internal conflict and division.

A solution in unity

Lisa Wedeen points out that Yemeni nationalism was a construct of the early twentieth century, but by the 1960s it was an idea that had taken root in the minds of all Yemenis and had become a political reality.[2] Yemeni nationalism, like Arab nationalism, does not necessarily mean that all Yemenis or all Arabs should be in the same state, but the political elites in both the south and the north aspired to form a single state from the two 'halves' of Yemen even if they did not share a common vision of how that state should be governed.

Was union inevitable, as the leaders of both parts of Yemen kept proclaiming? It would have been difficult for two Yemeni states to live in peace and cooperation if both put unity at the centre of their agenda while maintaining different political systems. In 1972 and 1979 the two Yemens had signed unity agreements, but in the immediate aftermath of border wars. There were only half-hearted efforts to follow this up. Each state felt strong enough to hold out for a form of unity that would suit its political system and interests. During the 1970s and early 1980s, the PDRY was at least as strong as the north. By late 1989 the PDRY was weakened by internal disputes and was about to lose the support of the Soviet Union at a time when the north had a relatively strong and stable regime, and was enjoying a period of relative economic prosperity.

By 29 November 1989, the PDRY leaders had concluded that a form of unity was probably unavoidable. They had initiated a study of how union might be achieved, and concluded that the PDRY should opt for a gradual process, starting with what they called confederation. As envisaged in the study, this would have seen the setting up of an all-Yemeni government with limited powers as the first step. It would have allowed the YSP to carry on governing the south and implementing the profound political and economic reform programmes recommended in other YSP studies of the late 1980s. The YSP leaders were aware of their weaknesses: a loss of legitimacy after 1986; reduced state capacity; mounting economic difficulties; the virtual disappearance of their main international sponsor; and a deepening unpopularity in the country. The PDRY's superior military and government strength of the 1970s had receded as the YAR enhanced its regime, army, economy and state capacity in the 1980s.

Ali Abdullah Salih perceived, even if the southern leaders did not, that he might not get a better opportunity to press for unity. He, like al-Bidh, needed a domestic success to bolster his political fortunes, and he understood the implications of the fall of the Berlin Wall for the PDRY leaders. The dynamics of the crucial meeting between Ali Abdullah Salih and Ali Salim al-Bidh on 30 November are uncertain. There is some evidence that al-Bidh may have acted out of fear that his YSP colleagues were planning to unseat him, and that he had put a similar proposal to Ali Abdullah Salih before 29 November without informing his divided colleagues. Al-Bidh calculated after his meeting with Ali Abdullah Salih that unity would be immensely popular, and his rivals within the leadership could not openly oppose the idea. He must also have been attracted by what he got from unity: the vice presidency in the Republic of Yemen, an apparently equal voice in the running of Yemen, and a place in a future pantheon of Yemeni heroes. Unity was more than the least bad way out of the PDRY's difficulties.

Al-Bidh's colleagues still believe that other options were open to them. For example, the PDRY could have completed the programme of political and economic reform it had recently drawn up. This would have broadened democracy and opened up the system to new political forces. The socialist model would have been modified and foreign policies realigned. This was theoretically possible, but it is difficult to see how a weakened, divided and unpopular leadership with uncertain legitimacy could have hoped to implement such drastic changes without major dislocation and opposition from within the YSP and the armed forces; and it would presumably have had to put all this through while trying to negotiate a federal or confederal relationship with a confident northern government. Some of the southern leaders feared a possible war, especially if Ali Abdullah Salih had – as he threatened to do – gone back to Sana'a on 30 November and vented his anger from there. Aden had few real friends in the region and it had little to offer the West at 'the end of history'. Ironically, however, the PDRY might have escaped Saudi and Kuwaiti retribution for Sana'a's stand when Iraq occupied Kuwait in August 1990: the PDRY had poor relations with Saddam Hussein.

Al-Bidh and Salih had different concepts of what unity meant. They made the fatal mistake of agreeing to unity without first negotiating the details. The south approached it as a form of federation in which the YSP regime would remain intact in the south, and use the electoral system to acquire a major say in northern and thus national politics, bearing in mind the significant support for the NDF. Salih, like a majority of the northern political leaders since 1967, saw the north absorbing Yemen's lost southern and eastern regions. It was convenient for both leaders to encourage greater openness and democracy in the other state, and to try to prevent these freedoms subverting their authority in their halves of Yemen. The two regimes entered this union with opposed visions and, in the case of the south, confused aims. From the perspective of 2013, it seems that President Salih had deceived and outmanoeuvred al-Bidh and the other leaders. He enticed them into a union with promises, and then used northern power and numbers to isolate and weaken the southern leadership. The failures were only too obvious in the civil war of 1994, which led to the destruction of the PDRY's residual power and the dismantling of what was left of its regime. The northern half of Yemen, as Ali Nasir had feared, swallowed the south. Others will say that Yemen was united again.

Could a southern state re-emerge?

The regime used its victory to eliminate the final traces of the YSP-led regime and bring the south under its full control. Salih's political system of co-opting the loyalty and support of local elites through mediation and patronage was extended to the south. The southern provinces were controlled in the same way as those in the Shafi'i north. Loyalty was rewarded by position, contract and favour. For southerners it meant a levelling down of administration and government services to those of the north, and an extension to the south of the corruption, 'clientelism' and poor governance that even Yemeni ministers acknowledge distort decision-making and lead to abuse by the powerful and well-connected. Northern control was in effect legalized through changes to the Constitution that vested power in the presidency. The army and security forces of the south were disbanded, and there were purges of southerners from government departments and agencies. This was balanced in the mid 1990s by the co-opting of people associated with Ali Nasir Muhammad and those southerners who opposed the setting up of the DRY. However, towards the end of the 1990s a number of these co-opted politicians were marginalized: they might have positions in government, but not much power. All this took place against a background of economic crisis in the immediate aftermath of the civil war, and Yemen was obliged to implement an IMF-backed austerity programme in the 1990s.

Some southerners have edited memories of a utopian PDRY; others recall its failures. Very few of the youthful demonstrators in southern cities will have actual memories of an independent south. There is a feeling that no one is listening to their demands. The YSP boycotted the 1997 parliamentary elections, and when it did compete in the flawed 2003 elections it won only eight seats, compared with the fifty-six achieved in the 1993 elections.[3] It is part of the transitional government set up in 2011, but few now regard it as the true voice of the south, while many accuse it of bargaining for a share of the spoils of power. The YSP leaders argue that they can do more for the south by playing a constructive role in the transition, and seek to change regime policy from within, not oppose it from outside.

Discontent began to express itself outside the normal political process in the late 1990s in demonstrations arranged by local committees in parts of the south, which loosely coalesced in 2001 in an organization called Sons of the South. This drew quite widespread support from current and former southern leaders (including the then vice president, Abd Rubbuh Mansur Hadi). Its activities peaked before the 2003 elections, and then faded. Al-Hiraak started in 2007, when local committees of former military and security personnel organized demonstrations calling for improvements to their pension arrangements and the provision of alternative employment. They formed a coordinating council, and were soon joined by others protesting at the lack of jobs and absence of government services. The movement spread to most parts of the old PDRY. It was most obvious in Lahij and Dhala, and in Abyan as well as Aden, but by 2010 was active in all parts of the old PDRY. The movement proclaimed its non-violence, but there were deaths and injuries when security forces broke up demonstrations and arrested some of its leaders. The regime closed down Aden's long-established *al-Ayyam* newspaper. In 2010 there were increasing reports of small-scale attacks on security forces in Dhala, Lahij and Abyan – the same areas where the rebellion against the British had begun in the 1960s. The story of the PDRY shows that these regions have much more influence on southern politics than either Aden or the Hadhramaut.

In mid 2012, al-Hiraak was a grassroots movement without an overall leadership, though there were rival committees claiming to represent it. Muhammad Ali Ahmad, who wants a federal Yemen, was trying to unite leaders into a group that could take part in the national dialogue. Partisans of Ali Salim al-Bidh were campaigning in Aden for secession. Al-Hiraak bore the hallmarks of the PDRY: based on regional groups who could not agree on an overall leadership, aims or strategy, and showing signs of falling back on regional power bases. In the late 2000s, Ali Nasir Muhammad sponsored meetings to overcome tensions between groups from Dhala/Lahij and Abyan – an indication that they still existed. In 2012, Some Hadhramis are calling for a separate Hadrami region within Yemen or an independent south. The major grievances were as follows:

1) demands by the organized committees of former senior military, security and police officers for better pension arrangements, and either reinstatement or the offer of alternative jobs;
2) protests over the lack of employment opportunities throughout the south;
3) complaints that Aden was neglected – it was supposed to be the commercial capital of Yemen, but development spending, it was claimed, was focused on the north;
4) numerous complaints over property rights – this is a complicated issue linked to the expropriations and nationalizations of the early days of the PDRY, and moves in its last days and in the united Yemen to restore property to previous owners; the legal situation is often not clear, and claimants normally petition for their rights – a process that can lead to endless delays; in addition, rich north Yemenis, some with connections to the innermost parts of the regime, have acquired land by methods many in the south regard as an abuse of power;[4]
5) southern resources had been 'stolen' to support the regime in Sana'a – a reference to the fact that Yemen's most productive oilfields are in the south, where the oil and LNG terminals are also located; there were accusations that north Yemenis linked to the regime had won most of the contracts providing services to the oilfields.

Southerners summed this up as 'northern occupation'. At first there was a demand for decentralization or a return to the federal system discussed by the YSP in the run-up to the unity negotiations In 1989. As the movement developed there were growing calls for self determination. By the end of 2010 a majority wanted secession, though a minority argued against this as a betrayal of the popular desire for unity and as unrealistic – given the will and power of a regime determined to maintain the unitary state. The former PDRY leaders in exile had by the end of 2010 failed to overcome their past differences and found it difficult to make their voices heard. The international community that is helping to manage the transition process was working with President Hadi to persuade southerners to join the national dialogue, arguing that it was the only game in town. They would prefer that the south remains part of Yemen, but accept that this might require Yemen to become a federal state – either one with a northern and southern region or one with several regions to accommodate the aspirations of al-Huthi in the northwest but also potentially of a separate Hadhramaut in the south.

What is clear is that very few people want a return to the PDRY regime of the 1967–90 period. The PDRY was a child of the nationalism and Marxism of the 1960s, which died of self-inflicted wounds just as the Soviet system was approaching collapse. The PDRY regime was not cohesive enough to overcome the regionalism and tribalism that destroyed the country's unity. These forces may now be stronger than in the late 1980s, encouraged by the former Salih regime, which knew how to manage tribalism through co-option and divide-and-rule tactics in order to stay in power. Al-Hiraak, perhaps without being conscious of it, aspires to the reformed democratic PDRY that Jarallah Umar and others were calling for in the 1980s, which was partially implemented just before and after unity. It also suffers, it seems, from the same internal divisions as the PDRY.

The legacy of the PDRY is best summed up in the assessment of southern politicians such as Yassin Sa'id Nu'man. They acknowledge their responsibility for failing to build a viable state, but believe that the shared experience of the PDRY nurtured a distinctive southern identity. Others see the PDRY as an unfinished experiment, and believe that if they can learn from their mistakes they can create a modern, well-run state serving its people effectively. There are those who see the PDRY as a totalitarian state whose leaders destroyed its economy and the lives of many of its citizens before turning their guns on each other: it was a failed state that had to be rescued by the north. The majority believe that the 'southern personality' should have expression in a new south, though they disagree on what form it should take: decentralized southern provinces, confederation, federation or secession. The PDRY and YAR leaders made the error in 1989 in agreeing to full unity and a centralised system. There may now be a chance to revisit the question of federation, which most southerners would accept. Even the secessionists do not want to go to back to the PDRY of the 1970s and 1980s. To them, the PDRY was not a state that failed but rather a regime that failed its people.

APPENDICES

APPENDIX A

THE PRINCIPAL TRIBES IN LAHIJ, ABYAN AND SHABWA

Most tribes in PDRY were small compared with those in the YAR, and the two largest south Yemeni tribes – the Yafi'i and the Awlaqi – were not as influential in PDRY politics as some of the smaller ones. Politicians in the power struggles of the PDRY looked for support from their home provinces, building on traditional alliances among groups of tribes, which had often belonged to the same sultanate or amirate before 1967. These rivalries were taken into the PDRY armed forces and the People's Militia. On the other hand, politicians from Hadhramaut were mostly Saada, and did not form a cohesive group but acted as individuals, reaching the highest ranks in the state. They stood aside from – and in some cases looked with disdain on – the 'Bedouin' in Abyan and Lahij. Most of the prominent politicians from Aden were of north Yemeni origin, and were often referred to as 'northerners' by their rivals in the south. Map A shows the location of tribes and pre-1967 political units.

Before 1967 the Sultanate of Lahij (along with the Sultanate of Fadhli, in Abyan) was comparatively rich, controlling significant agricultural lands and close enough to Aden to be influenced by its politics. Its population was estimated at around 40,000 in 1960. The largest tribe in 1967 was the Abdali (24,000 people), from which the sultans were drawn. The other larger tribe was the Subayhi (12,000). Tribalism among the Abdali and Subayhi had broken down before 1967, and in the PDRY they did not exert much influence – though individuals from these tribes held important positions. Qahtan al-Sha'bi and Faysal al-Sha'bi were Saada from the Subayhi area. Dr Yassin Sa'id Nu'man was prime minister from 1986 to 1990. The Hawshabi (3,100 people) was a sultanate composed of a single tribe, and was nominally a vassal of the Sultan of Lahij. The small Alawi shaikhdom was in a similar position.

The most significant and coherent tribes in the Lahij province in the PDRY were those living within the amirate and town of Dhala (25,750 people), from which Ali Antar came; the shaikhdom of Shu'ayb (5,000), the home of Salih Muslim and Ali Shaya Hadi; and what the

British called the independent tribes of Radfan (37,000), principally the Qutaybi and Halmayn. Men from these groups were recruited into the armed forces by Ali Antar and Salih Muslih, and dominated the army after 1986.

The Yafi'i had a history of martial endeavour both in fighting imams and Ottomans and as mercenaries for the Hadhrami sultans as well as the Nizam of Hyderabad, but they were not a coherent unit in 1967. They were divided into the Sultanates of Lower Yafi'i and Upper Yafi'i. Most of Upper Yafi'i and part of Lower Yafi'i were in difficult, mountainous terrain, and were what the British called 'unadministered' in 1967; they had rarely been visited. Though the Sultanate of Lower Yafi'i had some coherence under its Afifi sultans, the tribes of Upper Yafi'i were mostly independent of the nominal sultan. There were wild variations in British estimates of the size of these sultanates because of the lack of knowledge of the 'unadministered' areas. Thus the Aden Handbook[1] estimated (admitting that the figures were probably exaggerated) the population at 120,000 for Lower Yafi'i and 70,000 for Upper Yafi'i; but estimates made in 1965, probably more accurate, gave figures more than 50 per cent lower.[2]

PDRY politics included important Yafi'i politicians, including Salim Salih Muhammad and Muti'a, but the Yafi'i did not function as a cohesive group and their influence was limited. There had been traditional alliances with the tribes of Dhala and Radfan which continued in PDRY, as did their longstanding rivalry with the Fadhli tribe in Abyan. The PDRY government, presumably by design, divided the Yafi'i between Lahij and Abyan, placing the majority in the latter. Yafi'i soldiers and militias sided with Lahij politicians in their disputes with Salmin in the 1970s and Ali Nasir in the 1980s. There had been a strong tradition of emigration from the Yafi'i tribes and there are significant communities in the Gulf, and even the UK.

In Abyan, people from the former Sultanate of Fadhli (55,000 people), close to Aden, were highly influential in PDRY politics. Salmin was a Fadhli, and cultivated close relations with the main tribes of the region. Abd Rubbuh Mansur Hadi – vice president of Yemen from 1994 to 2011 and president since 2012 – is a Fadhli. Tariq al-Fadhli, one of the leaders of the southern secession movement in 2009, is from the old ruling family.

The Awdhali tribe (15,000 people) was prominent in the Federal Regular Army before independence, and continued to make an unusually large contribution to the armed forces after 1967. The Awdhali were supporters of Ali Nasir Muhammad. The most prominent among them in the PDRY was Muhammad Ali Ahmad.

The Dathina Federation (something of a British fiction) was a comparatively prosperous area in 1967, with about 12,000 people. It had a state council, whose presidency rotated among the three largest tribal groups, including the Hassani (the home of Ali Nasir Muhammad) and Maysari (the home of Muhammad Ali Haytham, prime minister from 1969 to 1971). The Dathina tribes had once been attached to the Awlaqi and at other times had been subject to rule by the Fadhli sultan.[3] In the PDRY there were good relations between these three groups, particularly under Ali Nasir.

There were three Awlaqi entities before 1967: the Upper Awlaqi sultanate (19,000 people), the Lower Awlaqi sultanate (14,000) and the Upper Awlaqi shaikhdom (12,000) – a 1953 creation of the British designed to weaken a particularly uncooperative sultan. A significant part of the officer corps of the Federal Regular Army was recruited from the Awlaqi, who were mostly supporters of FLOSY before independence. In the PDRY, Awlaqi politicians usually sided in internal disputes with leaders from Abyan. The former ruling family of the Upper Awlaqi shaikhdom, the Ahl Muhsin bin Farid, were major opponents of the PDRY from exile. In the PDRY, Lower Awlaqi was included in Abyan and the Upper Awlaqi in Shabwa, in a move to weaken Awlaqi solidarity.

The well-organized Amirate of Bayhan (28,000 people) was before 1967 a frontier state subject to the attentions of the imam's agents and provided in Sharif Haydar al-Habili, the first Arab commander of the FRA (when it became the South Arabian Army in June 1967). He also led one of the main groups fighting the PDRY from exile, and is now a member of the Upper House in the Yemeni parliament. Bayhan usually supported Ali Nasir. There were two main tribes in Bayhan – the Balharith and the Massabain.

APPENDIX B

LIST OF PROMINENT PERSONALITIES

This list includes those mentioned in the text and groups them according to their regional origin or affiliation. Details of their careers are found in the text, but for the lesser-known politicians I have made a brief note of their key position.

PRSY Leaders

Faysal Abd al-Latif al-Sha'bi (died 1971)
Muhammad Ali Haytham (1940–93)
Qahtan al-Sha'bi (1920–81)
Sayf al-Dhala'i (died 1973)

PDRY Leaders

Politicians from Lahij (Second Province), including Yafi'i from Abyan and Lahij
Ali Ahmad Nasser Antar al-Bishi (1937–86), from Dhala
Ali As'ad Muthana (died 1986), from Shu'ayb
Ali Shaya Hadi (1945–86), from Shu'ayb
Fadhl Muhsin Abdullah, from Yafi'i, brother-in-law of Abd al-Fattah Isma'il
Haytham Qasim Tahir, from Radfan, chief of staff, 1986–90, and minister of defence in the ROY, 1990–94
Husain Qumatah (executed 1982), from Yafi'i, commander of the People's Militia in the 1970s
Muhammad Salih Yafi'i (Muti'a) (executed 1980), from Upper Yafi'i

Sa'id Salih Salim (died late 1980s), from Radfan, minister of state security after 1986
Salih Muslih Qasim (1943–86), from Shu'ayb.
Salih Ubayd Ahmad, from Dhala, minister of defence, 1986–90, and deputy prime minister in the ROY, 1990–94
Salim Salih Muhammad (born 1947), from Upper Yafi'i
Sayf Sayl Khalid, from Lahij, leader of the 'Fattahiyin', 1986–90
Yassin Sa'id Nu'man (born 1947), prime minister of the PDRY, 1986–90

Politicians from Abyan (Third Province)
Abd Rubbuh Mansur Hadi, deputy chief of staff in 1986, vice president of ROY, 1994–2012, and president from 2012
Ahmad Abdullah Muhammad Hassani, commander of the navy, 1980–86
Ali Salih Ubad (Muqbil)
Ali Salim Law'ar (executed 1978), head of Salmin's office in the 1970s
Ali Nasir Muhammad (born 1937)
Ja'am Salih (executed 1978), an ally of Salmin and Politburo member in the 1970s
Muhammad Abdullah al-Battani, minister of interior, 1981–86
Muhammad Ali Ahmad, governor of Abyan, 1979–86
Muhammad Haydarah Masdus
Salim Rubayya Ali (Salmin) (1935–78)

Politicians from Shabwa (Fourth Province)
Abdullah Ali Ulaywa, chief of staff in 1986
Ahmad Musa'id Husain, minister of state security, 1980–86
Muhammad Salih Awlaqi (died 1973), minister of defence under Qahtan and minister of foreign affairs in 1973

Politicians from Hadhramaut (Fifth Province)
Abd al-Qadir Ba Jamal (born 1946), a PDRY minister and prime minister of the ROY, 2001–07
Abdullah al-Bar, a leader of the extreme left Hadhrami administration, 1967–68
Ali Salim al-Bidh (born c. 1940)
Faraj Sa'id bin Ghanim (1937–2007), a PDRY minister, and prime minister of the ROY, 1997–98
Faysal al-Attas, leader of the extreme left in Hadhramaut, 1967–68
Hassan Ba'um, ally of Salmin and one of the leaders of the Southern Mobility Movement.

Haydar Abu Bakr al-Attas (born 1939)
Salih Munassir al-Siyayli (died 1994), from a shaikhly not a Sayyid family
Salih Abu Bakr Bin Husainun (1936–94)
Salim Muhammad Jubran, a politburo member after 1986

Adeni politicians of north Yemeni origin – often called 'northerners'
Abd al-Aziz Abd al-Wali Nashir
Abd al-Aziz al-Dali
Abd al-Fattah Isma'il al-Jawfi (1939–86)
Abdullah al-Khamiri
Ahmad Abdullah Abdillahi
Mahmud Ushaysh (died 1986)
Muhammad Sa'id Abdullah al-Sharjabi ('Muhsin')
Rashid Muhammad Thabit
Sultan Muhammad al-Dawsh, secretary general of the Trade Unions

The Northern Branch of the YSP
Abd al-Wahid Muradi
Ahmad Sallami
Jarallah Umar (1942–2002), secretary general of the Northern Branch and of the NDF
Muhammad al-Thawr
Sultan Ahmad Umar, head of the NDF, but did not have a formal position in the YSP
Yahya al-Shami, from the northern branch of al-Tali'a

Communists (Members of the People's Democratic Union – PDU)
Abdullah Abd al-Razzaq Ba Dhib (died 1976)
Abu Bakr Abd al-Razzaq Ba Dhib
Ali Abd al-Razzaq Ba Dhib, the leading communist after the death of his brother Abdullah

Ba'athists (Popular Vanguard Party – al-Tali'a)
Abd al-Ghani Abd al-Qadir
Anis Hassan Yahya, leader

NOTES

Chapter One

1. There is a very large body of works covering the period. The best summary is Gavin, *Aden under British Rule*.
2. Yemenis at the time of the PDRY referred to the northern and southern states as 'halves' (*shatrain* in Arabic) of one nation. The term came into formal use in the revised PDRY constitution of 1978.
3. Willis, 'Making Yemen Indian': pp. 23–38.
4. These were the Abdali, Amiri (Dhala) Fadhli, Awlaqi, Yafi'i, Hawshabi, Alawi, Aqrabri and Subayhi.
5. The Master of Belhaven, *The Kingdom of Melchior*: p. 2.
6. The figures quoted are drawn from two publications by the British authorities in Aden: the 'General Handbook on Aden Colony and the Protectorate' (dated about 1960) and 'A Survey of Aden and the Protectorates of South Arabia' (August 1965). The latter said that the figures 'are rarely more than an intelligent guess and, depending on the context in which they are used, will almost certainly be disputed'.
7. Stephen Day quoted two anecdotes to the author, attributed to tribal leaders, on their attitude to the British:

    1) Sharif of Bayhan: 'In any dealing with the British it is better to be their enemy than their friend. If you are their friend, they will sell you. If you are their enemy there is a good chance they will buy you.'
    2) Sultan Nasir of Fadhli: 'I have studied the history of Britain in the Middle East and do not believe your government will keep a single word of its promises. But I will trust you.'

8. International Fund of Agricultural Development, *Report of the Special Programming Mission*: p. 67.
9. The NLF and its Ba'athist and communist associates will be considered in later chapters.
10. The British believe that the NLF exploited it; the NLF insists it inspired it.
11. There are several accounts of this. See for example Jones, *Britain and the Yemeni Civil War*.
12. Nashir, *Yahya al-Mutawakil*: pp. 94–6.

Chapter Two

1. Muhammad, *Dhakriyat wa Ahadith*: p. 20.
2. Naumkin, *Red Wolves of Yemen*: p. 67.
3. PDRY Ministry of Culture and Information, *Aden's Bloody Monday*: p. 35.
4. Stephen Day, then a political officer in the Sultanate of Fadhli, recalls arresting Salmin and al-Sallami around the time for organizing a strike, and was surprised to find codes and other incriminating material in their possession. It suggests that MAN was planning action even before the formation of the NLF.
5. Dresch, *History of Modern Yemen*: p. 91.
6. Muqbil, *Uktubar*.
7. The others were Nasir Saqqaf, Abdullah Majali, Muhammad Ali Dumani, Thabit Ali Mansuri, Muhammad Ahmad al-Duqm, Ahmad Abdullah al-Awlaqi, Aidrus Husain al-Qadi, Ali Muhammad al-Kazimi and Abdullah Muhammad al-Salahi.
8. Naumkin, *Red Wolves of Yemen*: p. 82.
9. Halliday, *Arabia without Sultans*: p. 191.
10. Muhammad, *Dhakriyat*: p. 21, and in conversation with the author, June 2009.
11. Carapico, *Civil Society in Yemen*: pp. 94–5. Paul Dresch notes that this organization based its constitution on the Holy Qur'an – see *History of Modern Yemen*: p. 98. Naumkin also refers to the Organization of South Yemen which was a secret group within a legal organization called the Yafi'i Youth League – see *Red Wolves of Yemen*: p. 83.
12. Muqbil, *Uktubar* (quoting Muhsin Ibrahim): p. 82.
13. Kostiner, *Struggle for South Yemen*: p. 67.
14. See Harding, *Roads to Nowhere* for a vivid account of his contacts with tribes in Radfan during and after the campaign, esp. pp. 215–43.
15. There is a detailed description of the NLF organization, leaders and activities in Arabic in Muhammad Sa'id Muhammad Abdullah (Muhsin), *Adan Kifah Sha'b wa Hazima Imbaraturiya* (Beirut, 1989).
16. FCO documents: *PDRY Leadership: Political Philosophy and the Power Structure* (1977), National Archives, FCO 8/2967.
17. Interview with Abdullah al-Asnaj, London, December 2008.
18. Interview with Muhammad Ali Ahmad, March 2010.
19. It was drafted by Salim Zayn, who was from the right wing of the NLF.
20. Muqbil, *Uktubar*: p. 206.
21. *Ibid.*: pp. 181–2.
22. Halliday, *Arabia without Sultans*: p. 208.
23. Naumkin, *Red Wolves of Yemen*: p. 162.
24. Many of the NLF fighters in the rural areas were illiterate tribesmen. See Muqbil, *Uktubar*: pp. 182–200. He also talks of a reorganization of internal forces and gives details of the membership and operations.
25. These were: Abd al-Karim Muhsin from Radfan; Muhammad al-Bishi from Dhala; Ahmad al-Sha'ir from Aden; Haydarah Mutlaq from Halmayn; Ali Midayr from Yafi'i; Salih Muslih from Shu'ayb; and Ali Nasir Muhammad from the Central District.
26. Halliday, *Arabia without Sultans*: p. 202.

NOTES TO PAGES 26–37

27 These were said to be Abd al-Nabi Madum, Mayyub Ali Ghalib, Salih Ba-Qish, Muhammad Sa'id Abdullah ('Muhsin') and Abdullah al-Khamiri) – see Muqbil, *Uktubar*: p. 206.
28 FCO documents: letter from D.J. McCarthy to Ivor Lucas of the Middle East Department of the FCO, dated 30 January 1977, National Archives, FCO/2967.
29 Interview with Muhammad Ali Ahmad, March 2010.
30 The Upper Yafi'i Sultanate, which had not joined the federation, did not become part of PRSY until March 1968.
31 The NLF 'government' in Abyan despatched a small group to assist the NLF in Hadhramaut – consisting of six people in two vehicles, according to Muhammad Ali Ahmad in an interview, March 2010.
32 Interview with Haydar al-Attas, November 2009.
33 Trevelyan, *Middle East in Revolution*: p. 266. Many Yemenis educated under the British might disagree.

Chapter Three

1 Quoted in Dresch, *History of Modern Yemen*: pp. 118–19.
2 Halliday, 'People's Democratic Republic of Yemen': p. 43.
3 PDRY Ministry of Cultural and Guidance, *Aden's Bloody Monday*: p. 6.
4 Interview with Abdullah al-Asnaj, January 2009.
5 Faysal al-Attas has said that Aden feared that Hadhramaut might seek independence – with the help of Saudi Arabia. See Day, 'Power-sharing and Hegemony'.
6 FCO Documents: J. Phillips, *Southern Yemen: Annual Review for 1969*, National Archives, FCO 8/1447.
7 The others were Adil Mahfuz Khalifa (justice and awqaf), Faysal bin Shamlan (public works and communications), Abd al-Malik Isma'il (labour and social affairs), Muhammad Abd al-Qadir Ba Faqih (education), Ahmad Sidqi (health) and Sayyid Umar Akbar (local government and agriculture).
8 Interview with Abdullah al-Asnaj, January 2009.
9 The First Province included Aden, Bir Ahmad, and Dar Sa'ad, Omran, Perim, Kamaran and Socotra. The Second Province included Lahij, Subayhi, Dhala, Hawshabi, Alawi, Radfan, Shu'ayb, Halmayn and Maflahi. The Third Province included most of Upper and Lower Yafi'i, Fadhli, Awdhali, Dathina and Lower Awlaqi. The Fourth Province included Bayhan, Upper Awlaqi, Wahidi and the North West tribal area of Hadhramaut. The Fifth Province was the heart of Hadhramaut and the Sixth was Mahra.
10 At this period the HBL in Hadhramaut was a separate force.
11 Naumkin, *Red Wolves of Yemen* (New York and Cambridge, 2004): pp. 290–1.
12 Interview with Haydar al-Attas, November 2009.
13 Interview with a person who later became a Politburo member, May 2010.
14 The 1973 census gave the population figures for provinces as follows: Aden: 291,000; Lahij: 273,000; Abyan: 311,000; Shabwa: 162,000; Hadhramaut: 492,000, and Mahra: 61,000.
15 Naumkin points out that Isma'il claimed that the figures were unrepresentative of the size of the NLF in Lahij and Aden and the right had inflated the

size of the contingent from Abyan. *Red Wolves of Yemen*: 296. Salim Salih Muhammad said in an interview in July 2009 that the NLF membership in Hadhramaut was very small at this time.
16 Naumkin, *Red Wolves of Yemen*: p. 296.
17 Interview with Politburo member who was working with Qahtan in 1968, May 2010.
18 Interview with one of those arrested, July 2010.
19 Salmin told one of his colleagues that the left would need to regroup, learn the lessons and wait for a better opportunity. Author interview with the colleague, August 2009.
20 Naumkin, *Red Wolves of Yemen*: p. 322.
21 Russian diplomat speaking to the author in Aden in 1970.
22 Faysal al-Sha'bi and others on the right had earlier agreed that the NF should be much more active in instilling within the armed forces the NF's ideology to counteract the influence of senior conservative officers. One leading figure on the left told the author (July 2010) that this education programme had helped the left spread its influence within the army and paradoxically had undermined the potential support for Faysal's pragmatic socialism.
23 Interview with one of Faysal's colleagues, May 2010.
24 In an interview in July 2010 with one of the left-wing leaders of 1969 he said that the left were surprised at the ease with which they took control. For example, they sent only 20 men to take over the radio station. Qahtan and Faysal had failed to mobilise support or prepare for the confrontation. They seemed to see themselves as indispensible.
25 Phillips, *Southern Yemen*.
26 Naumkin, *Red Wolves of Yemen*: p. 323.
27 Phillips, *Southern Yemen*.
28 Alaini, *50 Years in Shifting Sands*: p. 197.
29 See, for example, Nashir, *Yahya al-Mutawakkil*.
30 Page, *The Soviet Union and the Yemens*: p. 20.
31 Primakov, *Russia and the Arabs*: p. 84.
32 Behbehani, *China and the People's Democratic Republic of Yemen* gives full details of the minutes of meetings held by the PRSY delegation.

Chapter Four

1 Interview with Yassin Sa'id Nu'man, former PDRY prime minister and Politburo member, March 2010.
2 Interview with an Arab minister who met Salmin many times in the 1970s, and said that Salmin did not have a Marxist or Maoist thought in his head, but acted out of instinct.
3 Haydar al-Attas, who accompanied him on a visit to Moscow in 1972, believed that Salmin was at that stage open to other forms of Marxism, but his visit was mishandled by Soviet officials, who twice denied him a meeting with Russian premier Leonid Brezhnev. Salmin felt slighted both as an individual and as president, and this appeared to reinforce an interest in Maoism that had developed during a visit to China during the height of the Cultural Revolution. Moscow learned its lesson, and treated him better next time. Interview with Haydar al-Attas, November 2009.

4　Interview with Ali Nasir Muhammad, January 2010.
5　Interview with Salim Salih Muhammad, June 2009.
6　Nashir, *Yahya al-Mutawakkil*: p. 150.
7　Jallul, *Al-Yaman*: 149, quoting Karen Brutents, former senior CPSU official.
8　Interview with Mohsin Alaini, May 2009.
9　Halliday, *Arabia without Sultans*: p. 239.
10　Curiously, one of the members represented PORF, the FLOSY fighting arm that had been recruited mostly from members of the NLF.
11　Al-Ashmali, *Al-Wahda wa al-Siraa al-Siyasiya*: p. 143.
12　Anthony, 'The Communist Party of the People's Democratic Republic of Yemen: p. 233.
13　Unlike some of his ministerial colleagues, he would meet British diplomats in the early 1970s in his office and talk freely on any political subject.
14　Interview with Politburo member, May 2010. Several other leading figures agree with this.
15　The names of those elected as full members were Abdullah al-Khamiri (minister of state for the Cabinet), Mahmud Ushaysh (ambassador), Rashid Muhammad Thabit (minister of information), Abd al-Rahman Atiq (deputy minister of interior), Awadh al-Hamid (governor of Lahij), Ali Salim Law'ar (head of external relations in the party), Aida Ali Sa'id (head of the Union of Yemeni Women and of Ali Nasir's private office, Mahdi Abdullah Sa'id (president of the General Union of Workers), Abdullah Salih al-Bar, Mansur al-Sarari (People's Defence Committee), Muhsin, Husain Muhammad Qumatah (head of Peoples Militia), Sultan al-Dawsh (secretary for the mass organizations), Sa'id Askari (governor of Mahra), Ahmad Abdullah Abd al-Illah (deputy minister of foreign affairs), Hassan Salih Ba'um (an ally of Salmin's from Hadhramaut), Muhammad Haydara Masdus, Ahmad Musa'id Husain, Mohammad Sa'id Abdullah and Ahmad Salim Mikhbal.
16　Interview with former members of the Politburo, 2009.
17　Interview with Hadhrami Sayyid and a colleague of al-Bidh, November 2009.
18　FCO documents: letter from the British embassy in Aden to R. M. Hunt of 2 June 1973. National Archives, FCO 8/2034.
19　Interview with Ali Nasir, January 2009. He was able to produce the minute of a meeting he had held with the British ambassador in 1972 that could easily have been written by the ambassador himself.
20　Interview with a Yemeni businessman who established a factory in the early 1970s and found himself facing pressures from the top NF and government leaders, and had to use his access to Ali Nasir to keep going.
21　For details of the judicial system, see Shamiry, 'Judicial System in Democratic Yemen'.
22　Interview with Muhammad Ali Ahmad, governor of Abyan for over ten years from the mid 1970s, April 2010.
23　Muhammad, *Dhakriyat wa Hadith an al-Nidhal al-Watani wal Wahdawi*.
24　Molyneux et al., 'Women and Revolution in the People's Democratic Republic of Yemen'. It elected six delegates to the SPC.
25　The main opponent was the National Union Forces, belonging to the United National Front of South Yemen, which combined elements of FLOSY, SAL,

former army officers and former sultans and their supporters. This was backed by the Saudi government, which provided money, a base at al-Sharura, and a radio station – which proved rather more effective than the regime in getting its version of events into the Arab media. It was led by Abdullah al-Asnag.
26 Haytham at a press conference on 1 January 1970.
27 Interview with Haydar al-Attas, May 2009.
28 FCO Documents: A. R. H. Kellas, letter to A. A. Acland (10 March 1971), National Archives, FCO 8/1698.
29 Interview with former deputy minister of the interior, June 2009.
30 Bidwell, *Two Yemens*: p. 266.

Chapter Five

1 A leading figure in Soviet foreign policy had earlier noted that the NF 'was trying to force reforms in all spheres of the nation's life even though there was no real ground for such a radical approach'. See Primakov, *Russia and the Arabs*: p. 82.
2 The author vividly recalls being summoned to meet Mahmud Ushaysh, minister of economy, in early 1970, and being asked to explain why the two banks only appeared to have overdrafts and debts. He could not accept the explanation that the NF had been saying for months that it would nationalize the banks, and that the banks' management might have taken some pre-emptive action.
3 Several former officials working in the PDRY in the early 1970s have commented how ministers, including Ali Nasir Muhammad and Mahmud Ushaysh, would protect those with experience and skills from the wilder men who wanted to get rid of anyone inherited from the previous regime.
4 The NLF had kept links with Yemeni communities abroad, and Ali Salim al-Bidh was one leader who had visited East Africa before 1967 to seek funds for the NLF.
5 The author remembers one case in Aden, for example, where five co-workers 'took over' a retail store from its unfortunate Parsee owner.
6 World Bank, *People's Democratic Republic of Yemen*.
7 Lackner, *People's Democratic Republic of Yemen*: p. 157.
8 The World Bank estimated that PDRY received around $250 million in external aid up to 1977, two thirds of which came from the Soviet Union and its allies. However, at the end of 1977 there were aid commitments of $432 million of which $232 million was from international agencies and Arab countries. External debt at the end of 1977 stood at $432 million and debt servicing in 1977 was $1.5 million. World Bank, *People's Democratic Republic of Yemen*: pp. 24–5.
9 Peterson, 'Tribes and Politics in Yemen': p. 8. NF sources estimated in the early 1970s that around 10 per cent of the population was nomadic.
10 Dresch, *History of Modern Yemen*: p. 142.
11 Cigar, 'Islam and the State in South Yemen': pp. 185–223.
12 When peasants demonstrated against the 1977 law, they were sentenced to death (later commuted).
13 See Molyneux, *State Policies and the Position of Women Workers*.
14 Dahlgren, 'Islam, Custom and Revolution in Aden: pp. 327–46.

NOTES TO PAGES 74–88

15 Interview with Ali Nasir Muhammad, January 2010.
16 Alaini, *50 Years in Shifting Sands*: p. 197.
17 The YAR government said they had been lured over the border to a banquet and murdered. The PDRY said he had launched an attack on its territory. See Halliday, *Revolution and Foreign Policy*: p. 116.
18 Alaini, *50 Years in Shifting Sands*: p. 259.
19 Interview with Mohsen Alaini, who said that he had reached the agreement with Ali Nasir, but insisted that Abd al-Fattah Isma'il join the talks to ensure that the regime in Aden would accept the outcome.
20 Alaini, *50 Years in the Shifting Sands*: pp. 265–72.
21 The NDF consisted of the Revolutionary Democratic Party, the Organization of Yemeni Resisters, the Popular Democratic Union (that is, the north Yemeni PDU), the Popular Vanguard Party (the north Yemeni al-Tali'a), and the Labour Party.
22 Interview with Mohsen Alaini, May 2009.
23 Gause, *Saudi–Yemeni Relations*: p. 112.
24 Charbal, 'Ali Nasir Remembers', *Al-Wasat* 184 (7 August 1995): p. 27.
25 Primakov, *Russia and the Arabs*: pp. 82–4.
26 Ozoling and Andreasyan, 'Some Problems': p. 9.
27 Victoria Clark gives a slightly different perspective based on interviews with Vladimir Naumkin and a former Soviet ambassador to Aden, in which both speak more positively of the Soviet attitude to the PDRY in its early days. See Clark, *Yemen: Dancing on the Heads of Snakes*: pp. 113–14.
28 FCO Documents: J. G. W. Ramage, *People's Democratic Republic of Yemen: Annual Review for 1973*. National Archives, FCO 8/2606.
29 Charbal, 'Ali Nasir Remembers', *Al-Wasat* 184 (7 August 1995): p. 28.
30 See Page, *The Soviet Union and the Yemens*: pp. 60–1.
31 *Ibid.*: p. 74.
32 Behbehani, *China and the People's Democratic Republic of Yemen* gives a detailed account of the 1968 visit to China by a PDRY delegation.
33 The author witnessed this odd ritual.

Chapter Six

1 FCO Documents: Secret Annex to 'PDRY Leadership: Political Phil-osophy and Power Structure Security Organisations', 1977. National Archives, FCO 8/2967.
2 Yemeni Socialist Party, *Critical and Analytical Document*.
3 Ramage, *People's Democratic Republic of Yemen*
4 Isma'il, *Hawl al-'Ihawra*: pp. 477–86.
5 See Yemeni Socialist Party, *Critical and Analytical Document*.
6 The writer recalls two meetings with Salmin in 1976. At the first, Salmin was filling his car with petrol in a garage in Aden – just like anyone else. He was alone without a driver or bodyguards. On the second, Salmin was walking alone in the late evening in fields near Zingibar, and stopped for a chat.
7 Halliday, 'Yemen's Unfinished Revolution: p. 18.
8 FCO Documents: J. G. W. Ramage, letter to Ivor Lucas (6 May 1975), National Archives, FCO 8/2482.
9 *Ibid.*

10 Helen Lackner, *People's Democratic Republic of Yemen*: p. 71.
11 The members of the Politburo were (in order of the votes they achieved at the Congress) Abd al-Fattah Isma'il, Salim Rubayya Ali, Ali Nasir Muhammad, Ali Salih Ubad ('Muqbil'), Muhammad Salih Muti'a, Ali Salim al-Bidh, Salih Muslih, Ja'am Salah Muhammad and Abd al-Aziz Abd al-Wali – two northerners, four from Abyan (including Muqbil), three from Lahij, and one from Hadhramaut.
12 Embassy of the People's Democratic Republic of Yemen, London, *Present and Future*.
13 Ibid.
14 Embassy of the People's Democratic Republic of Yemen, London, *Political Report*.
15 *Ibid*.: pp. 14–15.
16 *Ibid*.: p. 19.
17 Isma'il, *Hawl al-Thawra* : pp. 477–86.
18 Embassy of the People's Democratic Republic of Yemen, London, *Political Report*: p. 25.
19 *Ibid*.: p. 33.
20 The government estimated that Bedouin tribes accounted for ten per cent of the population in the early 1970s.
21 Isma'il, *Hawl al-Thawra*: pp. 477–86.
22 Halliday, 'Yemen's Unfinished Revolution'. One of these was Hassan Ba'um, who is now a figure in the south Yemeni secessionist movement.
23 FCO Documents: Secret Annex to 'PDRY Leadership: Political Philosophy and Power Structure Security Organisations', 1977. National Archives, FCO 8/2967.
24 Isma'il, *Hawl al-Thawra*: pp. 477–86.
25 Embassy of the People's Democratic Republic of Yemen, London, *Political Report*: p. 16.
26 Isma'il, *Hawl al-Thawra*: pp. 477–86.
27 Embassy of the People's Democratic Republic of Yemen, London, *Political Report*.
28 Interview (March 2010) with Hassan Ba'um, a close ally of Salmin at this time, and a member of the Central Committee. See Hadi, *17 Sa'at tarikhiya 'ind Bab al-Yaman*.
29 Interview with former PDRY official.
30 Interview (May 2009) with former minister who described how Salmin tried to force him to build a power station in a remote part of the country even though there was no fuel, infrastructure or even money available. Salmin could not be budged, and it took some deft manipulation by Ali Nasir to save the minister his job.
31 Interview with former deputy minister, June 2009.
32 Page, *The Soviet Union and the Yemens*, quoting A. Vasilev, 'Nadezhdy Iuzhnugo Iemena', *Pravda*, Moscow (14 September 1969): p. 23.
33 There is a vivid account of the incident from an eyewitness in al-Salami, *Tears of Sheba*: pp. 167–70.
34 Interview with Muhammad Ali Ahmad, March 2010.
35 Muhammad, *Dhakriyat*: p. 114.

36 Ibid.
37 Isma'il, *Hawl al-Thawra*: p. 483. In an interview, Muhammad Ali Ahmad said that Salmin had agreed to resign and fly to Addis Ababa with $270,000.
38 Muhammad Ali Ahmad believes that Salmin had intended to leave for Addis Ababa, and that the attempted coup was the work of his supporters, who acted without Salmin's knowledge, presumably understanding that they would lose their positions and possibly their freedom once he had gone. Salmin's surviving supporters say that he was the victim of a plot by colleagues who feared he would join Muhammad Ali Haytham and others in opposition.
39 Isma'il, *Hawl al-Thawra*: p. 483.
40 Ali Sarraf, *Al-Yaman al-Janubi* (London, 1992): p. 400.
41 Hadi, *17 Sa'at tarikhiya 'ind Bab al-Yaman*, gives a current and thorough account of the events leading up to Salmin's death.
42 Muhammad, *Dhakriyat*: p. 116.
43 Halliday, 'Yemen's Unfinished Revolution'.
44 Nashir, *Yahya al-Mutawakkil*: p. 134.
45 Interview with the Central Committee figure in 2010. His view was that Salmin and Muslih had organized the assassination. He claims that the assassin had been told to carry a concealed weapon, and was to use this to kill al-Ghashmi as soon as he opened the briefcase.
46 Interview with former assistant to Abd al-Fattah Isma'il.
47 In interview in July 2010 a PDRY official described how he met a dishevelled Qahtan al-Sha'bi in June 1978 when he emerged briefly from house arrest in the midst of the fighting around the presidential palace to point out that his left-wing opponents were now killing each other – as he had long expected.
48 Isma'il, *Watha'iq al-Mu'tamar*: p. 51.
49 Al-Sururi, *Tajraba*: p. 52.

Chapter Seven

1 I have drawn on books by Fred Halliday, Tareq and Jacqueline Ismael, Paul Dresch, Helen Lackner, Ali Sarraf and Faysal Jallul (see bibliography) and others in writing this chapter supplemented by interviews, YSP documents and media reports from this period.
2 Yemeni Socialist Party, *Al-Mu'tammar*: pp. 49–55.
3 Ibid.
4 Ibid.
5 Al-Sururi, *Tajraba*: p. 54.
6 Abd al-Fattah Isma'il and Ali Nasir had signed an agreement on 12 September 1978 with Abd al-Bari Tahir and Abd al-Wahab Ghalib of the Yemen Labour Party; Sultan Ahmad Umar and Jarallah Muhammad Umar of the Revolutionary Democratic Party; Yahya Muhammad al-Shami and Abd al-Aziz Muhammad Sa'id of the Yemeni Popular Vanguard Party (the northern version of al-Tali'a); and Husain al-Hummaza and Muhammad Salih Hadi of the Organization of Yemeni Revolutionary Resisters. See al-Sarari, *Al-Hizb al-Ishtiraki*: p. 151. The northern version of the PDU was also a member.
7 See <www.al-bab.com/yemen/biog/jarallah.htm>.

8   Interviews with ex-PDRY leaders who say that the members were Jarallah Umar, Ahmad Sallami, Yahya al-Shami, Muhammad al-Thawr and Abd al-Wahid al-Muradi.
9   The other members of the Presidium were Sultan Muhammad al-Dawsh (trade union leader), Riyadh al-Akbari, Ay'dah Ali (the PDRY's leading lady from the days of the independence struggle), Sa'id Salih Salim (from Lahij), Mahmud Sa'id Madhi (a Hadhrami with a degree from LSE who had played an important role on handling the PDRY's economic and financial policies), Abdullah Ahmad Ghanim (secretary), Faris Salem Ahmad and Ali Sallami.
10 Interviews with former PDRY officials.
11 Al-Sururi, *Tajraba*: pp. 55–6.
12 See Chapter 5.
13 Abu Luhum, *Al-Yaman*, vol. 3: pp. 266–7.
14 Lackner, *People's Democratic Republic of Yemen*: p. 85.
15 Halliday, *Revolution and Foreign Policy*: p. 124.
16 Charbal, 'Ali Nasir Remembers', *Al-Wasat* 182 (24 July 1995): p. 29.
17 *Washington Post*, 4 December 1984: pp. 1, 44.
18 Some in the PDRY leadership believed that the Soviets would come to the PDRY's aid if the YAR had defeated them. See Clark, *Yemen: Dancing on the Heads of Snakes*: p. 121.
19 Abu Luhum, *Al-Yaman*, vol. 3: pp. 274–5.
20 Halliday, *Revolution and Foreign Policy*: pp. 197–207.
21 Page, *The Soviet Union and the Yemens*: pp. 86–99.
22 FCO Documents: *PDRY (South Yemen): Soviet Client in the Arab World*, FCO briefing document (September 1980), National Archives, FCO 972/112: p. 2.
23 Halliday, *Revolution and Foreign Policy*: p. 193.
24 World Bank, *People's Democratic Republic of Yemen: A Review of Economic and Social Development*, March 1979: pp. 24–5.
25 Interview with a former senior government official, July 2009.
26 They were soon released, as they had diplomatic immunity. The PDRY embassy in Baghdad was attacked. There were further problems the following year, when the PDRY arrested what it called Iraqi spies, and Iraq expelled some PDRY students.
27 Al-Sururi, *Tajraba*: p. 54.
28 YSP, *Critical and Analytical Document on the Revolutionary Experience in Democratic Yemen (1978–1986)* (Aden, after 1986): p. 38.
29 Ibid.
30 Sarraf, *Al-Yaman al-Janubi*: p. 298.
31 Al-Sururi, *Tajraba*: p. 56; interview with Muhammad Ali Ahmad, March 2010.
32 Ali Nasir Muhammad gave the author a copy of an article written by Sayf al-Din al-Dawri for the newspaper *al-Zaman* (date uncertain), in which he quotes Fadhl Muhsin Abdullah accusing Ali Nasir of manipulating and inciting the conflict between Ali Antar and Muhsin, and encouraging Ali Antar to believe that Abd al-Fattah Isma'il was backing Muhsin. Fadhl Muhsin adds that Isma'il had no involvement, and that this was part of an operation to engineer the resignation of Isma'il.

33 Tareq Y. Ismael and Jacqueline S. Ismael, *People's Democratic Republic of Yemen* (London, 1986): p. 71.
34 Gause, *Saudi–Yemeni Relations*: p. 141.
35 YSP, *Critical and Analytical Document*: p. 41.
36 *Ibid.*: pp. 41–2.
37 BBC Summary of World Broadcasts – ME/6365 (8 March 1980). Lahij was given the name Tuban, with four subdivisions: Lahij, Dhala, Lab'uth and Radfan – but the government subsequently referred to it as Lahij.

Chapter Eight

1 Interview with Mohsen Alaini, May 2009.
2 There were thirteen changes and five new ministers, including the following appointments: Ali Salim al-Bidh (deputy prime minister), Anis Hassan Yahya (Al-Tali'a, deputy prime minister and minister for fish wealth), Ali Abd al-Razzaq Ba Dhib (PDU, deputy prime minister), Ali Antar (minister of defence); Salih Munassir al-Siyayli (minister of state security), Salim Salih Muhammad (minister of foreign affairs), Salih Muslih (minister of interior), Abd al-Aziz Abd al-Wali (minister of state for cabinet affairs), and Haydar Abu Bakr al-Attas (minister of construction).
3 Interview with Haydar al-Attas, November 2009.
4 Interview with a member of the YSP Politburo of the period.
5 Interview with Muhammad Sa'id Abdullah (Muhsin), May 2010.
6 Interviews with former PDRY officials.
7 According to a senior official in the ministry of finance in 1980 Muti'a had agreed with a Saudi businessman of Yafi'i origin a deal whereby the businessman would invest in PDRY on favourable terms and help develop a number of potentially valuable projects in Aden. Interview with the official, May 2010.
8 YSP, *Critical and Analytical Document*: p. 43.
9 See for example Gause, *Saudi–Yemeni Relations*: p. 152.
10 Interview with a former PDRY diplomat based in India at the time.
11 Interview with a former official who was in the Ministry of Information in 1981.
12 Interview with Politburo member, May 2010.
13 YSP, *Critical and Analytical Document*: p. 46.
14 Day, *Power-Sharing and Hegemony*.
15 Muhammad, *Dhakriyat wa Ahadith 'an al-Nidhal al-Watani wa al-Wahdawi*: 136. Others have said that al-Dali was astonished to hear he was being made minister of foreign affairs.
16 One senior member of the Central Committee close to Ali Nasir at the time said that Qumatah was hanged for his part in a plot to overthrow Ali Nasir. Interview conducted in April 2010.
17 Jallul, *Al-Yaman*: p. 159.
18 *Middle East Contemporary Survey* (*MECS*) (Tel Aviv, 1984).
19 YSP, *Critical and Analytical Document*: p. 52.
20 Al-Sururi, *Tajraba* (Beirut, 2001): p. 65. Muhsin in an interview in May 2010 said that Ali Nasir had no intention of making al-Sururi a minister.
21 Interview with a former Central Committee member in June 2009.
22 Interview with Haydar al-Attas and other leaders in 2009.

23 The others were Abu Bakr Ba Dhib, Anis Hassan Yahya, Salih Munassir al-Siyayli, Salim Salih Muhammad and Ali As'ad Muthana.
24 Interview with Haydar al-Attas, January 2010.
25 BBC, Summary of World Broadcasts – ME/7877 (16 February 1985).
26 Interview with Haydar al-Attas, January 2010.
27 Jallul, *Al-Yaman*: p. 163.
28 Muhammad Ali Ahmad (governor of Abyan, an Awdhali); Muhammad Sulaiman Nasir (minister of agriculture, from Dathina), Ahmad Abdullah al-Hassani (the naval commander from Dathina), Abd Rubbuh Mansur Hadi (deputy chief of staff from Fadhli, now vice president of the Republic of Yemen), Muhammad al-Battani (minister of interior, an Awdhali), Faysal Rub (commander of 14 Brigade from Dhala), al-Khadr al-Danbur (a brigade commander from Fadhli), Abdullah Salih Ulaiwa (chief of army staff, an Awlaqi from Shabwa), Ahmad Musa'id Husain (the Awlaqi minister of state security), Salim Ali Qahtan (senior army officer, another Awlaqi), Abdullah al-Bar (a Hadhrami), and Abdullah Ahmad Ghanim (a minister of state from Aden). Jallul, *Al-Yaman*: p. 163. The role of these people in the events of January 1986 and interviews conducted in 2009 and 2010 confirm this assessment.
29 Interview with the officer (November 2009), now a leading member of the exile opposition. He gave the anecdote as an illustration of the divisions that existed in the PDRY Armed Forces at the time. It seems improbable that Salih Muslih had any serious intention of implementing his idea though another senior figure in the YSP said he had heard the same story from a different military source (interview in July 2010).
30 Halliday, *Revolution and Foreign Policy*: p. 40.
31 Al-Ashmali, *Al-Wahda wa al-Siraa al-Siyasiya*: p. 166; BBC Summary of World Broadcasts ME/8014 (27 July 1985).
32 Interview in November 2009 with former Politburo member who made this approach.
33 Interview with Politburo member who was told this by the new Soviet ambassador after January 1986.
34 At least one member of the Politburo believes that Mengistu urged Ali Nasir to eliminate his opponents as Mengistu had done in Addis Ababa. Interview with author in November 2009.
35 Al-Sururi, *Tajraba*: p. 71.
36 Noel Brehony, 'PDRY since 1967', unpublished paper presented at a seminar at the Centre for Middle East Studies, SOAS, in May 1986.
37 Interview with Haydar al-Attas, January 2010.
38 Gueyras, 'Last Days of Ali Nasir': pp. 37–40.
39 Al-Ashmali, *Al-Wahda wa al-Siraa al-Siyasiya*: p. 166.
40 Sarraf, *Al-Yaman al-Janubi*: pp. 383–98.
41 *Ibid.*: pp. 399–405.
42 Interview with a member of the Central Committee, June 2009.
43 Gueyras, 'Last Days of Ali Nasir': pp. 37–40.
44 Al-Sururi, *Tajraba*: p. 74.
45 Lackner, 'Postscript'.
46 Gueyras, 'Last Days of Ali Nasir': pp. 37–40.

NOTES TO PAGES 136–154 233

47 Some former PDRY leaders blame the Lebanese communist for misreporting this conversation to Ali Nasir in order to precipitate the crisis.

Chapter Nine

1 See Dresch, *History of Modern Yemen*: p. 168.
2 Katz, 'Civil Conflict in South Yemen': pp. 7–11.
3 This view of a utopian PDRY is shared by many south Yemenis today, even though few are old enough to remember what life was like in the early 1980s.
4 Al-Sarari, *Al-Hizb al-Ishtiraki*: p. 151.
5 Charbal, 'Ali Nasir Remembers', *Al-Wasat* 182 (24 July 1996): p. 29.
6 Halliday, *Revolution and Foreign Policy*: p. 129.
7 Gause, *Saudi–Yemeni Relations*: p. 139.
8 Interview with Politburo member, May 2009.
9 <www.al-bab.com/yemen/biog/jarallah.htm>.
10 Gause, *Saudi–Yemeni Relations*: p. 144.
11 Interview with Yassin Saʻid Nuʻman, March 2010.
12 Halliday, *Revolution and Foreign Policy*: p. 199.
13 Charbal, 'Ali Nasir Remembers', *Al-Wasat* 185 (14 August 1995): p. 20.
14 Halliday, *Revolution and Foreign Policy*: p. 195.
15 *Ibid*.: p. 197.
16 FCO, *Soviet, East European and Western Development Aid*: p. 22.
17 Charbal, 'Ali Nasir Remembers', *Al-Wasat* 184 (7 August 1985): p. 20.
18 *Ibid*.: p. 29.
19 *Ibid*.: p. 18.

Chapter Ten

1 Ali Salim al-Bidh told a friend later that he had feigned death before managing to get out of the room.
2 Some people do not accept that he was killed at the time, believing that he died two weeks later. The naval commander, whose ships fired the rocket, says that he heard from a daughter of Ismaʻil that Ismaʻil had contacted his family several days after 13 January. Ismaʻil's son says that his father died on 13 January.
3 Interviews with two military commanders, May 2009 and February 2010.
4 This figure is almost certainly an exaggeration. The total size of the PDRY armed forces in 1986 was under 28,000, with perhaps 15,000 in the People's Militia. Muhammad Ali Ahmad had recruited a militia of unknown size in Abyan.
5 Interview with former PDRY senior military officer, May 2009.
6 Interview with a top military commander on Ali Nasir's team, February 2010. The new minister of defence said on 22 June that most of the brigades outside Aden did not take part in the fighting.
7 Interview with Haydar al-Attas, May 2009.
8 *Ibid.*
9 Cigar, 'Soviet–South Yemeni Relations': pp. 3–38.
10 One of Ali Nasir's military supporters said in an interview with the author that the Russian ambassador had contacted him after this meeting to try to arrange mediation. The officer contacted Ali Nasir in Abyan, who agreed to provide a written statement of his demands. When the officer tried to deliver the Soviet

ambassador's response the officer went to Abyan, only to find that Ali Nasir had left for the north.
11 Interview with one of the officers present at this meeting, May 2009.
12 When the author visited Muhsin in his villa in Aden in May 2010 he noted that '1986' was carved over its entrance.
13 Ali Muhsin Hamid – note sent to author.
14 Roland Papp, quoting East German archives.
15 Their version is in the Final Statement of the Third Session of the Central Committee of the YSP, held in September 1986 (this is the Ali Nasir version of the Central Committee). The document was provided to author by Fred Halliday.
16 Other leading supporters of Ali Nasir were Muhammad Abdullah al-Battani (minister of interior and later a minister in YAR governments), Ahmad Musa'id Husain (minister of state security), Hadi Ahmad Nasir, Abd al-Qadir Ba Jamal, Muhammad Abd al-Qawi, Alawi Husain Farhan (deputy minister of state security), Muhammad Sulaiman Nasir and Abdullah Ulaywa (head of the air force).
17 Other key appointments included Salih Munassir al-Siyayli (deputy prime minister and minister of interior), Salih bin Husainun (deputy prime minister and minister of energy, a Hadhrami), Salih Ubayd Ahmad (minister of defence, from Lahij), Abd al-Aziz al-Dali (minister of foreign affairs, a northerner), Sa'id Salih Salim (a previous head of the Peasants' Union, minister of state security from Lahij), Faraj bin Ghanim (minister of planning, a Hadhrami), Rashid Muhammad Thabit (minister of state for unity affairs, a northerner), and Mohammad Sa'id Madhi (minister of finance, an LSE-educated Hadhrami technocrat).
18 Day, *Power-Sharing and Hegemony*.
19 Interview with Yassin Sa'id Nu'man, March 2010.
20 Al-Sururi, *Tajraba*: pp. 124–5.
21 He had taken a wounded colleague to a hospital in Aden, where he was murdered.
22 PDRY Ministry of Culture and Guidance, *Aden's Bloody Monday*: p. 30.
23 Yemeni Socialist Party, *Proposed Political Solution* and *Al-Biyan al-Siyasi al-Khatamy al-Sadir*. It is not clear where these documents were published. Both were given to the author by Fred Halliday.
24 BBC Summary of World Broadcasts, ME/8186 (18 February 1986).
25 Halliday, *Revolution and Foreign Policy*: p. 42.
26 This is disputed by some of Ali Nasir's military supporters, who claim that some of the aircraft attacking them were piloted by Soviets.
27 Lackner, 'Postscript'.
28 Ali Sarraf, *Al-Yaman al-Janubi* (London, 1992): pp. 360, 361.
29 Interview with senior YSP official, August 2009.
30 See *Middle East Contemporary Survey* (*MECS*) (Holmes and Mayer Tel Aviv for 1986–1988).
31 Interview with Politburo members, 1986–89, in 2009.
32 Interview with a businessman who helped manage their patronage networks in the PDRY and outside.
33 Interview with an official who worked for al-Bidh in 1986.

34 BBC Summary of World Broadcasts, ME/8211 (19 March 1986).
35 One of Ali Nasir's advisers says he was present at a meeting arranged by President Hafiz al-Assad in Damascus in 1986 or 1987 between Ali Nasir and Yassin Sa'id Nu'man to discuss a possible reconciliation. There was a second meeting a month later at which Nu'man said that the Politburo had rejected the idea. President al-Assad was upset and warned Nu'man against passing sentences of death on Ali Nasir and his men.
36 BBC Summary of World Broadcasts, ME/8526 (26 March 1987).
37 Ali Nasir spent an increasing amount of time in Damascus from late 1986 but his close associates remained in the YAR and continued to try to undermine the regime in the south.
38 Robert D. Burrowes, 'Oil Strike and Leadership Struggle in South Yemen: 1986 and Beyond', *Middle East Journal* 43: 3 (Summer 1989): pp. 437–54. This article gives a very clear analysis of the situation in PDRY in the period 1986-88 (and an excellent summary of the pre-1986 period). In writing this chapter I have drawn on this article but taken into account the facts that emerged later and the interviews conducted with some of those involved.
39 Yemeni Socialist Party, *Critical and Analytical Document on the Revolutionary Experience in Democratic Yemen (1978–1986)*, (Aden, after 1986).
40 Names given in the conference report include Ali Salih Ubad 'Muqbil', Ali Abd al-Razzaq Ba Dhib and Abd al-Qadir Ba Jammal among those sacked. Ba Jammal was imprisoned after the January 1986 events.
41 BBC Summary of World Broadcasts ME/8371 (23 July 1986).
42 Charles Dunbar, 'The Unification of Yemen: Process, Politics and Prospects', *Middle East Journal* 46: 3 (Summer 1992): pp. 456–76.
43 Robert D. Burrowes, 'The Yemen Arab Republic's Legacy and Yemeni Unification', *Arab Studies Quarterly* 14: 4 (Fall 1992): pp. 41–69.
44 Interview with Haydar al-Attas, Jeddah, May 2009.
45 Halliday, *Revolution and Foreign Policy*: p. 213.

Chapter Eleven

1 There are now many accounts of the politics of the period from the late 1980s to 1994 in English and Arabic. In writing this chapter I have taken account of those in the bibliography but I have tried to tell the story from the perspective of the south, supplementing the literature by looking at the record of what leading southern figures said at the time and by interviewing southern politicians involved in these events.
2 Economist Intelligence Unit, *Country Profile: Yemen* (London, 1994–95): p. 50.
3 Dunbar, 'Unification of Yemen: pp. 456–76.
4 Interview with a former deputy minister in both PDRY and ROY governments.
5 Middle East Contemporary Survey 1989/90.
6 Graz Liesl, 'South Yemen waits for unity', *Middle East International*, 16 March 1990.
7 Interview with a former PDRY deputy minister of interior, June 2009.
8 Quoted by Paul Dresch, *A History of Modern Yemen* (Cambridge, 2000): p. 172.

9 Al-Ashmali, *Al-Wahda wa al-Siraa al-Siyasiya*: p. 176. Other sources give a lower figure.
10 Interview with the adviser in May 2010 who left the PDRY with Ali Nasir in 1986 when he said the debt was $3.5 billion.
11 *Middle East Contemporary Survey (MECS)*, 1989/90.
12 Interview with Central Committee member for 1986–90, who attended meetings of the Politburo as a party secretary.
13 Interview with Yassin Saʿid Nuʿman, March 2010.
14 BBC Summary of World Broadcasts, ME/0193 (2 July 1988).
15 In early 1990, a candidate supported by Sayf Sayl defeated one backed by Salim Salih Muhammad in a bitterly contested local election in Aden.
16 <www.al-bab.com/yemen/biog/jarallah.htm>. See also Jarallah Umar, *Watani aw la Watan* (Sanaʿa, 2003).
17 Jarallah Umar had been educated at Islamic schools before turning to socialism and his former colleagues say that he was seen as an authority on Islam within the YSP.
18 Ali Salih Obad, 'Democracy, the Inexperienced', in Joffe et al., eds, *Yemen Today*: pp. 71–4.
19 Interview with the head of the working party, June 2009.
20 The Central Committee statement is available at <www.al-bab.com/yemen/pol/yspl.htm>.
21 BBC Summary of World Broadcasts, ME/0493 (27 June 1989).
22 Lisa Wedeen, *Peripheral Visions: Publics, Power and Performance in Yemen* (Chicago, 2008): p. 53.
23 BBC Summary of World Broadcasts, ME/0582 (9 October 1989).
24 Interview with Salim Salih Muhammad and with another member of the committee in June 2009.
25 Ali Muhammad al-Sarari, *Al-Hizb al-Ishtiraki wa al-Wahdat al-Yamaniya* (Beirut, 1999): pp. 86–7.
26 Al-Ashmali, *Al-Tarikh al-Siyasiya*: p. 167.
27 Brian Whitaker, *The Birth of Modern Yemen* (e-book): 25 – available at <www.albab.com/yemen/birthofmodernyemen/default.htm>.
28 Interview with a former senior Saudi diplomat, February 2010.
29 Dunbar, 'Unification of Yemen: pp. 456–76.
30 BBC Summary of World Broadcasts, ME/0146 (27 March 1989).
31 See Dunbar, 'Unification of Yemen: pp. 456–76 for a first-hand account by the then US ambassador on the politics of the YAR at the period.
32 BBC Summary of World Broadcasts, ME/0589 (17 October 1989).
33 Interview with Salim Salih Muhammad, June 2009.
34 BBC Summary of World Broadcasts, ME/0623 (25 November 1989).
35 Interviews with Politburo members, 2009.
36 Interview with a deputy minister, February 2010.
37 Interviews with Haydar al-Attas, Salim Salih Muhammad and a member of the Central Committee during 2009.
38 Sinan Abu Luhum gives accounts of conversations he had with Salim Salih Muhammad and other PDRY leaders shortly after the fall of the Berlin Wall. He says that Salim Salih made a brief visit to Moscow and came back quite depressed. Abu Luhum, *Al-Yaman*, vol. 4: p. 25.

39 The idea had been put privately to the PDRY leaders in the late summer of 1989 – see Dunbar, 'Unification of Yemen': pp. 456–76.
40 BBC Summary of World Broadcasts, ME/0623 (24 November 1989).
41 BBC Summary of World Broadcasts, ME/0623 (24 November 1989).
42 The northern delegation thought that al-Bidh, Salim Salih and Muhsin favoured a gradual process while Yassin Sa'id Nu'man, al-Attas and Sa'id Salih favoured a faster process (though from author interviews this assessment was not correct). Luhum, *Al-Yaman*, vol. 4: p. 23.
43 Carapico, Dresch, Burrowes and Dunbar are among those writing in English to describe the background to the unity discussions. There are now several books in Arabic, which give different and sometimes conflicting accounts. Each of the people I interviewed gave slightly different accounts of events. My version takes these others into account and I believe is as accurate as I can make it.
44 Al-Sarari, *Al-Hizb al'Ishtiraki*: pp. 95–107.
45 *Ibid*.
46 Interview with Salim Salih Muhammad, June 2009, and Haydar at-Attas, November 2009.
47 This is not evident from the photograph of the two Ali's signing the agreement in front of smiling ministers from both the YAR and the PDRY.
48 See for example Wedeen, *Peripheral Visions*: p. 235.
49 Interviews with Politburo members of the time in 2009 and 2010.
50 Others have said that Sa'id Salih Salim, the minister of state security, also objected.
51 Interview with Haydar al-Attas, May 2009.
52 BBC Summary of World Broadcasts, ME/W0119 (13 March 1990).
53 BBC Summary of World Broadcasts, ME/0742 (19 April 1990).
54 *Ibid*.
55 The ministers from the south included Salih Ubayd Ahmad (deputy prime minister and minister of security and defence affairs), Muhammad Haydarah Masdus (deputy prime minister for manpower and administrative reform), Salih Munassir al-Siyayli (minister of expatriate affairs), Salih Abu Bakr Bin Husainun (minister of oil), Fadhl Muhsin Abdullah (minister of supply and trade), Muhammad Sa'id Abdullah ('Muhsin' – minister of local administration), Abd al-Aziz al-Dali (minister of state for foreign affairs), Rashid Muhammad Thabit (minister of state for the house of representatives), Faraj bin Ghanim (minister of planning and development) and Haytham Qasim Tahir (minister of defence).
56 BBC Summary of World Broadcasts, ME/0795 (20 June 1990).

Chapter Twelve

1 I have used as background for this chapter the writings of Paul Dresch, Robert Burrowes, Sheila Carapico, Lisa Wedeen and Brian Whitaker, who describe and analyse the events of the period in far greater detail than I have done. While drawing on their works, I have tried to use statements by southern leaders during the period and what I have been told in interviews to complete in this chapter the story of PDRY. I have also used some of the more recently

published work in Arabic. However, it is a summary of the complicated and difficult politics of the period and those interested in getting a fuller picture should read Carapico, *Civil Society in Yemen*; Dresch, *History of Modern Yemen*; Burrowes, 'The Yemen Arab Republic's Legacy'; and Whitaker, *Birth of Modern Yemen*.

2. There is a good summary of the way that Ali Abdullah Salih built up his regime in Burrowes, 'The Yemen Arab Republic's Legacy.'
3. Bonnefoy, 'Salafism in Yemen': pp. 245–62.
4. Carapico, *Civil Society in Yemen*: pp. 17–18.
5. Yemen was the only Arab state on the UN Security Council in 1990, and joined King Hussain of Jordan's call for an 'Arab solution' to the Iraqi occupation. Saudi Arabia and Kuwait saw this as an endorsement of the Iraqi actions. One reason why Kuwait and Saudi Arabia supported the south in the 1994 fighting in Yemen was because al-Bidh had told Saddam Hussein 'to his face' to withdraw from Kuwait at a meeting in Baghdad in 1990. While Iraqi influence had often been strong in the YAR, the PDRY had had difficult relations with Saddam's regime, as noted in earlier chapters of this book.
6. There was some redistribution of lands following the changes of leadership in the PDRY in the 1970s and 1980s, adding to the complications. See Dresch, *History of Modern Yemen*: p. 187.
7. *Ibid.*
8. BBC Summary of World Broadcasts, ME/0954 (3 January 1991).
9. Dresch, *History of Modern Yemen*: p. 191.
10. Interview with an adviser to President Salih from 1990 to 1994, May 2010.
11. BBC Summary of World Broadcasts, ME/1055 (23 April 1991).
12. Dunbar, 'Unification of Yemen': pp. 456–76.
13. Al-Qa'ida had not yet been created, but the ideas that inspired it were present among the many Yemenis who had fought in Afghanistan.
14. Interview with Haydar al-Attas, November 2009.
15. In an interview with a leading supporter of Ali Nasir, he described how he himself had organized some of the attacks on southern opponents, but says that he did so with the help and encouragement of northern security officials. No other sources have reported this.
16. BBC Summary of World Broadcasts, ME/1567 (18 December 1992).
17. Whitaker, 'National Unity and Democracy in Yemen: p. 21–7.
18. Interview with Haydar al-Attas, November 2010.
19. I have used the figures given in Whitaker, *Birth of Modern Yemen*: pp. 138, 139. Other sources give slightly different figures.
20. BBC Summary of World Broadcasts, ME/1868 (10 December 1993).
21. <www.al-bab.com/yemen/pol/eighteen_points.htm>.
22. Haytham died of a heart attack on 9 July 1993.
23. Whitaker, *Birth of Modern Yemen*: p. 144.
24. BBC Summary of World Broadcasts, ME/1744 (19 July 1993).
25. BBC Summary of World Broadcasts, ME/1815 (9 October 1993).
26. Alaini, *50 Years on the Shifting Sands*: pp. 365–7.
27. In October, a nephew was killed in what appeared to be an operation targeting two of Bidh's sons, Adnan and Yanuf, in Aden. A month later there was a further attack on Adnan (who was a police chief in Aden).

NOTES TO PAGES 193–217

28 BBC Summary of World Broadcasts, ME/1828 (23 October 1993).
29 Reuters, 16 October 1993, quoted in Whitaker, *Birth of Modern Yemen*: pp. 149.
30 BBC Summary of World Broadcasts, ME/1854 (November 1993).
31 Hurd and Noakes, *North and South Yemen*: p. 48.
32 BBC Summary of World Broadcasts, ME/1867 (9 December 1993).
33 For a lively and detailed discussion of this period see Carapico, *Civil Society in Yemen*: pp. 170–86.
34 There is a copy of this remarkable document at <armiesofliberation.com/document-of-pledge-and-accord>.
35 Interview with two former PDRY military commanders who made these approaches.
36 Interview with the foreign official, February 2009.
37 For a detailed description and analysis of the civil war see Whitaker, *Birth of Modern Yemen* (Chapter 12), and al-Suwaidi, ed., *The Yemeni War of 1994*.
38 BBC Summary of World Broadcasts, ME/1930 (24 February 1994).
39 Saif, *Strengthening Parliaments*.
40 BBC Summary of World Broadcasts, ME/1984 (29 April 1994).
41 BBC Summary of World Broadcasts, ME/2004 (23 May 1994).
42 Al-Bidh later said that it was Abd al-Rahman al-Jifri that pushed him into secession. See Dresch, *History of Modern Yemen*: p. 196.
43 BBC Summary of World Broadcasts, ME/2004 (23 May 1994).

Chapter Thirteen

1 After 1994 there were changes to the boundaries of the former PDRY provinces, and to some of the adjacent former YAR provinces. Dhala was a new province carved out of the old Lahij and some former YAR territory.
2 Wedeen, *Peripheral Visions*: pp. 23–38.
3 The YSP and Islah had an electoral pact under which they agreed not to compete with each other in some constituencies. The YSP argues that the electoral system is biased against it. Elections due in 2009 were postponed to allow for a dialogue between the GPC and JMP over changes to the electoral process.
4 See for example Thomas Pritzat, 'Land Distribution'.

Appendix A

1 Colonial Office, *General Handbook*.
2 'A Survey of Aden and the Protectorates of South Arabia' (August 1965).
3 British Residency in Aden, *Arab Tribes*: p. 34.

SELECT BIBLIOGRAPHY

The main books and articles I have drawn on are listed below. In addition, I have made extensive use of BBC Summaries of World Broadcasts and the annual series produced by Holmes and Meier of New York in the Middle East Contemporary Survey (MECS) sections on the The People's Democratic Republic of Yemen. I have also drawn on documents available at the British National Archives and the extensive documentary records of the Arab World Documentation Centre of the Institute of Arab and Islamic Studies at Exeter University, as well as private papers kindly provided by the late Fred Halliday, Helen Lackner and John Shipman. I have also used the online documents of Brian Whitaker at <www.al-bab.com/yemen>.

Abu Luhum, S., *Al-Yaman, Haqaiq wa wathaiq ashtiha* (Sana'a, vol. 1, 2004, vols 2 and 3, 2006, vol. 4, 2008).
Abu Talib, H. A., *Al-Siraa shatray al-Yaman: Judhurhu wa taturathu* (Cairo, 1979).
Alaini, M., *50 Years in Shifting Sands* (Beirut, 2004).
Al-Ashmali, M. A., *Al-Wahda wa al-Siraa al-Siyasiya* (Cairo, 2006).
——— *Al-Tarikh al-Siyasi lil-Dawlat al-Haditha* (Cairo, 2002).
Al-Ashtal, A., 'PDRY, Politics in Command', *Race and Class* 17: 3 (1976): pp. 275–80.
Al-Habshi, M. U., *Al-Yaman al-Janubi, siyasiya, iqtisadiya wa ijtima'iya* (Beirut, 1968).
Al-Jifri, A. R., 'No substitute for a Nationally United Yemen', in Joffe et al., eds, *Yemen Today*.
Al-Kuhali, J. U., *Watani aw la Watan, Mawadi maskut anha* (Sana'a, 2003).
Al-Mutawakel, Y., 'Yemeni Unity – Economic Prospects, Yemen Studies', *Korean Journal of Yemeni Studies*, available at <hopia.net/kyc/book/y_perd_e2.htm#1>.

Al-Rasheed, M. and Vitalis, R., *Counter-Narratives: History, Contemporary Society, and Politics in Saudi Arabia and Yemen* (New York, 2004).
Al-Salami, K., *Tears of Sheba: Tales of Survival and Intrigue in Arabia* (London, 2003).
Al-Sarari, A. M., *Hawl al-Wahda al-Yamaniya wa al-intihazia al-Siyasiya wa al-Hizb al-Ishtiraki al-Yamani* (Beirut, 1981).
——— *Al-Hizb al-Ishtiraki wa al-Wahda al-Yamaniya* (Beirut, 1999).
Al-Shu'aybi, M. A., *Jumhuriya al-Yaman al-Dimuqratiya al-Sha'biya, Dirasat fi al-Tanmiya al-Iqlimiya wa mushkilha* (Aden, 1971).
Al-Sururi, A., *Tajraba al-Yaman al-Dimuqratiya* (Beirut, 2001).
Al-Suwaidi, J. S., ed., *The Yemeni War of 1994: Causes and Consequences* (Abu Dhabi, 1995).
Ali, H. and Whittingham, K., 'Notes towards an Understanding of the Revolution in South Yemen', *Race and Class* 16: 1 (July 1974): pp. 83–110.
Ali, S. R., *An Important Speech Delivered on the Tenth Anniversary of Glorious National Independence* (Aden, 1977 – in Arabic).
Amin, S. H., *Law and Justice in Contemporary Yemen: People's Democratic Republic of Yemen and Yemen Arab Republic* (Glasgow, 1987).
Amnesty International, *The People's Democratic Republic of Yemen* (London, 1976).
Anthony, John Duke, 'The Communist Party of the People's Democratic Republic of Yemen: An Analysis of its Strengths and Weaknesses', in Pridham, ed., *Contemporary Yemen*.
Arif, M., 'People's Democratic Republic of Yemen Seeks to Develop Productive Capacity of Economy', *IMF Survey*, April 1983: pp. 119–22.
Behbehani, H. S. H., *China and the People's Democratic Republic of Yemen* (London, 1985).
Belhaven, The Master of, *The Kingdom of Melchior* (London, 1949).
Bidwell, R., *The Two Yemens* (Harlow, 1983).
Blaustein, A. P. and Flanz, G. M., 'People's Democratic Republic of Yemen', Constitutions of the Countries of the World Series (New York, 1972).
Bonnefoy, L., 'Salafism in Yemen', in al-Rasheed, M., ed., *Kingdom without Borders* (London, 2008): pp. 245–62.
British Residency in Aden in 1986, *Arab Tribes in the Vicinity of Aden* (London, 2008).
Bujra, A. S., *The Politics of Stratification: A Study of Political Change in a South Arabian Town* (Oxford, 1971).

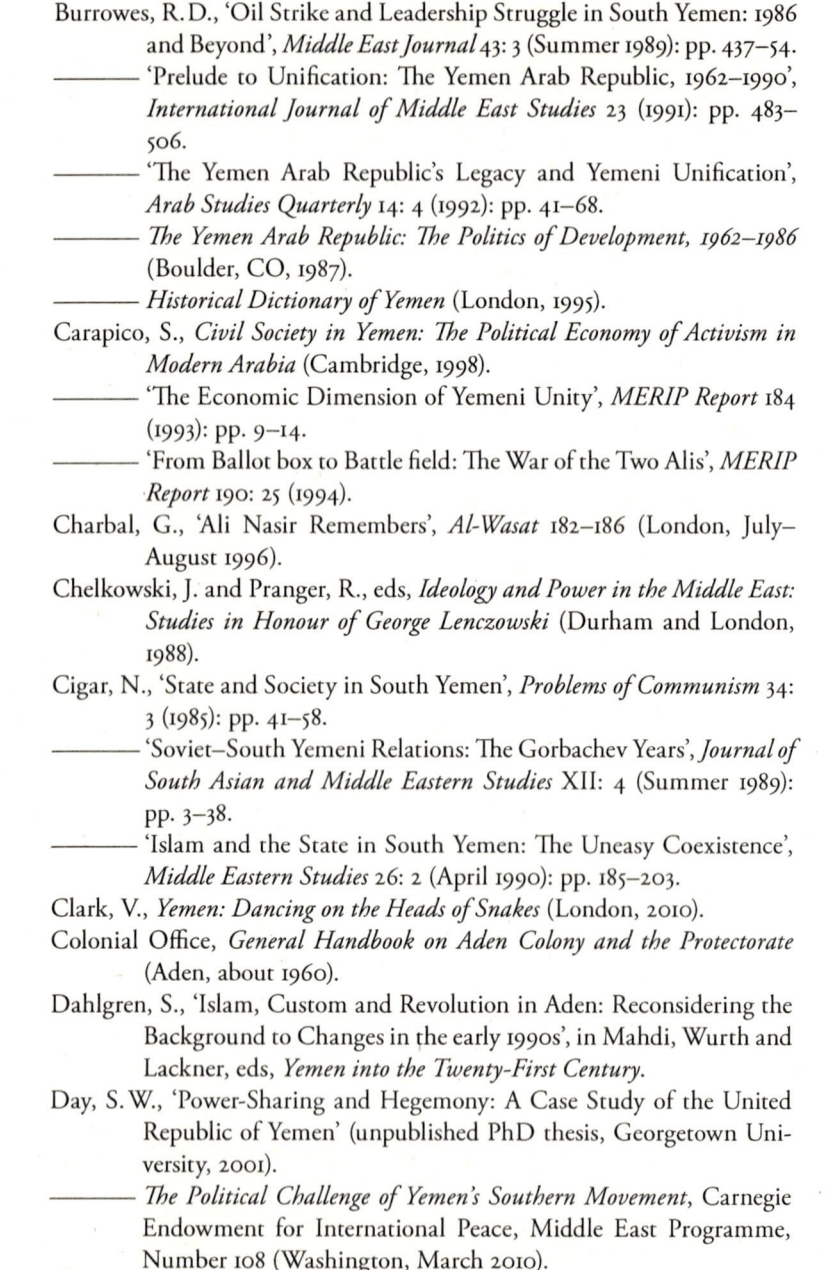

Burrowes, R.D., 'Oil Strike and Leadership Struggle in South Yemen: 1986 and Beyond', *Middle East Journal* 43: 3 (Summer 1989): pp. 437–54.
—— 'Prelude to Unification: The Yemen Arab Republic, 1962–1990', *International Journal of Middle East Studies* 23 (1991): pp. 483–506.
—— 'The Yemen Arab Republic's Legacy and Yemeni Unification', *Arab Studies Quarterly* 14: 4 (1992): pp. 41–68.
—— *The Yemen Arab Republic: The Politics of Development, 1962–1986* (Boulder, CO, 1987).
—— *Historical Dictionary of Yemen* (London, 1995).
Carapico, S., *Civil Society in Yemen: The Political Economy of Activism in Modern Arabia* (Cambridge, 1998).
—— 'The Economic Dimension of Yemeni Unity', *MERIP Report* 184 (1993): pp. 9–14.
—— 'From Ballot box to Battle field: The War of the Two Alis', *MERIP Report* 190: 25 (1994).
Charbal, G., 'Ali Nasir Remembers', *Al-Wasat* 182–186 (London, July–August 1996).
Chelkowski, J. and Pranger, R., eds, *Ideology and Power in the Middle East: Studies in Honour of George Lenczowski* (Durham and London, 1988).
Cigar, N., 'State and Society in South Yemen', *Problems of Communism* 34: 3 (1985): pp. 41–58.
—— 'Soviet–South Yemeni Relations: The Gorbachev Years', *Journal of South Asian and Middle Eastern Studies* XII: 4 (Summer 1989): pp. 3–38.
—— 'Islam and the State in South Yemen: The Uneasy Coexistence', *Middle Eastern Studies* 26: 2 (April 1990): pp. 185–203.
Clark, V., *Yemen: Dancing on the Heads of Snakes* (London, 2010).
Colonial Office, *General Handbook on Aden Colony and the Protectorate* (Aden, about 1960).
Dahlgren, S., 'Islam, Custom and Revolution in Aden: Reconsidering the Background to Changes in the early 1990s', in Mahdi, Wurth and Lackner, eds, *Yemen into the Twenty-First Century*.
Day, S.W., 'Power-Sharing and Hegemony: A Case Study of the United Republic of Yemen' (unpublished PhD thesis, Georgetown University, 2001).
—— *The Political Challenge of Yemen's Southern Movement*, Carnegie Endowment for International Peace, Middle East Programme, Number 108 (Washington, March 2010).

Dresch, P., *Tribes, Government and History in Yemen* (Oxford, 1989).
——— 'The Tribal Factor in the Yemeni Crisis', in al-Suwaidi, ed., *The Yemeni War of 1994*.
——— *A History of Modern Yemen* (Cambridge, 2000).
Dresch, P. and Haykel, B., 'Stereotypes and Political Styles: Islamists and Tribesfolk in Yemen', *International Journal of Middle East Studies* 27: 4 (1995): pp. 405–31.
Dunbar, C., 'The Unification of Yemen: Process, Politics and Prospects', *Middle East Journal* 46: 3 (Summer 1992): pp. 456–76.
Efrat, M., 'The People's Democratic of Republic of Yemen: Scientific Socialism on Trial in an Arab Country', in Wiles, ed., *New Communist Third World*: pp. 165–201.
Embassy of the People's Democratic Republic of Yemen, London, *The Present and Future of the People's Democratic Republic of Yemen* (London, c. April 1975).
——— *The Political Report Presented by Comrade Abdel Fattah Isma'il to the Unification Congress* (September 1977).
Enders, K., Williams, S., Choueiri, N., Sobolev, Y. and Walliser, J., eds, *Yemen in the 1990s: From Unification to Economic Reform* (New York, 2002).
Executive Committee of the National Front, *Kayf nafham tajraba al-Yaman al-Janubiya al-Sha'biya?* (Beirut, 1968).
Foreign and Commonwealth Office, *Soviet, East European and Western Development Aid, 1976–1982* (London, 1983).
Foster, D., *Landscape with Arabs: Travels in Aden and South Arabia* (Brighton, 1969).
Gause, F.G., 'Yemeni Unity: Past and Future', *Middle East Journal* 42: 1 (1988): pp. 33–47.
——— *Saudi–Yemeni Relations: Domestic Structures and Foreign Influence* (New York, 1990).
Gavin, R.J., *Aden under British Rule, 1939–1967* (London, 1975).
Groom, N., *Sheba Revealed: A Posting in Bayhan in the Yemen* (London, 2002).
——— 'A Passage to Yafa (1891–1967)', *British Yemeni Society Journal* (London, 2007), available at <www.al-bab.com/bys/articles/editor07.htm>.
Gueyras, J., 'The Last Days of Ali Nasir', *MERIP Report* 141 (July–August 1986): pp. 37–40.
Hadi, N., *17 Sa'at tarikhiya and Bab al-Yaman* (Beirut, 1978).
Halliday, F., *Arabia without Sultans* (London, 1974).

────── 'The People's Democratic Republic of Yemen', in White et al., eds, *Revolutionary Socialist Development in the Third World* Sussex, 1983).

────── 'The Third Inter-Yemeni War and its Consequences' *Asian Affairs* 26: 2 (1985): pp. 131–40.

────── 'Catastrophe in South Yemen' *Middle East Report* 139 (1986): pp. 37–9.

────── 'Yemen's Unfinished Revolution: Socialism in the South' *MERIP Report* 81 (1989): pp. 3–20.

────── *Revolution and Foreign Policy: The Case of South Yemen, 1967–1987* (Cambridge, 1990).

Harding, J., *Roads to Nowhere: A South Arabian Odyssey, 1960–1965* (London, 2009).

Hawatmah, N., *Azmat al-Thawra fi al-Janub al-Yamani* (Beirut, 1968).

Haykel, B., *Revival and Reform in Islam: The Legacy of Muhammad al-Shawkani* (Cambridge, 2003).

Hickenbotham, T., *Aden* (London, 2003).

Hinchcliffe, P., Ducker, J. T. and Holt, M., *Without Glory in Arabia: The British Retreat from Aden* (London, 2006).

Hopwood, D., ed., *The Arabian Peninsula: Society and Politics* (London, 1972).

Hurd, Robert and Noakes, Greg, *North and South Yemen: Lead-up to the Break-up*, Washington Report on Middle East Affairs, July–August 1994.

Ingrams, H., *Arabia and the Isles*, 2nd edn (London, 1952).

────── *The Yemen: Rulers and Revolutions* (London, 1963).

International Development Agency, *Yemen: Southern Governorates Development Project* (New York, 1997).

International Fund of Agricultural Development, *Report of the Special Programming Mission to Peoples' Democratic Republic of Yemen* (Rome, June 1983).

International Monetary Fund, *PDRY: Recent Economic Developments* (1972, 1974, 1976, 1977, 1978).

────── *Staff Report for Consultation*: (1972, 1973, 1976, 1977, 1978, 1979).

Ishiyama, J., 'The Sickle and the Minaret: Communist Successor Parties in Yemen and Afghanistan after the Cold War', *Middle East Review of International Affairs* 9: 1 (March 2005).

Ismael, T. and Ismael, J., *The People's Democratic Republic of Yemen: Politics, Economics and Society: The Politics of Socialist Transformation* (London, 1986).

Isma'il, Abd al-Fattah, 'How We Liberated Aden', *MERIP Report* 1971.
────── *Political Report of the National Front Political Organisation* (Aden, 2 March 1972).
────── *Al-Taqrir al-Siyasi li-Lajna al-Markaziya ila al-Mu'tamar al-Am al-Sadis lil-tanthim al-Siyasi al-Jabha al-Qawmiya alidhi madam al-Amin al-Am lil-Lajna al-Markaziya* (Aden, 1975).
────── *The Present and the Future of the People's Democratic Republic of Yemen* (PDRY Embassy, London, 1977).
────── *Watha'iq al-Mu'tamar al-Ula lil-Hizb al-Ishtiraki al-Yamani* (Beirut, 1979).
────── *Al-Mu'tamar lil-Hizb al-Ishtiraki al-Yamani, October 1978* (Aden, 1979).
────── *Hawl al-Thawra al-Wataniya al-Dimuqratiya wa afaqiha al-Ishtirakiya* (Beirut, 1979).
Jallul, Faysal, *Al-Yaman: al-Thawratan, al-Jumhuriyatan, al-Wahda 1967–1994* (Beirut, 1999).
Joffe, E. G. H., Hachemi, M. J. and Watkins, E. W., eds, *Yemen Today: Crisis and Solutions* (London, 1997).
Johnson, C. H., *The View from Steamer Point* (London, 1964).
Jones, C., *Britain and the Yemeni Civil War 1962–1965* (Sussex, 2004).
Katz, M. N., 'Civil Conflict in South Yemen', *Middle East Review* (Fall 1986): pp. 7–11.
────── 'Yemeni Unity and Saudi Security', *Middle East Policy* 1: 1 (1992): pp. 117–35.
Kelly, J. B., 'Hadhramaut, Oman, Dhufar: The Experience of Revolution', *Middle Eastern Studies* 12: 2 (May 1976): pp. 213–30.
Khimov, B. J. and Gosarov, F. I., *Iqtisad Jumhuriya al-Yaman al-Dimuqratiya al-Sha'biya* (Aden, 1981).
Kostiner, J., 'Arab Radical Politics: al-Qawmiyyun al-Arab and the Marxists in the Turmoil of South Yemen', *Middle Eastern Studies* 17:4 (1981): pp. 454–77.
────── *The Struggle for South Yemen* (London, 1984).
────── *South Yemen's Revolutionary Strategy, 1970–85: From Insurgency to Bloc Politics* (Jerusalem, 1990).
────── *Yemen. The Tortuous Quest for Unity, 1990–94* (London, 1996).
Lackner, H., *People's Democratic Republic of Yemen: Outpost of Socialist Development in Arabia* (London, 1985).
────── unpublished paper, 'Postscript: 13 January 1986, before and after'.
Landau, J. M., 'Soviet Works on the Arabian Peninsula', *Middle Eastern Studies* 21: 1 (January 1985): pp. 89–92.

Leveau, R., Mermier, F. and Steinback, U., *Le Yemen Contemporain* (Paris, 1999).
Little, T., *South Arabia: Arena of Conflict* (London, 1968).
Luqman, A. M., 'Education and the Press in South Arabia', in Hopwood, ed., *The Arabian Peninsula*.
Mahdi, K. A., Wurth, A. and Lackner, H., eds, *Yemen into the Twenty-First Century: Continuity and Change* (Reading, 2007).
Makkawi, A., *Shihad fi al-Tarikh* (Cairo, 1979).
Mannea, E., 'Yemen, the Tribe and the State', paper presented to the International Colloquium on Islam and Social Change at the University of Lausanne on 10–11 October 1996, available at <www.al-bab.com/yemen/soc/manea1.htm>.
Mawby, S., 'From Tribal Rebellions to Revolution: British Counter-Insurgency Operations in Southwest Arabia 1955–67', *Electronic Journal of International History*, available at <www.history.ac.uk/resources/e-journal-international-history/mawby-paper>.
Molyneux, M., *State Policies and the Position of Women Workers in the People's Democratic Republic of Yemen (1966–77)*, (Geneva, 1982).
Molyneux, M., Yafai, A., Mohsen, A. and Ba'abad, N., 'Women and Revolution in the People's Democratic Republic of Yemen', *Feminist Review* 1 (1979): pp. 4–20.
Mondesir, S. L., *A Select Bibliography of the Yemen Arab Republic and the People's Democratic Republic of Yemen* (Durham, c. 1975).
Muhammad, A. N., *Al-Mu'tamar l-Istithnafi lil-Hizb al-Ishtiraki al-Yamani* (Aden, 1980).
Muhammad, S. S., *Dhakriyat wa ahadith 'an al-Nidhal al-Watani wa al-Wahdawi* (Sana'a, 2004).
——— *Al-Gharba lays Watanna* (Sana'a, 2007).
Muqbil, A. S., *Uktubar: al-thawra al-tahriri al-Musalaha fi al-Janub (1963–1967)*, (Sana'a, undated).
Mylroie, L., *Politics and the Soviet Presence in the People's Democratic Republic of Yemen: Internal Vulnerabilities and Regional Challenges* (Washington, 1983).
Nashir, S., *Yahya al-Mutawakkil, Hudur fi Qalb al-Tarikh* (Sana'a, 2003).
Naumkin, V. V., *Red Wolves of Yemen: The Struggle for Independence* (New York and Cambridge, 2004).
Obad, A. S., 'Democracy: The Inexperienced', in Joffe et al., eds, *Yemen Today*.
Ozoling, V. and Andreasyan, R. N., 'Some Problems Arising in the Process of Noncapitalist Development of the PDRY', paper presented

at the International Symposium on Contemporary, Yemen, Exeter University, 1983.
Page, S., *The Soviet Union and the Yemens: Influence in Asymmetrical Relationships* (New York, 1985).
PDRY Ministry of Culture and Information, *Aden's Bloody Monday* (Aden, 1986).
PDRY Petroleum and Minerals Board, *Petroleum Opportunities in Yemen* (Aden, c. 1983).
Peterson, J. E., 'Conflict in the Yemens and Superpower Involvement', Centre for Contemporary Arab Studies, Occasional Papers Series (Washington, 1981).
—— 'The Yemen Arab Republic and the Politics of Balance', *Asian Affairs* CII: 3 (October 1981).
—— 'Yemen: The Search for a Modern State', in Pridham, ed., *Contemporary Yemen*.
—— 'Tribes and Politics in Yemen', Arabian Peninsula Background Note No. APBN-007, published on <www.JEPeterson.net>, December 2008.
Pridham, B. R., ed., *Contemporary Yemen: Politics and Historical Background* (Kent, 1984).
—— *Economy, Society and Culture in Contemporary Yemen* (London, 1985).
Primakov, Yevgeniy, *Russia and the Arabs* (New York, 2009).
Pritzat, T., 'Land Distribution after Unification and its Consequences for Urban Development in Hadramawt', in Mahdi et al., eds, *Yemen into the Twenty-First Century: Continuity and Change* (Reading, 2007).
Saif, A. A., *Strengthening Parliaments in Conflict/Post-Conflict Situations: Case Study on Yemen* (UNDP publications, 2005), available at <www.pogar.org/governance/publications.asp>.
—— *The Politics of Survival and Structural Control in the Unified Yemen, 1990–1997*, MA Dissertation at the University of Exeter, 1988, available at <www.al-bab.com/yemen/unity/saif1.htm#Introduction>.
Sarraf, A., *Al-Yaman al-Janubi: al-Hayat al-Siyasiya min al-Isti'mar ila al-Wahdah* (London, 1992).
Schmitz, C. P., *State and Market in South Yemen* (unpublished PhD thesis, University of California, Berkeley, 1997).
Sergeant, R. B., *The Sayyids of Hadhramaut* (London, 1957).
—— 'The Two Yemens: Historical Perspectives and Present Attitudes', *Asian Affairs* 60: 1 (February 1973): pp. 3–16.

—— 'Both Sides of al-Mandab', *Swedish Research Institute in Istanbul, Transactions*, vol. 2 (13 May 1988).
Shaif, A. G., *The Yemeni Civil War of 1994: A Crisis of Leadership* (Sheffield, 1995).
Shamiry, Naguib A. R., 'The Judicial System in Democratic Yemen', in Pridham, ed., *Contemporary Yemen*.
Shipman, J., 'The Hadhramaut', *Asian Affairs* 15: 2 (June 1984).
Stanzel, V., 'Marxism in Arabia: South Yemen Twenty Years After Independence', *Aussenpolitik* 39: 3 (1988): pp. 265–77.
Stevenson, T., 'Yemeni Workers Come Home: Reabsorbing One Million Migrants', *MERIP Report* 181 (1993): pp. 15–20.
Stookey, R. W., *South Yemen: A Marxist Republic in Arabia* (Colorado, 1982).
Stork, J., 'Socialist Revolution in Arabia: Report from the People's Democratic Republic of Yemen', *MERIP Report* 15 (March 1973): pp. 1–25.
Trabulsi F., *Wu'ud Adan: Rihlat Yamaniya* (Beirut, 2000).
Trevaskis, K., *Shades of Amber* (London, 1967).
Trevelyan, H., *The Middle East in Revolution* (London, 1970).
Unified Political Organization of the National front, *Al-Mu'tamar al-Tawhidi* (Beirut, 1975).
Van Hear, N., 'The Socio-Economic Impact of the Involuntary Mass Return to Yemen in 1990' *Journal of Refugee Studies* 7: 1 (1990): pp. 18–38.
Walker, J., *Aden Insurgency: The Savage War in South Arabia 1962–67* (London, 2005).
Wedeen, L. 'Seeing Like a Citizen, Acting Like a State: Exemplary Events in Unified Yemen', *Comparative Studies in Society and History* 45: 4 (2003): pp. 680–713.
—— *Peripheral Visions: Publics, Power, and Performance in Yemen* (Chicago, 2008).
Weir, S., 'A Clash of Fundamentalisms: Wahhabism in Yemen', *MERIP Report* 204 (1997): pp. 22–6.
Welton, M., *The Establishment of Northern Hegemony in the Process of Yemeni Unification* (1997), available at <www.al-bab.com/yemen/unity/mw0.htm>.
Wenner, M., 'Ideology versus Pragmatism in South Yemen, 1968–1986', in Chelkowski and Pranger, eds, *Ideology and Power in the Middle East: Studies in Honour of George Lenczowski* (Durham and London, 1988).
Whitaker, B., 'National Unity and Democracy in Yemen: A Marriage of Inconvenience', Joffe et al., eds, *Yemen Today*.

——— *The Birth of Modern Yemen* (2009) e-book, available at <www.albab.com/yemen/birthofmodernyemen/default.htm>.
White, G., Murray, R. and White, C., eds, *Revolutionary Socialist Development in the Third World* (Sussex, 1983).
Wiles, P., ed., *The New Communist Third World: An Essay in Political Economy* (New York, 1982).
Willis, J.M., 'Making Yemen Indian: Rewriting the Boundaries of Imperial Arabia', *International Journal of Middle East Studies* 41: 1 (February 2009): pp. 23–38.
World Bank, *People's Democratic Republic of Yemen: A Review of Economic and Social Development* (Washington, 1979).
——— 'Structural Economic Reforms in the Republic of Yemen', paper presented to Consultative Group Meeting for Yemen (Brussels, 19–20 January 1997).
Yemeni Socialist Party, *Bayan Sadir an al-Lajna al-Markaziya lil-Hizb al-Ishtiraki al-Yamany Hawl al-Awda al-Rahina* (Aden, 1978).
——— *The Constitution of the PDRY* (Aden, 1978).
——— *Al-Mu'tamar al-Ula lil-hizb al-Ishtirakiya al-Yamani* (Beirut, 1979).
——— *Critical and Analytical Document on the Revolutionary Experience in Democratic Yemen (1978–1986)*, (Aden, after 1986).
——— *Salih Muslih Qasim fi Rihab al-Khalidin* (Aden, 1986).
——— *Proposed Political Solution to the Crises Existing in the Yemeni Socialist Party in the People's Democratic Republic of Yemen* (Aden, 1986).
——— *Al-Bayan al-Siyasi al-Khatamy al-Sadir an umal al-dawra al-thalatha lil-jabha al-Markaziya lil-Hizb al-Ishtiraki al-Yamani* (Aden, 1986).
——— *Sajil al-Khalidin min Shuhada al-Hizb fi 13 Yanair al-Dami* (Aden, 1986).
——— *Political Report to the 1987 Conference* (English translation in typescript).

INDEX

No attempt has been made to find an equivalent of the European 'surname' to index on, so personal names should be looked up as written (A'yda Ali al-Yaf'i appears just so). However, if actors are sufficiently well known to be generally referred to using a single name (e.g. al-Attas), they are listed under this name (e.g. al-Attas, Haydar). Titles (President, Colonel, Shaikh, etc.) have been omitted.

13 January violence (1986) 151–62

A'yda Ali al-Yaf'i 72
Abbud Brigade 57, 119
Abd al-Aziz Abd al-Ghani 193
Abd al-Aziz Abd al-Wali 38, 58, 109, 110, 124, 128
Abd al-Aziz al-Dali 129, 134, 154–6, 163, 169
Abd al-Ghani Abd al-Qadir 109, 121
Abd al-Majid al-Zindani 180, 184, 188, 193
Abd al-Malik Isma'il 38
Abd al-Qadir al-Amin 17
Abd al-Qadir Ba Jamal 131, 134, 175, 197
Abd al-Qawi Makkawi 11, 105, 113, 196–7
Abd Rubbuh Mansur Hadi 210, 212, 216
Abd al-Rahman al-Iryani 75–6
Abd al-Rahman al-Jifri 185, 196, 198
Abd al-Wakeel al-Sururi 106–7, 130
Abd al-Wasi Sallam 188
Abdali tribe 215
Abdullah Abd al-Alim 77
Abdullah al-Ahmar 184, 188, 190, 192–3
Abdullah al-Ashtal 38, 196
Abdullah al-Asnaj 5, 11–12, 14, 20, 34, 196
Abdullah al-Sallal 9, 13
Abdullah Salih Ulaywa 153, 162
Abdullah Ba Dibh School for Scientific Socialism
  see Higher School of Scientific Socialism
Abdullah Bukair 154
Abdullah Salih al-Awlaqi 29
Abu Bakr Abd al-Razzaq Ba Dhib 56, 63, 120, 123, 134, 196, 220
Abyan xi, 3, 21, 27, 31, 36, 37, 40, 41, 46, 53, 54, 57, 58, 61, 64, 66, 71, 72, 95–8, 100, 101, 105, 110, 121, 125–33, 140, 152–3, 156, 162, 170, 187–8, 190–2, 194–5, 201–3, 205, 210–11, 215–17, 218, 219
Aden, as port 5, 66; British and xviii, 4-13; coup of 14 October (1966) 26; sacked by Islah 198; shanty towns 140; terrorist incidents 25
Aden Protectorate Levies (APL) 4, 6, 9–10
Aden Trade Union Congress (ATUC) 5, 11, 19, 22, 23
agriculture 64–6, 68, 137, 138
Ahmad Abdullah Abdillahi 124, 128
Ahmad Abdullah al-Hassani 126, 128, 155, 162

INDEX

Ahmad Abdullah Muhammad Hassani 153
Ahmad al-Ghashmi 76–7, 94, 97
Ahmad al-Sallami 196
Ahmad Husain Musa 162
Ahmad Musa'id Husain 128, 131, 134, 162, 197
al-Attas, Haydar 68, 109, 124, 131, 134, 147, 154–6, 159, 162, 168, 170, 178, 179; al-Bidh and 160; appointed premier of PDRY (1985) 131; appointed president of PDRY 151; appointed premier of ROY (1990) 182; attacked (1992) 188; DRY and 196; in exile 201–2; on Nasir 137; retains premiership (1993) 192; Soviet Union and 165–6; on unity 173
al-Attas, Umar Ali *see* Umar Ali al-Attas
al-Bidh, Ali Salim 26, 27, 28, 29, 33, 37, 38, 57, 96, 109, 118, 123, 130, 131, 132, 144, 151, 155, 156, 159, 180, 181, 193, 210; after 13 January 159–62; al-Attas and 160; appointed Secretary General of the YSP 151; appointed vice president of the Republic of Yemen 182; coup (March 1968) and 39–40; disillusioned with unity 193–4; and DRY 196; flees 198; in exile 201–2; lone survivor 169–71; meets imams 164; reform and 172; returns 129; signs Pledge (1994) 194–5; suspended 125; unity and 176–7, 189–90, 208–9; visits United States 193
al-Hiraak *see* Southern Mobility Movement
al Huthi rebellion xix, 203
al-Kathiri 7–8
al-Khamiri, Abdullah 23, 24, 35, 38, 46, 96, 123–4, 128, 134, 156, 163
al-Qu'ayti 7–8
al-Qa'ida in the Arabian Peninsula (AQAP) xix, 203
al-Tali'a (Popular Vanguard Party) 14, 38, 88, 91, 106–7, 127, 135

Alawi Husain Farhan 162
Algeria 167
Ali As'ad Muthuna 109, 157
Ali Ba Dhib 105, 109, 123, 220
Ali bin Naji al-Kadr 75
Ali Nasir Muhammad *see* Muhammad, Ali Nasir
Ali Salih Ubad *see* Muqbil
Ali Salim al-Kindi 46
Ali Salim Law'ar 99; rehabilitated 182
Ali Shaikh Omar 159
Ali Shaya Hadi 16, 61, 98, 215; killed 151; versus Nasir 134–5
amnesty (1990) 182
Amnesty International 63
Andropov, Yuri 145
Anis Hassan Yahya 56, 101, 109, 134, 162
Antar, Ali 16, 19, 23, 24, 36, 38, 40, 45, 48, 61, 83, 101, 109, 110, 111, 118, 123, 144, 155, 202, 205, 215–16; departs 125–6; killed 151; versus Nasir 128-136; versus Salmin 95–6
Arab League 10, 20–1, 23, 32, 79–80, 112
armed forces/army 18, 32–43, 46, 49, 53, 58, 60–1, 65, 76, 85, 91, 96–8, 112, 119, 122, 125, 127, 132, 152, 170, 177; *see also* Popular Defence Forces
assassinations after unity 188–9
Awdhali tribe 4, 19, 27, 43, 54, 101, 127, 216
Awlaqi tribe 4, 6, 7, 9, 26–7, 29, 41–2, 44–5, 69, 74, 127–8, 197, 202, 215, 217, 219

Ba Dhib, Abdullah Abd al-Razzaq 15, 56, 65, 105
Ba Dhib, Abu Bakr 120, 123–4, 134, 196
Ba Dhib, Ali 105, 109, 123–4
Ba'ath Party 14–15, 33, 38, 156, 191; *see also* al-Tali'a
Bahrain 93
Bayhan 217
Barre, Siad 80, 83

INDEX

Berlin Wall falls (9 November 1989) 177, 208
bombing 70
Brezhnev, Leonid 81–2, 116, 143–5
Britain 84–5; aid to Yemen 29, 33, 43
British Petroleum (BP) 23, 64, 65

Cable & Wireless 65
Carapico 195
Carter, President Jimmy 113
Castro, Fidel 84, 158
Chernenko, Konstantin 145
China 18, 25, 48, 53, 66, 77, 82, 84, 85, 87, 116
civil war 195–8
COMECON (Council for Mutual Economic Assistance) 115
Communism 32, 46, 55, 56, 59, 65, 80, 84, 101, 117–18, 156, 205–6
Communist Party 33, 156
Communist Party of the Soviet Union (CPSU) 18, 73, 81,115–16, 165–6, 206
Corrective Move *see* Glorious Corrective Move
coups: 14 October 1966 26; 20 March 1968 39–40
Cuba 61–2, 83; events of 13 January and 158–9; *see also* Castro, Fidel

Dathina 9, 19, 27, 42, 43, 45, 54, 101, 217
DDR *see* East Germany
Debray, Régis 25
Democratic Republic of Yemen (DRY) 196–7, 209
Dhala xix, 9, 11, 19, 23, 26–7, 37, 43, 58, 201
Dunbar, Charles 175, 180, 188

East Germany 62, 83, 116; demands repayment 168; support for State Security 62, 82, 83, 206; violence of 13 January and 159
Eastern Aden Protectorate (EAP) 5, 10
economic policies
    Under Qahtan al-Sha'bi 43
    Under Salmin 64–8, 92
    Under Abd al-Fattah Isma'il 111
    Under Ali Nasir Muhammad 137–40
    1986–90 164, 180
education 22, 72, 92
Egypt 80, 81, 146, 166, 204; June War (1963) 12–13; Nasser and 8–9; NLF and 23–4; Syria and 14
elections: 1986 162, 172; 1993 190–1
Ethiopia 80, 83, 97, 116, 147, 159, 167
expulsions from Saudi Arabia (1990) 185

Fadhl Muhsin Abdullah 101, 170, 196, 202
Fadhli 6, 9, 53, 58, 95, 98, 101, 105, 188, 190, 198, 201, 202, 210, 215–17
Fahd bin Abd al-Aziz, King 146
Fanon, Frantz 25
Faris *see* Ahmad Umar
Faruq Ali Ahmad 162
Fattahiyin 163, 165, 170, 171
Faysal Abd al-Latif al-Sha'bi 15–17, 21, 26, 29, 33–4, 37, 38, 42, 48, 215; resignation 44; shot 46, 63; rehabilitated 182
Faysal al-Attas 37
Faysal bin Shamlan 34, 197, 202
Faysal, King 78
Findlay, Paul 85
fishing 67–8, 138–9, 143
five-year plans 137–9, 164
floods 138, 142–3, 145
food prices 66, 164, 168, 170, 186
foreign policy 73–4; under Qahtan al-Sha'bi 47–9; under Salmin 77–85, 92–3; under Abd al-Fattah Isma'il 112–17; under Ali Nasir Muhammad 143–7; 1986–90 158, 166
Federal Regular Army (FRA) 10, 217
France 84–5
freedom of expression 63
Front for the Liberation of South Yemen (FLOSY) 11–12, 20, 23–4, 25–7, 32, 41, 48, 217; in defeat 29, 31

General People's Congress (GPC) xv,

INDEX

179, 181–91, 193,
Glorious Collective Move (22 June 1969) 45, 46, 53, 56, 57, 59–61, 65, 81, 84, 85–7, 89–90,147
Gorbachev, Mikhail 159, 166
Guevara, Che 25

Habbash, George 15, 16, 80, 130
Hadhramaut 6–8, 12, 28, 32, 37, 57, 70, 159, 168, 191
Hadhrami Bedouin Legion (HBL) 8, 28, 29
Hadi Ahmad Nasir 123, 126, 128, 131–2; death sentence 162
Halliday, Fred xxi, 25, 99, 144
Hassan al-Bayumi 11
Hawi, George 84
Haytham Qasim Tahir 132, 136, 152, 155, 156, 161, 163, 180, 187, 195, 198
health 22, 73, 92
Higher School of Scientific Socialism 56, 80, 81, 88, 91, 95, 106, 117, 127, 206
Hiswa power station 144, 166
housing 73
human rights 63, 95
Husain Qumatah 97–8, 101, 128; suicide 129
Hussain, King 194
Hussein, Saddam 146, 208

Ibrahim al-Hamdi 76, 93–4, 99
illiteracy 39, 73, 90
Imam Badr 9
Ingrams, Harold 8
International Monetary Fund (IMF) 209
Iran 81, 146, 167
Iraq 80, 117, 146, 167
Islah (Yemeni Congregation for Reform) 184, 188, 190–2
Islam 22, 35, 70–1, 164, 171, 173, 183, 190
Sunnis and Shi'a 3; see also Salafism, shariah law, Wahhabism
Isma'il, Abd al-Fattah 7, 16, 17, 21, 23, 24, 27, 29, 33, 36, 38, 39, 43, 55, 56–8, 61, 69, 75, 81, 105, 109, 121,134, 154, 155, 156, 206; at Sixth Congress 88–91; Brezhnev and 116; critique of Nasir's government 131–2; foreign policy and 74; as general secretary 45, 54; as president 105–21; killed 151–2; Kosygin and 116; Marxism of 54; Nasir and 117–21, 129–32, 134–5; on Islam 70–1; on NF 56; plot to restore 129–30; rebellion of May 1968 and 41–2; removal of 120–1; Salmin and 86–91, 93–7, 100–1; after Salmin 110; at YSP launch 106; see also Fattahiyin
Israel: June War (1963) 12–13

Ja'am Salih Muhammad 58, 99; rehabilitated 182
Jarallah Umar 107, 124, 165, 169, 170–1, 173, 178, 190, 192, 197

Khalid Muhammad Abd al-Aziz 29
Kosygin, Alexei 115–16
Kurds 117
Kuwait 67, 79, 138, 166

Lahij xi, xix, 3, 6, 8, 9, 10, 12, 19, 21, 25, 26, 27, 31, 37, 41, 57–8, 61, 64, 66, 71–2, 96, 101, 121, 125–8, 130, 132, 133, 140, 152–3, 155–7, 159, 161, 163, 170–1, 177, 192, 197, 201, 205, 210–11, 215–16, 218, 219
liberalization 173–4, 180, 184–5
Libya 75–6, 79–80, 113, 147, 165

Mahdi Ahmad Salih 99
Mahra x, 1, 6, 11, 18, 27–9, 37, 71, 77, 119, 121, 127
Maoism 37, 41, 66; Salmin and 53–4, 86–7
Marhaba see Nasir Muhammad, Ali
Marxism 16, 21, 22, 31, 36, 212; Isma'il and 54; NLF and 25; see also Communism, Communist Party, Maoism, Soviet Union

Mengistu Haile Mariam 147, 154, 159, 167
Mohammed Ahmad al-Bishi 29
Mohsen Alaini 47, 74, 75
Movement of Arab Nationalists (MAN) 15–18
Mu'ammar al-Qadhafi 165
Mubarak Salim Ahmad 162
Muhammad Abdullah al-Battani 128, 131, 154, 162
Muhammad al-Sadi 202
Muhammad Ali Ahmad 21, 98, 101, 127–8, 140, 156, 161, 194, 196, 211, 216; death sentence 162
Muhammad Ali Haytham 2, 25, 33–4, 26, 42–6, 55, 74, 105, 146, 192, 217
Muhammad Haydarah Masdus 156, 163, 192, 196
Muhammad Haytham Qasim 156
Muhammad Salih Awlaqi 42, 44, 45, 74
Muhammad Salim Akkush 28
Muhammad Sulaiman Nasir 196
Muhsin Alaini 55
Muhsin (Muhammad Sa'id Abdullah) 58, 62, 96, 109, 109, 110, 128, 129, 155–6, 161, 170, 196; arrested 129; conflict of January 1986 and 154; dismissed 118–19; returns to cabinet 130–1
Muhsin Ibrahim 15
Muhsin Muhammad Abu Bakr bin Farid 196–7
Muhsin Muhammad Farid 159
Mujahid al-Kuhhali 112
Muqbil (Ali Salih Ubad) 23, 36, 38, 40, 57
Muqbil al-Wad'i 184
Muslim Brotherhood 70–1, 184
Mutawakkalite Imamate xviii–xix, 3
Muti'a, Muhammad Salih 57, 63, 78, 85, 101, 105, 109, 119, 120, 123, 146, 216; shot 124

Najib al-Sha'bi 202
Nasir Muhammad, Ali ('Marhaba') 21, 36, 43, 45, 54–5, 56–8, 61, 69, 74–5, 81, 83, 101, 105, 109, 136, 156, 197, 205, 209, 217; Abyan power base 126–7, 132; Antar versus 128–36; appointed prime minister 55; appointed president and secretary general 105; meets Brezhnev 82; at COMECON 115; civil service and 58–9; conflict of January 1986 151–5; criticism of 140; death sentence 162; economic policy 137–41; in exile 157–9, 161–2, 202; explains violence of January 1986 155; Isma'il and 117–21, 129–32, 134–5; opposition to 129; received by Salih 194; resigns as prime minister 131; Salmin and 94–6; after Salmin 109–10; Saudi Arabia and 145–7; Soviet Union and 143–5; as supreme leader (1980–82) 122–9; unity and 181; YAR and 140–3
Nasser, Gamal 8–9, 13, 14, 47–8
National Democratic Front (NDF) 94, 99,107, 109–15, 122, 124, 141–2, 147, 165, 170, 178, 184, 190–1, 209, 220
National Front (NF, formerly NLF) 31–8; armed forces and 35; left factions of 36; Fifth Congress (March 1972) 56; Sixth Congress (March 1975) 88–90, 92
nationalization 59, 65, 73
National Liberation Front (NLF, later NF) xviii, 10, 11–13; foundation of (March 1963) 17; First National Congress (June 1965) 22–3; Second Conference (June 1966) 24–5; Third Congress (November 1966) 26; Fourth National Congress (March 1968) 37–9, 81–2; Fifth Congress see NF; Sixth Congress see NF; alliances 14–17; British and 20; Egypt and 23–4; Islam and

INDEX

35; left/right struggle in 20–1, 31–2; MAN and 17–18; Radfan campaign 11–12; seizes power 29–30; tribalism and 34–5; unions and 23
Naumkin, Vitaly 35–6
Nayif Hawatmah 15, 16, 37, 38, 80, 130, 158, 204
North Korea 84
Nuʿman, Yassin Saʿid 131, 156, 160–1, 170, 179, 190, 192, 202
on PDRY 212

oil 81, 93, 116, 139, 159, 164, 168, 169, 174–6, 202, 204
Oman 77–8, 81, 95, 117, 145–7, 158, 159

Palestine Liberation Organization (PLO) 145, 146
People's Democratic Republic of Yemen (PDRY) (1970–90); as 'failing' xx, 203; historical origins of 3–4; legacy of 212; new Constitution (1970) 55; significance of xviii–xix; support for international terrorism of 84, 85
People's Democratic Union (PDU) 15, 23, 38, 88, 91, 127, 135
People's Republic of South Yemen (PRSY, 1967–70) xx, 3, 6, 13, 20, 28, 31–49, 74, 77–8, 202, 204, 218; becomes PDRY 55
People's Socialist Party (PSP) 11–12, 18, 19, 22, 23
perestroika 169, 171, 207; see also pluralism
planning 67; see also five-year plans
pluralism 170–1
Politburo 17, 56, 57–8, 60, 67, 72, 73, 79, 88–9, 92, 97–9, 101, 107–10, 112, 118, 120, 121–35, 141, 142, 151–3, 155–7, 159–64, 169–74, 177–80, 205, 206, 219, 220
Popular Defence Committees 62, 63, 90
Popular Defence Forces (PDF) see armed forces/army

Popular Democratic Front for the Liberation of Palestine (PDFLP) 15, 16, 80, 154, 158
Popular Front for the Liberation of Oman and the Arabian Gulf (PFLOAG) 77–8, 81, 82
Popular Front for the Liberation of Palestine (PFLP) 15, 16, 80
Popular Vanguard Party see al-Taliʿa

Qahtan al-Shaʿbi 10, 15, 17, 21, 24, 26, 27, 29, 31, 33–4, 36, 37, 38, 39, 49, 91, 202, 204, 215; autocratic style 42–3, 101; coup (March 1968) and 39–40; foreign policy and 47–8; rebellion of May 1968 and 41–2; rehabilitated 182; resignation of 44
qat 71
Qatar 93
Qutaybi rebellion (1963) 11–12, 19

Radfan campaign (1963) 11–12, 19
Radfan 11, 12, 18, 19, 22, 26, 152
radio 9, 14, 15, 39, 152
Rajib Labuzah 19
Ramadan War (1973) 80
Rashid al-Kaff 175
Rashid Muhammad Thabit 109
rebellion (14 May 1968) 40–1
remittances 66, 68, 69, 73, 111, 138, 158, 168, 186
Republic of Yemen (ROY) 179, 182
Revolutionary Security Organization see State Security

Saada (sing. Sayyid) 7
Saʿid Salih Salim 132, 151, 155, 156
Sadat, Anwar 93, 80
Salafism xix, 71, 184
Salih Abu Bakr bin Husainun 128, 135, 161, 194–5, 196
conflict of January 1986 and 154; killed 198
Salih Munassir al-Siyayli 118, 123, 134, 156, 173; versus unity 179; dies 198
Salih Muslih Qasim 38, 57–8, 61,

95–6, 98, 101, 109, 110, 111, 125, 128, 131–2, 132–3, 134, 141, 153, 205, 215–16; dismissed 119; killed 151
Salih Ubayd Ahmad 155, 156, 161, 163, 170, 196
Salih, Ali Abdullah xix, 77, 112–14, 132, 136, 141–3, 152, 154, 165, 179, 180, 181, 192–3, 202; on 1993 elections 191; defeats southern forces 198; patronage system of 183–4; signs Pledge (1994) 194–5; unity and 175, 177, 178, 208–9; on YSP 197
Salim Muhammad Jubran 163, 190
Salim Rubayya Ali *see* Salmin
Salim Salih Muhammad 18, 73, 99, 109, 119, 129, 132, 134, 135, 151, 155–6, 160, 170, 171, 173, 178, 179, 193, 196–7, 202, 216
Salmin (Salim Rubayya Ali) 36, 38, 40, 42, 45, 56–8, 69, 82, 205, 216; Abd al-Rahman al-Iryani and 75–6; as chairman 53; China and 84; downfall of 86–7, 91–2, 94–101; foreign policy and 73–4; Islam and 70; land reform and 66–7; rehabilitated 182; Saudis and 78–9
Saudi Arabia 78–9, 93, 164, 166, 175, 184, 206; in Yemen's civil war (1994) 196, 197; Nasir and 145–7; Salmin and 78–9
Sayf Sayl Khalid 163, 165, 170
Sayf al-Dhala'i 29, 33–4, 38, 48
Sayyid (pl. Saada) 7, 28, 123, 220
Sayyid Bubakr al-Kaff 8
'Seven Glorious Days' (July 1972) 87
'seventy days' 13, 32
Shabwa xi, 37, 41–2, 98, 105, 119, 121, 133, 152–3, 156, 159, 162, 164, 170, 174, 175, 187, 191, 195, 197, 202, 203, 217, 219
shariah law 180, 188
Sharif Haydar al-Habili 217
Shu'ayb 9, 26, 27, 37, 213, 216, 219
Sinan Abu Luhum 179
Somalia 80–3, 147, 185; recognizes DRY 197
Sons of the South 210
South Arabian League (SAL) 6, 10, 15, 21, 32, 41, 185
Southern Mobility Movement ('al-Hiraak') xix, 201–2
Soviet Union 48, 73, 81–4; aid from 67, 69, 138; as inspiration to PDRY 205–7; Isma'il's removal and 120; military aid 61, 115–16; Nasir's regime and 143–5; after Nasir 165–6; YSP and 115–16; violence of 13 January and 159; *see also* Communism, Marxism, perestroika
Stasi 62
State Security 62, 105, 109, 118, 123, 128, 131, 155, 162, 170, 205, 219
Sultan Ahmad Umar ('Faris') 23, 38, 165
Supreme People's Council (SPC) 38, 55, 67, 71, 90, 96, 107–8, 109, 120, 121, 156, 162, 172–3, 181–2
Suez Canal 9, 204; opening (1869) 3; closure (June 1967) xviii, 31; reopens (1975) 64, 68
Subayhi 21, 26, 131, 156, 215
Sulaiman Nasir Mas'ud 154
Sulaiman Nasir Muhammad 162, 196
Sultan Ahmad Umar 23, 38, 165
Syria 80, 146, 167

Tariq al-Fadhli 188, 190, 198, 201
trade unions 65, 92, 106
 see also Aden Trade Union Congress
Trevelyan, Humphrey 27, 29–30
tribalism 69–70, 159, 163, 183, 192, 205, 212, 215–17;
 NLF moves against 34–5
Trotskyism 36

Umar Ali al-Attas 156
unions *see* trade unions
United Arab Republic (UAR) 14
United Political Organization of the National Front (UPONF) 88; *see also* National Front

INDEX 257

United States 85, 117, 167
Ushaysh, Mahmud Abdullah 23, 33, 45, 109, 110, 131, 157; arrested 129; returns to cabinet 130–1

Vance, Cyrus 85
Vietnam 84

Wahhabism xix, 7, 184
Western Aden Protectorate (WAP) 4, 6, 10–12; NLF and 19
Wedeen, Lisa 207
women 22, 55, 55, 60, 71, 72, 183, 206; in NF 106; veil and 173
World Bank 67, 68, 82, 111

Yafi'i tribe 4, 7, 9, 17, 18, 19, 35, 58, 61, 69, 73, 97, 98, 101, 123–4, 128, 160, 195, 202, 215–16, 218, 219
Yahya al-Shami 178
Yahya al-Mutawakkil 99
Yemen Arab Republic (YAR) 32, 74–6, 95, 112–13, 165; presidency of Abd al-Rahman Iryani 75, 76; presidency of Ibrahim al-Hamdi 76, 93–4, 99; presidency of Ahmad al-Ghashmi 76–77, 94, 97; presidency of Ali Abdullah Salih *see* Salih; National Democratic Front (NDF) – see National Democratic Front; Hashid tribal confederation 114, 176, 184; Bakil tribal confederation 75, 114, 190; support for opposition in PDRY 41, 60, 75, 77, 113–14; Kuwait agreement on unity xv, 113, 114, 140–1, 178; Tripoli agreement on unity xv, 114;
Cairo agreement on unity xv, 75, 78, 114, 140; China and 48; Soviet Union and 48, 116; British aid to 29, 33, 43; China and 48; infrastructure of 64–5; partition of (1904) 3; revolution (1962–63) 11–12, 16; Soviet Union and 48; Sunnis and Shi'a 3; territorial conflicts 74–7; Wars with PDRY 75, 113; 1979 Unity talks with PDRY 174–80
Yemen, Republic of (ROY) 182–212; Aden agreement on unity 177–82; economic problems 185–7; elections (1993) 190–1; Document of Pledge and Accord 194–6; civil war (1994) 195–6; after 1994 201–3; unity 173–82, 207–9
Yemeni People's Unity Party (YPUP) 114–15, 124, 141–2
Yemeni Socialist Party (YSP) before foundation 18, 61, 70, 76, 87, 96, 106, 87; First Congress (October 1978) 106–8, 111, 112, 115; Exceptional ('Second') Congress (October 1980) 122–4; Third Congress (1985) 133; Exceptional Congress (1987) 162–3; 1993 elections and 190–1; civil war (1994) and 195–6; class composition of 127; Islah alliance 202; Nasir and 141; rejected 210; unity and 173–4, 179, 203
Yom Kippur War *see* Ramadan War

Zaydis xv, 3, 13, 75, 114, 131, 141, 187, 203